C000243881

BEREAVEMENT
AND
ADAPTATION

SERIES IN DEATH EDUCATION, AGING, AND HEALTH CARE
HANNELORE WASS, CONSULTING EDITOR

ADVISORY BOARD
Herman Feifel, Ph.D.
Jeanne Quint Benoliel, R.N., Ph.D.
Balfour Mount, M.D.

Bard—*Medical Ethics in Practice*
Benoliel—*Death Education for the Health Professional*
Bertman—*Facing Death: Images, Insights, and Interventions*
Brammer—*How to Cope with Life Transitions: The Challenge of Personal Change*
Corless, Pittman-Lindeman—*AIDS: Principles, Practices, and Politics, Abridged Edition*
Corless, Pittman-Lindeman—*AIDS: Principles, Practices, and Politics, Reference Edition*
Curran—*Adolescent Suicidal Behavior*
Davidson—*The Hospice: Development and Administration, Second Edition*
Davidson, Linnolla—*Risk Factors in Youth Suicide*
Degner, Beaton—*Life-Death Decisions in Health Care*
Doty—*Communication and Assertion Skills for Older Persons*
Epting, Neimeyer—*Personal Meanings of Death: Applications of Personal Construct Theory to Clinical Practice*
Haber—*Health Care for an Aging Society: Cost-Conscious Community Care and Self-Care Approaches*
Leenaars, Wenckstern—*Suicide Prevention in Schools*
Leng—*Psychological Care in Old Age*
Leviton—*Horrendous Death, Health, and Well-Being*
Leviton—*Horrendous Death and Health: Toward Action*
Lindeman, Corby, Downing, Sanborn—*Alzheimer's Day Care: A Basic Guide*
Lund—*Older Bereaved Spouses: Research with Practical Applications*
Papadatou, Papadatos—*Children and Death*
Prunkl, Berry—*Death Week: Exploring the Dying Process*
Riker, Myers—*Retirement Counseling: A Practical Guide for Action*
Samarel—*Caring for Life and Death*
Sherron, Lumsden—*Introduction to Educational Gerontology, Third Edition*
Stillion—*Death and the Sexes: An Examination of Differential Longevity, Attitudes, Behaviors, and Coping Skills*
Stillion, McDowell, May—*Suicide across the Life Span—Premature Exits*
Vachon—*Occupational Stress in the Care of the Critically Ill, the Dying, and the Bereaved*
Wass, Berardo, Neimeyer—*Dying: Facing the Facts, Second Edition*
Wass, Corr—*Childhood and Death*
Wass, Corr—*Helping Children Cope with Death: Guidelines and Resources, Second Edition*
Wass, Corr, Pacholski, Forfar—*Death Education II: An Annotated Resource Guide*
Weenolsen—*Transcendence of Loss over the Life Span*

IN PREPARATION

Corr, Stillion, Wass—*Death in the Lives of Children: A Guide for Helping*
Doka—*The Dread Disease*
Neimeyer—*Death Anxiety Handbook: Research and Applications*

BEREAVEMENT
AND
ADAPTATION

A Comparative Study of the Aftermath of Death

Marc P. H. D. Cleiren

Department of Clinical and Health Psychology
Leiden University

⬤HEMISPHERE PUBLISHING CORPORATION
A member of the Taylor & Francis Group

Washington   Philadelphia   London

USA	Publishing Office:	Taylor & Francis
		1101 Vermont Avenue,N.W., Suite 200
		Washington, DC 20005-2531
		Tel: (202)289-2174
		Fax: (202)289-3665
	Distribution Center:	Taylor & Francis
		1900 Frost Road, Suite 101
		Bristol, PA 19007-1598
		Tel: (215) 785-5800
		Fax: (215)785-5515
UK		Taylor & Francis Ltd.
		4 John Street
		London WC1N 2ET, UK
		Tel:071 405 2237
		Fax: 071 831 2035

First edition published in 1991 by DSWO Press, Leiden University, under the title "Adaptation after Bereavement."

BEREAVEMENT AND ADAPTATION: A Comparative Study of the Aftermath of Death

Copyright © 1993 by Hemisphere Publishing Corporation. All rights reserved. Printed in the United States of America. Except as permitted under the United States Copyright Act of 1976, no part of this publication may be reproduced or distributed in any form or by any means, or stored in a database or retrieval system, without the prior written permission of the publisher.

1 2 3 4 5 6 7 8 9 0   B R B R   9 8 7 6 5 4 3 2

Cover design by Michelle Fleitz.
A CIP catalog record for this book is available from the British Library.
∞ The paper in this publication meets the requirements of the ANSI Standard Z39.48-1984(Permanence of Paper)

Library of Congress Cataloging-in-Publication Data

Cleiren, Marc P. H. D.
  Bereavement and adaptation : a comparative study of the aftermath
of death / Marc P. H. D. Cleiren.
     p. cm.
  Includes bibliographical references and index.
    1. Bereavement—Psychological aspects—Longitudinal studies.
  2. Death—Psychological aspects—Longitudinal studies.
  3. Adaptability (Psychology)—Longitudinal studies.   4. Grief—
Longitudinal studies.   I. Title.
  BF575.G7C55   1992
  155.9'37—dc20   92-26136
  ISBN 1-56032-279-9   CIP
  ISSN 0275-3510

To Laurence

Table of Contents

Preface

Over the past five years, when telling someone that bereavement was the principal subject of my research, I frequently encountered a remarkable reaction. Even with virtual strangers the response was that they disclosed their personal experiences about the loss of someone close to them with strong emotion and in great detail. These occasions taught me that grief and bereavement are an integral part of the lives of many people. Often this part is invisible in daily life but it is always there hidden just beneath the skin.

Although bereavement is generally regarded to be one of the most stressful events in adulthood, we still know relatively little about its influences on life. Exactly *how* devastating is it and for whom? Most research in this area has hitherto concentrated on the widowed, but what about other family members? Is their grief any less? Are certain individuals more at risk for developing problems than others? Can we determine which bereaved are most likely to lose their 'joie de vivre' and to sink into depression without recovering? What about the influence of the mode of death? Is dealing with a loss due to a fatal accident or suicide more difficult than bereavement after a fatal disease? All these questions have, until now, hardly been answered on an empirical basis. During the past century, the social sciences have come up with a number of theories on the human grief process. What intrigued me during my work on this project was that the stories of the bereaved themselves often bore little resemblance to the often neatly ordered processes suggested in several grief theories. It seemed to me as if there was a wide gap between theory and the every day experience of bereaved people.

This book hopes to offer some empirical answers to the above questions. Its creation was guided by the desire to increase our knowledge about factors that influence adaptation after a loss, by the need to determine which bereaved are most at risk for long-lasting problems, and by the wish to evaluate existing theory against the background of our empirical findings.

The first part of this publication offers a critical review of the main psychological theories on adaptation after loss followed by an elaborate overview of the results of the empirical research on bereavement. The second part of the book reflects a substantial part of the results of the Leiden Bereavement Study. This was a longitudinal comparative survey among more than 300 bereaved, designed to obtain insight in the role of mode of death and relationship to the deceased in the adaptation after loss. To this goal, population samples of bereaved from three distinct modes of death were contacted. These were the bereaved of people who died from suicide, of people who suffered a fatal traffic accident, and of people who died after a long-term disease. Elaborate structured interviews were held at four and at fourteen months after the loss. Participants were widowed, parents who lost a child, people who lost a sibling, and adults who lost a parent. Here the book discusses grief reactions and psychological, physiological and social functioning, all against the background of the sociodemographic situation, the relationship to the deceased, and the circumstances of death. It examines the predictive value of early adaptation for longer term functioning and identifies risk groups of bereaved. The last part of the book discusses the implications of the findings and puts the present empirical study in perspective with grief theory.

We live in a society where we are brought up to control, acquire, possess, and keep. Limitless growth and eternal youth are reigning collective fantasies. Death is a spoilsport in the game. Our daily life often pushes mortality back into the dark and neglected corners of our mind. This book shows that in bereavement these illusions are easily shattered. The extent to which our world collapses and our ability to rebuild it are not only dependent upon the type of loss we suffer but also upon the way we constructed and perceived our world in the first place. I hope that this book offers insight into how people cope with loss in our times and how families like our own are affected, cope, wrestle, and survive. In the end each story of bereavement and grief is not a story about 'them', but one about 'us'.

Marc P. H. D. Cleiren

Acknowledgments

This book is the result of the efforts of many people. First of all I want to thank the bereaved who took part in this study and took the time and trouble to help us by telling their story in so much detail, during such a difficult period in their lives.

Without the motivated help of the many interviewers, recording and ordering the accounts of the bereaved would not have been possible.

Three people have played a core role in moulding the book into its present form. During the entire process, Dr. Ad J. F. M. Kerkhof provided invaluable assistance by clarifying the ways to tackle the write-up of the study, garnished with superb pep-talk and moral support in the inevitable dark hours of the process. Prof. Dr. René F. W. Diekstra and Prof. Dr. Leo J. Th. van der Kamp contributed in an important and complementary way: Leo by helping me to get from raw data to results, René by meticulously reading and commenting on earlier versions of this manuscript. They have without any doubt increased the value of this work.

My other colleagues at the Department of Clinical and Health Psychology supported me by taking a sympathetic interest in my work and proceedings. In particular I want to thank Jan van der Wal, who started out on this project and who taught me the tricks of the trade, Nadia Garnefski for her methodological help and ready ear, Harold van Driel for handing me the right articles at the right time, Mary Jansen for her generous help both in Leiden and the USA, and Albert Mulder for the fruitful discussions on mutual problems.

I am indebted to Ad van Zoelen for his assistance during the last phase of the data acquisition, and to Llewelyn Brown for his quick and accurate corrections of my English.

I also wish to thank Wolfgang and Maggie Stroebc for their support and the stimulating discussions on our common area of interest. Dale Lund assisted me a great deal in finishing the write up of this study by his enthusiasm and knowledge. I am thankful for our continuing friendship.

I feel grateful to my close fiends and those special members of Vox Europae. Our meetings throughout the last years made me completely forget the lonely and lengthy process of writing this book and gave me a fresh look on my work upon returning to it. Coby, Orin and DaBen and many others helped me to put my work into perspective.

Last and therefore not least I thank Laurence for her love and putting up with me in these last eventful years. Our relationship has enriched our personal development.

Chapter 1

Introduction

This study concerns the effects of the death of a family member on the life of the surviving members of that family. We will examine how the bereaved react to the loss in different areas of functioning. Central in this publication are the role of the mode of death and the kinship relationship to the deceased in the adaptation of the bereaved after the loss. We will also focus in detail on how the situation before the death influences the adaptation and well-being of the bereaved afterwards.

In any given year in the past decade, the number of people that died in the Netherlands varied between 110,000 and 130,000 (CBS, 1983, 1988, 1989). Estimating that one death leaves five next of kin or close friends behind, every year more than half a million people (about 4% of the Dutch population) become bereaved. Most of them after some time are able to re-engage and function adequately in daily life. A minority however does not recover, or only marginally so, and continues to be debilitated in physical, psychological, and social functioning. Estimates of the magnitude of this group vary considerably, but it is generally assumed that at least 20% of all bereaved fall into it. Since the problems of people in this proportion may persist for much longer than one year, and in fact often last many years, the actual size of the problem will be much larger.

Although some knowledge exists about the factors that may determine functioning after a loss, much remains to be learned about their relative importance and interaction. If it is possible to determine in an early stage which individuals are likely to develop problems following loss, more adequate prevention and intervention strategies can be developed, and severe mental and physical health problems may be partially prevented.

1.1   The Leiden Bereavement Study

The study reported here was undertaken to assemble in-depth information on the role of the death with reference to specific situational and personal aspects that may influence adaptation after a loss of a family member. This requires a systematic, and preferably repeated assessment of the aspects involved.

The Leiden Bereavement Study is a controlled longitudinal study of 309 family members (parents, spouses, siblings and adult children) of people who died from three different causes of death: bereaved after suicide (n=91), a traffic accident (n=93) and people who died after a long-term disease (n=125). A standardized and elaborate interview was held approximately four months after the death occurred. A follow-up interview, mainly focussing on the events and changes since the first, took place fourteen months after the death.

Previous publications have reported part of the results of this study (Van der Wal 1986, 1987; Van der Wal & Cleiren 1988; Van der Wal, Cleiren & Diekstra 1988a,b). Van der Wal (1988) made a thorough analysis of the reactions of bereaved from suicide and the bereaved from a traffic accident, four months after the loss. His work is part of the basis of this publication.

In this book, these data are elaborated with a third mode of death: long-term disease, and the data of a follow up interview with the bereaved at fourteen months will be added. The focus of the present publication will be, on the one hand, on describing the characteristics of loss-reactions, health and social functioning after the loss, and, on the other hand on factors that may influence functioning, such as characteristics of the loss-situation, the relationship with the deceased, and sociodemographic factors. Throughout the study, we will systematically examine the role of the mode of death and the kinship relationship to the deceased.

Before giving a more detailed review of the literature and the design, method and results of our study, it is desirable to give a rough indication of our subject and to position it in its context. We also have to define the terminology we will use to discuss our subject. In the remaining sections of this chapter, we will first give a brief outline of the field under study. In the subsequent sections, a definition of the concepts involved will be given.

1.2   The context of bereavement

In our culture, the death of someone close is being regarded as one of the most pervasive events in human life. Although, as regards frequency, death has a less important place than in earlier times and in many other (third world) countries, it is still a common event in our society. The death of a family member, in particular, may constitute an important change of our world as compared to how it was before the loss. In order to be able to function in this new life-situation, we in turn need to adapt ourselves to this change.

The human reaction to bereavement seems to be characterized by a remarkable variety of feelings, thoughts and behavior. Grief or sadness is commonly regarded as the most generally experienced emotion, but it is by no means the only one. Yearning and pining for the deceased, symptoms of shock, numbness, hallucinatory experiences, feelings of anger, guilt, depression, meaninglessness, health problems, irritability, hyperactivity, but also relief and hope, may all be experienced in often rapid succession and alternation. The bereaved not seldom find themselves for a shorter or longer period of time 'out of control,' being swept from one state of mind to another. This process is often an exhausting experience, draining energy and attention away from the demands of daily life.

Although death and dying are universal phenomena in human beings, the experience of these events and the reactions they elicit are by no means universal. Not every bereaved person experiences all, or even the majority of the phenomena mentioned above.

Cultural influences

Death, and the experience of its consequences, takes place in a context. This context is, in its widest sense defined by one's culture. The cultural aspect of bereavement that draws most attention in this respect are the rituals and stories associated with death and dying. They are an important reflection of a society's attitude towards death, and can tell us about the social context of the loss. A culture, however, is more than its rituals.

In today's world, differences between cultures are increasingly associated with differences in well-being, poverty and death rate of the population. The extent to which death is a frequent, and relatively 'normal' phenomenon thus also differs widely from culture to culture, and may profoundly shape the social and personal context of a loss. People living in a country where children at an early age run a high risk of dying (e.g. from diseases or hunger) may have less trouble finding recognition and models for coping with the loss of their child than parents in our culture. They also may feel less 'abnormal' as a result of the death. Also within a culture there may be relevant differences in this sense between social classes.

In the present study we will limit ourselves to the consequences of bereavement as they can be found in our own culture, broadly defined as the modern Western culture. The literature which was consulted and referred to in this publication originates primarily from the Anglo-saxon tradition, with most of the studies being conducted in Great Britain and the United States. To a much lesser extent, literature from the Latin tradition was available and consulted. Of course further subdivisions on different levels are possible in terms of cultural traditions and nationalities. To the extent that we are aware of them, these differences will be mentioned and, where relevant, discussed. The limitation to these origins implies that no assertion is made about the possibilities of extending the findings to other cultures.

Situational and individual differences

Within our society, the reactions to a death differ widely according to the persons concerned. The situation (or the smaller context) in which the loss takes place also defines the subsequent processes.

Some reactions may be expected to be more pronounced with specific causes of death: survivors of suicide may be more prone to experience feelings of guilt. Bereaved who lose someone after a prolonged period of illness may show severe signs of exhaustion due to intensive caregiving, and in the case of homicide, feelings of anger towards the murderer(s) may be all-absorbing. If in addition to the loss, a person has or has had to cope with other problems, such as poverty, additional stressful events, or impaired physical health, this may increase the tension and impair adaptation.

The character and intensity of bereavement reactions are also determined by the relationship to the deceased. Here, not only the degree of emotional and social closeness to the deceased (e.g. a close friend versus a far-off acquaintance) may play a role, but also the nature of the relationship. The loss of ones young child is obviously different in nature from the death of a spouse.

Still, the impact of death seems to be not always determined by relationship, kinship or distance. People may react intensely to the death of an admired statesman, or a cherished pop-musician, who may have been an idol or considered as a far-off personal friend or supporter.

Individual reactions to death also differ considerably in seemingly identical situations. The reason for this is, first of all, that everyone carries with him a personal history of events. More or less stable personal characteristics or coping patterns that existed before the loss define, to a large extent, the way one deals with it.

In understanding the reactions to the death of a family member, it is thus imperative to take the context of the loss into account. This context is defined by cultural, situational and individual characteristics. In Chapter 3, empirical knowledge on these aspects will be discussed in more detail.

1.3   Definition of concepts

Like in many areas of daily life, a variety of terms is used to describe the processes associated with death and bereavement. In the literature we find terms like *loss, bereavement, grief, grieving, griefwork, bereavement process, mourning process, mourning*, and the like. Many of them are overlapping, or are used interchangeably. This conceptual overlap poses itself as a problem to the researcher. In order to be able to adequately describe the field from an empirical point of view, a clear definition of terms is necessary.

The concepts involved can be separated into a number of categories: those referring to the situation before the death occurred, those referring to the event of death itself, expressions referring to the adaptive processes following the death, and those referring to the situation that is considered to be the result of these processes. Each of these categories will be discussed hereafter.

Anticipation of the loss

If the death can in some way be expected or anticipated, the period before the death can be regarded as of influence on adaptation afterwards. The post-loss situation may be formed and influenced to a substantial degree by this knowledge or anticipation. The most generally used term for the processes during the time before the death is 'anticipatory grief'. The definition of anticipatory grief differs, however, considerably with the author and may comprise many different feelings (like anxiety, fear, or also relief) cognitive processes (like avoidance, hope, or role rehearsal) and behavior (like information seeking, intensified contact with the dying person). To what extent the stress in this period can be considered as valuable for adaptation to the death remains to be seen (see Cleiren et al. 1987). For this reason, we will make no assertions about the contents of this process, and henceforth prefer to speak of *anticipation of the loss* or *anticipation of the death*.

The loss event

A second category of terms refers to the objective situation. Words such as death, loss and bereavement all directly refer to the event that took place.

> *Bereavement* will be seen as the action of having something or someone go permanently out of one's control, possession or environment. In the context of this publication, *bereavement* will always pertain to death of a person.

The term *loss* will be used here as a synonym to bereavement. Thus, unless mentioned otherwise, 'loss' will be used here with the connotation of 'loss from death'. In this case, like bereavement, it also implies the irrevocable and definitive cessation of contact with a person.

The difference between the terms 'bereavement' and 'loss' on the one hand, and the term 'death' on the other, is that 'loss' and 'bereavement' are referring to the person who loses the object or person, while 'death' pertains to the person that was lost (the object of the loss). On the basis of this definition we can also define the term 'bereaved'.

The term *bereaved* as applied here, pertains to the person who has
sustained a loss by death of another person.

It must be added that there has to be a meaningful relationship to the deceased person,
at least in the ideation of the bereaved.

Processes after the loss

Next to terms referring to the loss situation *per se*, there are words that refer to the
experience of this situation.

To grieve can be seen as experiencing sorrow, pain, distress and sadness about a
loss. The noun *grief* has, however, gained a more elaborate meaning in the
bereavement literature (e.g. Parkes & Weiss, 1983), comprising a variety of emotions
as well as thoughts and behavior that occur after a loss. The term *grief*, as employed
here, also refers to the complex of feelings, cognitions and behavior of an individual
in reaction to a loss.

The processes in the individual after the loss are often indicated by adding
extensions like '-work' or '-process' to the terms 'grief' and 'bereavement'. These
extensions indicate that the situation after the loss is seen as characterized by changes,
rather than stability.

Another term to indicate bereavement processes is 'mourning'. Freud (orig.1917)
saw this as the process in which a person unwillingly has to withdraw libido from a
loved object. Later authors employ 'mourning' for the visible aspects of the reaction
to a loss, rather than for the intrapersonal aspects of the process. Averill (1968)
described it as the overt reaction to the loss prescribed by the community. Ramsay
(1979) conceived mourning as the behavior that occurs after bereavement. Parkes &
Weiss (1983) defined mourning as 'the observable expression of grief'.

Since we do not want to limit the study of the process neither to internal nor
behavioral processes, we will not use this terminology in the context of the present
study, and will prefer the more neutral term *bereavement process* , which will be used
in the same sense as *grief*.

Bereavement process will refer here to the cognitive, affective and
behavioral changes in the bereaved individual after the loss.

It must be noted that in this definition no specific direction of this process is assumed.
The term 'bereavement process' will thus mainly be used in a descriptive sense.
Although in the literature phases or steps in this process are often presumed, no
assumptions will be made here about its phasing or resolution.

Adaptation after the loss

In many studies of bereavement an attempt is made to assess the situation of the bereaved in terms of emotionality, physical and psychological health, or acceptance of the loss. Other indicators of functioning, like social integration are also considered.

Many different formulations are employed to describe virtually the same aspect. Psychological and physical ill-health after a loss are alternately indicated as 'poor recovery', 'bad outcome', 'unresolved grief', or 'poor functioning'. It is necessary to take a closer look at these concepts, since each of them can have a specific (theoretical) connotation.

The term *recovery* implies a return to the state as it was before bereavement in certain areas of functioning (Weiss, 1988). Strictly speaking, if one employs the term *recovery*, it implies a comparison with pre-bereavement functioning. Since in empirical research it is very rare that adequate measurement of the pre-bereavement situation is available, the term in most cases is not adequate to describe empirical findings. There is also considerable variety in the criteria for recovery employed in grief research.

The term *grief resolution* originates from psychodynamical theory. It assumes a process which leads to the resolution of grief, and implies counteracting processes or blockades that can prevent resolution and lead to 'unresolved grief'. The concept reflects a view, where some aspects are seen as productive and others as counter-productive. Since the term is related to the psychodynamical theoretical model, and we do not want to make assumptions about the processes, *grief resolution* has too specific a connotation for it to be useful as a description of the state of the bereaved.

The term *outcome of grief* refers specifically to the consequences of the loss, but implicitly ignores the fact that the phenomena observed are not solely the result of the loss event. Many other factors influence the observed state of the bereaved in terms of health or depression. In this sense the term 'outcome' is only appropriate if operationalized in terms of the loss itself, e.g. questions on ruminating over the loss or acceptance of the death.

The most neutral concept indicating the state of changes in the bereaved after the loss is *functioning after bereavement*. The term does not make any assertions on underlying dynamics, nor does it ascribe all changes that occur as due to the loss. *Adaptation after bereavement* is also a term which can be seen as referring to the loss itself, as well as the changed psychosocial situation. Adaptation *after* bereavement (rather than *to* bereavement) implies not only adjustment to the event of the loss, but also adjustment of all areas of life to the continued absence of the lost person. In this study, the terms 'functioning after bereavement' and 'adaptation after bereavement' will be used interchangeably as umbrella terms, comprising both functioning in different areas of life and loss-specific reactions.

Whereas the terms *grief* and *bereavement process* are suited to describe the overall situation of the bereaved, *functioning after bereavement* and *adaptation after bereavement* lend themselves better to more specific distinction between the aspects of grief. Functioning and adaptation can be operationalized in terms of reactions to the loss, as well as in terms of general health, substance-intake, or social integration.

1.4   The study of bereavement

Over the last decades there has been a growing interest in bereavement and grief. This has been marked by an increasing attention in the media, a growing awareness among caregivers, volunteers and the lay public, and a fast growing body of literature on grief and death related topics.

The literature on human grief can roughly be grouped in three clusters that have developed relatively independently from one another:

1)   *Case studies* in the form of autobiographical or biographical documents, or clinical observations.
  • *(Auto) biographical studies* often portray individual experiences, usually in the form of ego documents (e.g. diaries), written by people who have suffered an important loss, reflecting the authors' personal struggle in coming to terms with that loss (Forceville v. Rossum, 1978, 1982; Sen, 1988).
  • *Clinical studies*: Observations of someone or a small number of people suffering problems following the loss of a significant other, often obtained in a therapeutical context. (e.g. Hinton, 1971; Rynearson, 1987). Typically the dynamics of adaptation to the loss are described.

2)   *Groupwise studies* More or less systematic examinations of situation and symptomatology of bereaved persons. These studies can roughly be divided into two sometimes overlapping categories:
  • *Systematic observational studies*: Obtaining their data mostly directly from the bereaved. The goal is the examination of conditions and symptoms of groups of bereaved people, mostly using interviews or questionnaires. This type of study aims to uncover systematic relationships between the measured characteristics. (e.g. Maddison & Walker 1967; Parkes, 1975; Parkes & Weiss, 1983; Sanders, 1982-83, 1988; Lund et al. 1986, Stroebe & Stroebe, 1983).
  In recent years, physiological variables have been taken into account. More research has concentrated on psycho-epidemiological and neuro-endocrinological mechanisms in bereavement stress (e.g. Baron et.al.,

1990; Jacobs, 1987; Jacobs et.al. 1987a, 1987b; Irwin et al. 1987; Laudenschlager, 1988;).

- *Epidemiological studies*: Mostly large scale examinations of population, medical, and other registers. These studies are primarily aimed at identifying morbidity and mortality risk factors (e.g. Kaprio et al., 1987; Bowling, 1987; Levav et al., 1988).

3) *Grief theories*, seeking to provide explanatory frameworks for processes that follow bereavement. Authors attempt to integrate empirical findings and knowledge from diverse fields into a comprehensive conceptual framework. Most grief theories are linked to existing, more general psychological (e.g. Gauthier & Marshal, 1977) or biomedical theories (Boyden, 1987; Littlefield & Rushton, 1986). Several theories apply the concept of stages, components or tasks to be accomplished in order to regain a new equilibrium after the loss (e.g. Freud, 1957; Worden, 1982).

Case studies, and particularly accounts of individual experiences typically reflect the enormous and overwhelming impact the loss may have on the life of the bereaved. These are often accounts of people who successfully managed to come to terms with the loss, and give it a place in their life. This type of literature often serves as a source of recognition and a model for other bereaved persons. In the scientific area, it gives insight into the individual dynamical aspects of the bereavement process. However, those who finally successfully master their grief, and especially those who are able to put this process down in words form only a small minority of the bereaved. Thus it is uncertain whether or not the type of their experiences is shared by the bereaved in general.

Systematic observational and epidemiological studies of the bereaved have brought more insight into the prevalence of specific symptoms of grief and the differences between the bereaved in their adaptation to the loss. In most cases these studies have employed a more or less explorative or descriptive approach.

Groupwise studies seem to be the most appropriate in finding an overall image of grief, distinguishing between types of bereavement, and identifying risk-groups. An advantage of representative group studies is the opportunity to build prevention policies on them. A disadvantage may be that one easily loses track of the truly individual situation of the bereaved person. This aspect is better done justice in clinical (N=1) studies.

Despite considerable attention for the bereavement process, the development of a generally accepted and comprehensive theory has not yet materialized. Grief theories have often been developed from insights on the individual level, obtained in clinical studies, rather than from systematic observational study. Most of the theories have grown from their author's extensive experience in working with the bereaved, but are at the same time rooted in more general psychological theories. They often propose certain mechanisms and dynamics underlying the bereavement process from psychodynamical, behavioral and/or cognitive points of view. Shackleton (1984) in a review of some of the main theories in this area concludes that virtually all of them suffer from internal inconsistencies, lack of verifiability, or limitations in their scope. Still, as will be outlined in the next chapter, there is a development in the direction of more general theories on coping with loss and traumatic stress, which are related to cognitive theory.

The present empirical study is a combination of a systematic longitudinal observational study with case studies. Since no agreed upon explanatory theoretical framework for bereavement processes appears to be available (Shackleton, 1984; Wortman & Silver, 1989), we will not apply one here. Instead, we will present some of the major theories on bereavement processes without elaborate comment on each of them. The framework chosen for the present study will be a more or less general model for life-stress.

1.5   The further contents of this publication

The present publication consists of two sections: in the first four chapters, part of the literature on death-related bereavement and grief will be reviewed. Some theories on loss and the major findings and methodology of empirical studies are presented and discussed. This forms the framework for the second section: the description and discussion of a major part of the findings of the Leiden Bereavement Study, which was conducted at the Department of Clinical, Health and Personality Psychology of the University of Leiden in the Netherlands.

In the next chapter, we will discuss a number of the prevailing theories on grief and bereavement. At the end of the chapter, a framework is presented for the present study, which will also serve as an orientation to be applied in the discussion of the empirical literature.

The third chapter will present a review of the findings of systematic empirical studies into bereavement. The relationship between adaptation after bereavement and sociodemographic, situational, social and personal characteristics will be examined in a univariate and multivariate way. Results and methodologies of research will be critically examined, and we will deal with some of the major methodological problems in the study of bereavement.

In the fourth chapter, the design for the present study will be described. The background, method and specific goals of the Leiden Bereavement Study will be presented, together with the interview instrument and data on response, non-response and attrition.

Chapter 5 will offer a description of the properties of the measures of functioning used in the study. For each of these measures, we will discuss the situation for the sample as a whole. We will also systematically assess the quantitative and qualitative differences in functioning between modes of death and between family members. The change in functioning over time will be discussed.

In Chapter 6 the structure and interrelationships of the different aspects of outcome will be examined in a multivariate way. The dimensions of functioning will be put in perspective with each other and with the modes of death, kinship groups and sex.

In the seventh chapter, on the basis of the nature of the individual characteristics, the loss characteristics and the social context, statistical predictions will be made on adaptation of the bereaved at four months after the loss, and the change in functioning between four and fourteen months.

In the eighth and last chapter, conclusions will be drawn on the basis of the findings in the preceding chapters. On the basis of our findings we will look in retrospect to some of the theories on grief and how our observations may fit in with them. Also, practical implications of the findings for prevention of long-lasting health deterioration will be discussed, along with recommendations for further research.

Facts and circumstances in the casuistic material presented in this book which might indicate the identity of the bereaved have been modified to guarantee their anonymity and to safeguard the confidentiality of their communications. To this goal, cross-references between citations have been omitted as well.

Chapter 2

Theories on Adaptation after Bereavement

The goal of the present chapter is to show that although a number of theories have been developed to describe and explain the processes associated with bereavement, none of them can be fully adopted without limiting the aspects one has to take into consideration. Thus, if in the present study we opted for one particular theory, we would lose a relevant part of the information. In a comprehensive empirical study of bereavement, we have to choose for a broader orientation. To this goal, we will present a more elaborate framework which offers the possibility of incorporating, in a more or less eclectic manner, relevant aspects of psychodynamic, as well as behavioral theories.

In the following sections, a brief outline of some of the influential theories on the bereavement process will be discussed, together with their merits and limits in understanding the bereavement process. We choose to describe theories representative for the psychoanalytic, cognitive, behavioral and socio-biological view of grief. In the final sections of this chapter, a theoretical design will be proposed for the discussion of the empirical literature and as a background for the set-up for the empirical study.

2.1   Psychoanalytical theories on bereavement

Most of the initial theory on bereavement was directly based on psychoanalytic theory. This also meant a primary and sometimes exclusive focus on intra-psychic dynamical processes. Although a number of authors have contributed in this area (a.o. M. Klein, A. Freud), we will limit ourselves to two contributions of fundamental importance in this area, namely those of Sigmund Freud, and Lindemann.

Freud

One of the most influential theories is Freud's psychoanalytic theory. His views with regard to bereavement can mainly be found in his influential paper 'Mourning and Melancholia' (1957, orig.1917). Freud's views lie at the basis of many subsequent theories (e.g. Lindemann, 1944; Parkes, 1970 and Marris, 1958).

In Freud's view, the libido is attached (cathected) to the loved object and everything associated with it. When a person realizes that the object is irretrievably lost, he has to bring to consciousness all the thoughts concerning the object in order to detach the libido from them. This 'catharsis' is not easily brought about, and is a difficult and resisted task for the bereaved individual. When this 'grief work' has been accomplished, the ego is free again. According to Freud, melancholia (or depressive illness) is the result of a loss which remains unconscious. The repression of aggressive feelings with regard to the deceased means that some of the grief work is carried out in the unconscious instead of in the conscious. Failing to acknowledge the loss, the libido is withdrawn from it, but the ego identifies itself with the object. The disappointment and anger with the loved object are thus directed against oneself. By punishing oneself, one can punish the lost person without openly expressing hostility. Ambivalent feelings towards the loved object, in which both love and anger may be present, is thus, when repressed, an important cause for abnormal grief. According to Freud, the aggressive component of this state turns inward and causes melancholia.

With regard to the processes of bereavement, in 'Mourning and Melancholia,' Freud states that it is clear that withdrawing the libido is time consuming. According to him, it is difficult to say whether withdrawal of the libido starts in different places simultaneously, or follows a specific sequence.

Freud's theory concentrates on the intrapsychic aspects of bereavement. Freud himself was less concerned with death-specific characteristics or environmental factors. He was the first to propose a framework for the intrapersonal dynamics of the bereavement process.

Lindemann's theory

Lindemann (1944), starting from a (Freudian) psychoanalytic viewpoint, based his theory on careful observations during interviews with 101 relatives of thirteen people killed in a fire in the Boston Coconut Grove night club, and 88 killed in the second World War. He concluded that in the case of acute grief, bereavement reactions consist of a syndrome of five components: somatic disturbance, preoccupation with the image of the bereaved, guilt, hostility and disorganized behavior. He saw two abnormal grief syndromes: a delayed grief reaction, which could last for years, and what he called 'distorted grief', which could consist of social withdrawal, hypochondriacal development of the dead person's symptoms, psychosomatic illness and manic over-activity. Recovery from bereavement in his view is the emancipation from the relationship with the deceased, readjustment to the environment and formation of new relationships. To achieve this, analytic 'grief work' has to be done.

This comprises coping with the feelings of hostility and fear, the expression of a sense of loss and the verbalization of guilt feelings.

Lindemann's theory is valuable as it is the first to offer an observable categorization of the phenomena involved in reactions to sudden loss, many of which are nowadays seen as components of the Post Traumatic Stress syndrome (see DSM III-R, 1987). Lindeman's observations and theory are based on the study of deaths of a sudden and violent character. It therefore does not consider other mechanisms like anticipation, that may be involved in deaths resulting from (chronic) illness. He does not mention anticipatory stress, and feelings related to relief of stress after the loss.

Conclusion

Although metaphors like 'ego' 'libido' and 'unconscious' have been replaced by others in later psychodynamic theories, the notion that the course of grief is substantially dictated by intrapsychic processes has remained intact. Essential component of the psycho-analytic approaches to grief and bereavement is the notion that the bereaved identifies with the lost figure, which is seen as a compensation for the loss that was sustained. The process of identification has been questioned, but its essence: the major influence of the (introjected) form of the relationship with the deceased on the bereavement process, has become generally accepted in grief theory and research.

2.2 Psychoanalytic-cognitively oriented theories: Bowlby, Parkes and Marris

The theories outlined in this section have in common that they tend to accentuate cognitive functioning and goal-orientedness in adaptation after bereavement. In this section, we will outline the theories of Bowlby, Marris and Parkes. In a way, all three offer an alternative framework for the psychoanalytic one, but psychoanalytic elements are nonetheless still recognizable. Cathartic elements are particularly present in their view of the recovery process. First, the theory of Bowlby will be outlined, which has strongly influenced both Marris' and Parkes' views. Bowlby, on the other hand, has drawn from the elaborate empirical work of Parkes in validating his views on loss.

Bowlby

Bowlby (1969) formulated the first influential theory on attachment and loss, which in a number of aspects explicitly rejects Freudian theory. Nonetheless it can be considered to have strong roots in psychoanalytic thinking.

Like Freud, Bowlby presupposes unconscious processes and considers childhood experiences in bonding of importance in later development. Dissatisfied with some of the abstract concepts such as 'psychic energy' and 'drive' in psychoanalysis, Bowlby, especially in his later work, seeks to draw links with cognitive psychology. In his attachment theory he postulates that attachment behavior in human beings has a function of committing them to each other. The young child is extremely dependent on his environment. In order to survive, it has to make certain that it is cared for. This, it does by showing attachment behavior: behavior that serves to "...maintain certain degrees of proximity to, or of communication with, the discriminated attachment figure(s)." (Bowlby, 1969, p.40). Examples of such behavior are smiling when the attachment figure is present, crying or calling, to make the attachment figure appear, and searching behavior[1]. In attachment relationships (of which the first most often is the mother-child relationship) the individual is and feels protected. Attachment is thus goal-directed, and has a function in survival. Attachment behavior, also when expressed in adult life, is considered by him to be normal.

According to Bowlby, grief is essentially 'separation anxiety'. He draws an analogy between young animal's and children's reactions to separation from their mothers and reactions to loss in bereaved adults. He views bereavement as an unwanted separation from an attachment figure which gives rise to 'attachment behaviors' similar to those observed in animals and children. A brief period of protest is followed by a longer period of searching behavior. After some time these behaviors cease, as they prove to be ineffective in bringing back the attachment figure, and the bereaved enter a phase of despair and depression sets in. After that, a fourth and final stage is the 'reorganization' phase, in which the cognitive restructuring of ones situation takes an important place. Proceeding through these phases constitutes the 'grief work'. In contrast to Freud, Bowlby asserts that in a healthy bereavement process, the relationship with the deceased is often not broken. The bereaved may have a feeling of 'inner presence' of the deceased that is comforting and supportive in restructuring their lives.

Bowlby's model is a more or less an organic or medical one: it stresses the instinctual and congenital determination of the grief process. Like Freud's theory, it is a cathexis theory, where the childhood bond plays an important role as the model for later relationships. Recovery from loss is seen as analogous to recovery from a disease. There is some empirical basis for this theory. Behavior sequences, following the phases described above, have been found among animals in behavioral experiments (cf. Rosenblum, 1984) as well as in psychobiological research (Laudenslager, 1988).

---

[1]   We will not describe the different characteristics and types of attachment here. A detailed description can be found in Bowlby (1969).

A problem in Bowlby's theory is the assumption that identical processes in human and animal infants underlie similar behaviors and that childhood reactions to loss are essentially the same as adult responses. Although in empirical research similarities have been found between the reactions of young animals and those of children to (temporary) loss of the mother, the analogy is less clear with adult reactions to loss. In empirical observations it appears that anxiety and searching behavior, emphasized by the theory, are not a general aspect of the human grief process (Parkes, 1983). In later separation-experiments with animals it has been found that some species are more vulnerable to separation than others, and that reactions are strongly characterized by individual differences and situational characteristics (Rosenblum, 1984). A reliable indicator for psychological stress are immunobiological reactions. In some species, the loss of the mother itself is less indicative for these reactions than the degree of subsequent social isolation (Laudenslager, 1988). In humans, it is difficult to find empirical proof for the contribution of the loss itself to immunobiological reactions, since it is linked up with many stress-related factors, such as changes in sleep-patterns and circadian rhythms. Also behavioral aspects may change dramatically, such as changes in nutrition and use of psychoactive substances. All this may influence the reactions of the immune system (for a discussion: see Osterweis et al., 1984).

Parkes

Parkes' theory (1970, 1983) is partly influenced by Bowlby, with whom he has worked, but like Marris (discussed hereafter), he emphasizes the process of cognitive restructuring. Parkes in fact employs elements of different models to explain the nature of the bereavement process: a medical, a cognitive and, to some extent, a cathartic one. On one hand Parkes sees the social situation of the bereaved as essentially the same for the sick and the wounded. He seeks to classify grief in terms of medical diagnosis. On the other hand he views grief in terms of separation anxiety, and the bereavement reaction as an instinctive response to separation, following Bowlby in this respect. Cathartic elements can be found in his descriptions of the process of recovery. Although mainly formulating this in cognitive terms, Parkes assumes that in bringing the bereaved to fully experience his feelings of guilt or anger clears the way for alternative ways of thinking[2].

Parkes considers the normal reaction to bereavement to be a period of grieving, marked by distress and impaired functioning, followed by recovery. By recovery, he means the replanning of the life-situation and the attaining of a new, independent level of functioning. If recovery does not occur, the reaction is 'abnormal'.

---

2   cf. Parkes & Weiss, 1983, p.243.

According to Parkes the grief process consists of four stages, which resemble closely Bowlby's description. The first is centered around searching behavior. It is marked physiologically by high arousal, cognitively by illusions and dreaming of the dead person, and emotionally by anxiety. In the second stage, the loss becomes more and more 'real' to the person. Also, on an emotional level, he realizes that the loss is definitive. The intellectual knowledge, emotional acceptance, and behavior become congruent. The full recognition of the loss leads to a third stage: one of disorganization and despair. The 'assumptive world'[3] as it was known to the bereaved before the loss is scattered, impairing predictability of the world. The person becomes depressed and withdrawn. In the fourth stage, the bereaved constructs a new model of the world with which he restores predictability and control over his life.

Parkes stresses the importance of cognitive restructuring to come to terms with the new situation. In his view, the way to attain recovery is to go through the pain of the loss, and to bring to consciousness and express the feelings connected to it. Suppression of the pain may prolong or pathologize the grief process. In this respect Parkes holds a cathartic view, similar to Freud's. Pathological mourning is seen by him as a distortion or exaggeration of the normal process of grieving.

Although in the descriptions in his empirical work Parkes takes into account environmental and situational factors, his theory is largely intrapsychic. In employing three different models, the theory lacks a sense of unity. The use of three distinct frameworks gives it a jig-saw-like appearance and makes it lose transparency. Although testable hypotheses can be derived from them, the results can only corroborate or refute statements within each framework. In empirical research, the suggested massive cognitive disorganization has not been found among the bereaved.

Marris

The theory of Marris (1974) replaces Bowlby's notions on attachment-behavior and instinct by 'structures of meaning'. These can be seen as internal schemata in which the emotional attachment to others is represented, and by which involvement and interactions are defined. Although he originally adhered a psychoanalytic point of view similar to Lindemann's, he later put forward his cognitive grief theory, in which psychoanalytic notions remain strongly present. The latter theory will be discussed here.

With the loss of the deceased who occupied an important place in his environment, the life of the bereaved becomes less predictable: the loss of the familiar makes that new structures of meaning have to be established. Marris states that this predictability is central to survival: without it we cannot interpret the meaning of things that happen

---

[3]   Parkes defines this as '..an organized schema [...] which contains everything that we assume to be true on the basis of our previous experience.' (1988, p.56).

to us[4]. The bereaved thus finds himself in a situation of uncertainty, which he may try to resolve in two different ways: he can return in imagination to the time before death (yearning for the bereaved, reliving certain episodes, hallucinations, thoughts oriented towards the past) or he can forget or deny the issue (avoidance of thoughts about the deceased, thoughts oriented towards the future). Resolution of grief depends on the successful 'working out' of those conflicting tendencies. This is done partly by 'externalizing the ambivalence', which implies a catharsis of the conflicting tendencies, to facilitate the process of reestablishing meaning and to make the world predictable again. Marris stresses the importance of mourning rites in institutionalizing this ambivalence. Mourning rituals authorize the conflicting tendency in the bereaved: they allow the bereaved to care for the deceased and occupying oneself with the past, while, on the other hand, they allow recovery.

Important in his theory is the attention he draws to the impact death has on the whole life situation, and the conflicting (approach/avoidance) tendencies in the bereaved. Marris applies a more elaborate cognitive framework to the grief process than Bowlby does. This places the theory more in line with modern stress theory (see Section 2.6). The description of the recovery process and its mechanism, however, is unclear. Furthermore, empirical studies, so far, have not shown the claimed effect of mourning rituals on outcome in terms of health and well-being (Glick et al. 1974; v.d. Brink, 1989; cf. Shackleton, 1984).

2.3 Behaviorally oriented theories: Ramsay, Gauthier & Marshall

There is another category of theories which adopt a more behavioral view. They tend to see grief as a normal, natural process, which can be inhibited or reinforced by external, environmental stimuli. In contrast with the foregoing theories they are less concerned with the intrapsychic process of grief and its dynamics. Since their elements are more readily observable, they allow for a somewhat closer examination of their validity. The behaviorally oriented theories of grief are typically related to the clinical field, and concentrate on deviations in the grief process. Consequently they tend to concentrate more on pathological forms of grief and intervention strategies. Important in this area are the views of Ramsay (1979a,b), and Gauthier & Marshall (1977).

---

[4]   This closely resembles the view of Kelly (1963), who pointed out that the function and importance of forming constructs (structures of meaning) about ones world is to be able to predict and anticipate, as well as prepare actions for future events.

Ramsay

Ramsay adopts Averill's (1968) term 'bereavement behavior' to indicate the integral psychological and physiological response-pattern of a person after a significant loss. 'Grief' is seen as the general complex of psycho-physiological reactions with a biological origin, while 'mourning' is seen as the behavior that is defined by social conventions and customs. Ramsay (1979a) sees grief as a universal phenomenon among higher animals and humans. It is a complex but stereotyped response-pattern with physiological and psychological symptoms. Stimulus for grief is the real or imagined loss of a significant object. It ceases when new object relations are formed. The emotion is accompanied by severe psychological and physiological stress. Still, much of the behavior of the grieving subject during a period of grief is dysfunctional in establishing new relationships and alleviating the problems. The depressive mood he explains from a combination of theories. One is Seitz's (1971) low reinforcement theory: the depression is caused by a massive loss of formerly provided reinforcement (e.g. by the partner). The other is Seligman's theory of learned helplessness. The bereaved is powerless to change the situation: he cannot get the object back. This leads to a depressed mood in which potentially adaptive behavior does not occur.

The importance of Ramsay's approach lies in incorporating the role of reinforcement, environmental and situational factors such as social support into a theory of grief. Empirical evidence for the theory is scarce however, and largely provided by Ramsay himself on an impressionistic basis. One problem is that the theory is of little value for describing and investigating the 'normal' grief process, since it is only concerned with the disturbances of that process.

Gauthier & Marshall

Gauthier and Marshall (1977) in their theory ascribe a prominent role to the social environment in the genesis of pathological grief. The severeness of bereavement reactions is determined by disposition, abruptness of the loss, its significance, the availability of a replacement and social reinforcement for grieving or avoidance. In the course of a normal grief process the social environment initially reinforces grief. Later the reinforcement shifts to recovery and the development of new activities. The main cause of prolonged grief, according to Gauthier and Marshall, lies in inadequate or misplaced social reinforcement, grief symptoms being reinforced rather than adaptive behavior. They state that grief is reduced by appropriate manipulation of social reinforcement and prolonged stimulus exposure.

Like Ramsay's theory, Gauthier and Marshall's has a principally change-oriented scope on the grief phenomenon. It has a strong side in that it is coherent and does not suppose unobservable dynamic principles. It is however not a complete theory of grief, since it is not clear where the other-than-environmental factors fit in: factors which they too acknowledge to play a role in grief. Preexisting personal style factors may well play an equal or more important role than social reinforcement. There is some evidence that this is the case, and that it may interact with environmental reinforcement. De Boer & Van der Wal (1988) found that one of the important reasons for seeking the support of self-help groups rather than friends, was the pressure their friends exerted on getting well. Bereaved often felt they had problems in adjustment *because* the accent, in the contact with significant others, was placed on recovery. They felt they could not work things through at their own pace. Such an active rearrangement of the social network after the loss to obtain the desired 'reinforcement' makes the role of social reinforcement more complicated.

2.4   A sociobiological perspective

One of the rare theories that is particularly concerned with the role of kinship relationships in the impact of loss is the sociobiological approach. This perspective, to our knowledge only applied to bereavement by Littlefield & Rushton, asserts that the impact of death of a family member is related to the importance that person had for 'survival of the genes' of the bereaved. In fact, Littlefield & Rushton (1986) do not express a view on the nature and function of grief, but only consider the magnitude of problems after the loss to be ultimately determined by the degree of impediment of genetic survival[5].

Some of their predictions are that mothers would grieve more than fathers, healthy children will be more grieved for than unhealthy children, male children are more grieved for than female children, and that similar children were more grieved for than dissimilar children.

On the basis of Littlefield & Rushton's theory, we can also make predictions about the grief of other family members.

We would predict that children of the deceased would only suffer little or no loss at all in this respect, and thus evidence few problems. It could be argued that adult siblings sustain a somewhat greater loss than adult children of the deceased, since a sibling is more likely to contribute to the continuation of the genetic family line than older parents, who cannot have children anymore. On the other hand, parents losing a child would have the most problems, since they clearly lose a part of genetic survival. Spouses would take an intermediate position. Women suffer a considerably larger

---

5   Archer (1990) states that from a sociobiological point of view, Littlefield & Rushton's theoretical approach can be criticized for several reasons. Fundamental appears the fact that, whereas in sociobiology the adaptive function of behavior is considered crucial to its appearance, the behavior in grief seems to be counterproductive for survival, and to occur at the most as a byproduct of adaptation.

loss than men: while men, in theory, have greater chances of reproducing themselves, and are fertile until old age, a woman's fertility ends at a younger age, while pregnancy means a much heavier burden and risk to women, while demanding great sacrifices from them in terms of time and social position.

Age, in this sense, also is an important factor. Older parents and spouses sustain a greater loss, since their chances of reproducing their genes by having another child is more difficult or even impossible.

Taking the above aspects into account, it could be predicted that the ranking order of the kinship groups with regard to difficulties with bereavement would be as follows: parents would be most affected, followed by spouses, then siblings and finally children. Furthermore, it would be predicted that women will have more difficulties with a loss than men, while older age of the bereaved would be related to more difficulties.

Littlefield & Rushton (1986) conducted an empirical study to prove the validity of their theory. We will not go into the details of their findings, but point out that elaborate and fundamental comments have been provided by Archer (1990). A major problem seems their indirect method of assessing of grief intensity, by asking the parents to retrospectively rate the grief of all other family members. We will limit ourselves to Archer's conclusion that, although the results of the study partly seemed to corroborate their theory, it appears that alternative explanations are available, while method and explanation of the study are also subject to criticism (see Archer, 1990). Other research in this area to our knowledge has not been conducted.

2.5   Steps in the adaptation to bereavement

In the literature on bereavement, different models have been developed to systematically describe the grief process. We can distinguish two main types of models can be distinguished.

One is the category of stage, or phase models, which mainly describe the characteristics and order of intrapsychic states and behavior of the bereaved individual. Examples of these we find in Bowlby's (1969) and Parkes' (1970) theories, which were described in Section 2.2.

The other category considers adaptation after bereavement as the accomplishment of a series of tasks, and does not necessarily propose an order of occurrence of the phenomena. In this section, we will take a closer look at both types of models.

Phases and stages in the adaptation to bereavement

The phase or stage models usually attempt to chronologically order the reactions after a loss. Some of these models are linked to specific theoretical (dynamical) backgrounds, like Parkes' and Bowlby's, while others have a more descriptive character.

A well known model of this sort has been proposed by Kübler-Ross (1982). She developed her ideas about grief in her work with the terminally ill. Her model, although concentrating on the grief of the dying person, can also be applied to the bereaved. She distinguishes five stages through which the bereaved (and also the dying person) proceed. According to Kübler-Ross, the first stage is one of denial: 'It cannot be true'. The second is a phase of protest, where the question 'Why me?' is central. The third phase is marked by 'negotiating' with death: 'O.K., it is me, but if I do this, it will not happen.'[6]. From this, the person passes to the fourth phase: depression, in which he or she fully realizes the (impending) loss, and retreats from contacts with others. She also distinguishes a fifth phase in which the fate is accepted, and a new calm and detached attitude is found, and where personal growth has taken place. Although the model is somewhat different, it suggests roughly the same pattern as the ones proposed by Bowlby (1969) and Parkes (1970).

The strictness with which the stages or phases are separated from each other differs with each author. Most authors leave open the possibility that in individual cases phases may overlap, change in order, or even be skipped. Later, Parkes (1983,1988) also takes a more 'component' like point of view.

In the last decades, serious doubts have been raised about the validity of the stage or phase models. In virtually none of the empirical research has there been found evidence for the existence of distinct stages (e.g. Barrett & Schneweiss, 1980-1981). It must be added though, that a methodologically sound study of this is very difficult, because according to most theories, the length of each phase may differ considerably between individuals. This makes longitudinal study with short time-intervals necessary.

In most of the empirical research it is found that the diversity of grief symptoms decreases more or less quickly over time, with some symptoms disappearing faster than others (Zisook, Schuchter & Lyons, 1987).

The concept of distinct stages in the adaptation after bereavement seems untenable. Some authors have developed 'component' models in which the time-element is less compelling. Since it has been found that the emotions and behaviors in grief could overlap, change in order, be absent, or recur, Bugen (1977) stated that, more important than ordering grief symptoms on a time scale, is the recognition that grief is marked by a large variety of emotional states. He prefers to see these as 'components' rather than phases.

---

[6] This phase seems to be more pronounced in the dying person than in the bereaved.

Tasks in the adaptation after bereavement

In the literature on grief and bereavement there has been a development of a category
of task-models of grief (e.g., Spiegel, 1973; Schuchter, 1986; Worden, 1982; Van
der Wal, 1988; Weiss, 1988).

The common denominator for these models is the angle from which they look at
the bereavement process, rather than their contents. A characteristic of these models is
that they concentrate on the fact that the bereaved is actor in the adaptation to the loss
(Van der Wal, 1988). They are future or recovery-oriented, but on the whole do not
prescribe a fixed order of occurrence of phenomena. Whether certain grief responses
at a certain point in time have to be considered normal or pathological, a question
likely to play a role in the phase or stage models, is here avoided.

Although the contents of a task may be of a dynamical nature, the character of
these models is primarily descriptive, rather than explanatory. The process of
adaptation in this view is not an autonomous one, which unwinds itself in a 'natural'
series of changes. The changes have to be initiated and brought about by the bereaved
himself. Each task is formulated as a desired outcome in a certain area of functioning,
and accomplishment of each task can be seen as the goal of the process of adaptation.
The tasks have a *normative* character, being formulated as desirable (therapeutical)
outcomes. The bereaved is not necessarily conscious of these tasks, and may even
have other goals. The bereaved may, for instance, try to deny the reality of the loss,
when the latter is too painful to bear.

The various task-models often have different accents: Van der Wal (1988) accentuates
empirical verifiability of tasks. Others (Schuchter, 1986; Bugen, 1977) concentrate
more on tasks in the therapeutical work with the bereaved. Consequently, the contents
of the tasks differ with each author. Some commonly mentioned tasks are listed in
Table 2.1. They can be divided into two groups. Whereas the first four are related to
dealing with the loss- event itself, the latter three are pronounced goals pertaining to
general functioning of the bereaved.

In the background of some task-models (e.g. Spiegel, 1973), the tasks of dealing
with the loss event seem to be considered a *sine-qua-non* for achieving the tasks of
maintaining an acceptable level of general functioning.

Tasks a) through d) thus seem to function as subgoals on the way to adaptation,
and like in the phase- or stage models become assumptions about the necessary
processes to reach the goal of recovery. Whether experiencing grief has to be a
pronounced goal in recovery (task b) must particularly be questioned. This goal
seems to be introduced from a psychodynamical assumption that without catharsis,
resolution cannot take place. Although it is certainly possible that expression of grief
is important, putting it as a specific goal to attain for all the bereaved seems
premature. In strong contrast with this assumption is the finding in empirical research

that those who experience intense painful affect shortly after the loss, are also the ones who are worse off during the years that follow (Lund, 1985-1986; Vachon, Rogers e.a. 1982; Wortman & Silver, 1989).

Table 2.1
Tasks commonly mentioned in adaptation after loss.

(a) *Coming to terms with reality* : developing an image of the circumstances of death, recognizing the reality of the loss.

(b) *Experiencing and expressing the painful affects* : often concentrating on daring to undergo and express the conflicting and overwhelming diversity of feelings.

(c) *Finding means to modulate the painful affects* : finding adequate ways to regulate the pain in order to cope with the demands of daily life.

(d) *Emancipating from the bond with the deceased:* to integrate the changed relationship with the deceased spouse, often seen as giving a meaningful place in life to the relationship and the end of its interactive existence.

(e) *Conserving or adapting the social network* : maintaining or rebuilding meaningful and supportive relationships with others.

(f) *Conserving a positive self-image*, and perceiving oneself as being in control.

(g) *Maintaining or rebuilding psychological and physical health.*

A problem with some tasks is that their empirical operationalization is difficult, and that underlying processes are not observable. Examples are Spiegel's (1973) task of 'structuring the emotional chaos' and Worden's (1982) task of 'withdrawing energy and investing it in a new relationship'.

Another conceptual problem with many of the tasks listed is that they implicitly or explicitly define adaptation after the loss in terms of recovery (see also Section 1.3). They thus assume that the level of functioning of the bereaved before the death is the criterion to be attained at the end of the bereavement process. It is, however, probable that this situation is far from desirable to the bereaved. Prior to (and independent of) the loss, the bereaved may have had severe complaints in health, personal and social functioning. It may even be that living with the deceased had become unbearable (something which is likely to occur in suicide-bereaved) and that the death may *enable* the bereaved to function better than before the loss.

2.6   Cognitive stress theory

The above theories on bereavement and grief mainly concentrate on the dynamics of adaptation to loss. In this section, a more general, cognitive approach will be outlined which allows to look at bereavement from an information-processing point of view.

Over the last decennia, a more general cognitive approach to the reactions to loss has been developed on the basis of stress models (Lazarus, 1966; Lazarus & Launier, 1978; Horowitz, 1979). Central to these models is that they accentuate the combination and interaction of physical and psychological arousal, which is based on the perception of events, and which in turn influence perception. This approach is more closely linked to, and originates from experimental psychology (e.g. Neisser, 1976). Stress occurs when the demands on a person tax or exceed his adjustive resources (Lazarus, 1966). Of prime importance to this line of theory is also the notion that human beings perceive and interpret situations on the basis of past experience, and that this experience is organized in a systematic way.

Appraisal of events

Lazarus & Launier (1978) state that the interpretation of a (loss) situation rather than the situation itself determines the consequences for the individual. An individual confronted with a new situation immediately evaluates this situation. This activity is termed 'appraisal'. This can be seen as an immediate attempt to link what happens to one's schemata. Appraisal may occur on a conscious, but also on a more or less automatic level: an experienced driver reacts adequately to a whole range of traffic-situations, without pondering on which course of action to take.

Lazarus (1966) distinguished 'primary' and 'secondary' appraisal. When one is confronted with a new situation, primary appraisal takes place to assess its relevance to well-being. There are three main outcomes of appraisal: a situation may be judged as irrelevant, positive or stressful. If a situation is labeled as stressful, secondary appraisal takes place to decide on a plan for action to solve the problem. This involves taxation of the implications of the situation, ones own capacities to handle the situation, and the choice of adequate coping strategies.

In the case where the situation is judged as stressful, this may be interpreted again in three different ways: challenge, threat or pain. 'Challenge' means that the situation is perceived as an opportunity to grow, as a (positive) possibility for change. 'Threat' indicates that one anticipates a damaging situation which has not yet taken place, as may be constituted by the announcement that one's partner has a fatal disease. 'Pain' refers to damage that has already taken place, which is most clearly the case in the loss of someone close by death.

Primary appraisal also determines intensity and quality of the emotions in the situation: the situation elicits certain thought-processes which trigger specific emotions. A positive outcome of primary appraisal gives rise to feelings of joy or relief. An evaluation in terms of stress may result in more negative emotions. Anger may occur if the situation is perceived as a threat, and may be seen as instrumental in an attempt to change the situation or to avoid the looming damage. When the damage is done, this results in pain or grief. Since in a given situation changing appraisals may occur, the emotions may also alternate quickly.

Secondary appraisal refers to the ongoing assessment of the resources we have available to cope with a situation. In the secondary process, we attempt to choose the optimal course of action to take, in order to minimize damage. Primary and secondary appraisal are highly interrelated: when after secondary appraisal one concludes that insufficient resources are available, this may lead to a new (primary) appraisal of threat[7].

When we apply appraisal in this sense to bereavement reactions, it seems to parallel Bowlby's attachment theory, where the bereaved first protests against the (impending) loss, attempting to revert the situation with searching behavior and anger. Subsequent recognition of the impossibility of changing the situation (Bowlby: to bring back the lost attachment figure) leads to pain and grief.

The process of cognitive adaptation

Horowitz (1979) adopts the view that the individual needs to integrate new information with previous information. He postulates a tendency of the human mind to integrate new with existing information. This tendency causes the new information (= the stressful situation) to be repeatedly represented until the cognitive schemata are in accordance (congruent) with it.

According to Horowitz, the extent to which representation of the new information is repeated is regulated by certain 'controls'[8], a series of processes which select and interpret information, and tries to couple new information with existing schemata. The most important control processes appear to be regulatory, enabling facilitation or inhibition of the input of the new information to be processed. Control processes may comprise inhibiting intrusive thoughts about the event, searching for new information, changing the asserted meaning of the information and revising schemata. Adaptation after a stressful event is considered in terms of regaining optimal control. This involves optimal processing of new information, which in turn requires

---

7   In fact, the rank-order of both forms of appraisal is somewhat trivial, and in later work (e.g. Coyne, Aldwin & Lazarus, 1981) it is stressed there is a constant alternation between them.

8   In accordance with Brom & Kleber (1986) it can be stated that the status and structure of most of these controls remains unclear in the model.

alternation between allowing information in from active memory to be processed, and inhibiting the information flow when it interferes with immediate needs for functioning.

After a stressful event, both processes alternate, often in rapid succession. The victim may involuntarily reexperience the event in his mind's eye, often together with the emotional content. This may interfere considerably with daily functioning. To maintain control, he or she may avoid situations and thoughts which evoke the painful memories of the event. This may be done on a cognitive level (trying to banish it from from thought or memory) and may also manifest itself in behavior (avoiding places and people who are linked to the memories of the stressful event).

An unbalance between permitting the stressful information to be represented and inhibition can result in problems with adaptation. Too much control bars repeated representation in active memory, and invokes denial or 'numbing' which blocks further processing and thus hinders adaptation. Too low a level of control causes excessive emotions and the continual reappearance of the traumatic experience.

Adaptation after a stressful event is thus primarily considered in terms of cognitive restructuring. Horowitz's theory, offering an explanation for the processes observed after stressful life events, may also be applied to bereavement. The formalization of initial processes after the loss is particularly valuable. However, part of the mechanics of the model remains unclear. Except for the input-regulating control process for inhibition and facilitation of information, the way in which an individual makes decisions for a specific control mechanism is not made explicit. The main reason for this is that this is more a 'state' approach to stress. The theory is not concerned with the role of resources in the reactions to stress. Thus, differences in personal style, material resources, and the role of social support are not its primary concern.

2.7   Problems with the empirical application of theories on bereavement

Reviewing the theories that were discussed in the preceding sections, we can make some remarks on their suitability as a basis for the research on bereavement. As pointed out, virtually all the theories listed above have their value in understanding certain aspects of the bereavement process. At the same time, we can signal a number of problems which occur when we want to find a theory that offers a comprehensive framework for studying bereavement.

Empirical verification of theories

In order to employ a bereavement theory as a basis for research it has to meet certain standards. Ideally, a theory must enable us to make predictions from empirical observations and to explain relationships between those observations in terms of the theory. This subsumes a number of properties of such a theory.

In the first place, in research, the concepts employed in the theory must be observable, or unambiguously translatable into observable units. Psychodynamic theories in particular pose problems in this respect. Since similar behavior in individuals may be the result of different internal processes, and vice versa, it is likely that results of systematic observational group-study are subject to multiple psychodynamic interpretations.

Secondly, a theory has to be validated by empirical findings. Agreement between the findings of bereavement research and theory is rare however (Shackleton, 1984; Wortman & Silver, 1989). Many discrepancies between a theory's predictions and empirical findings question the external validity of the theoretical constructs. Often, theories are not supported by empirical evidence, and usually no attempts have been undertaken to adequately test them. In those cases where empirical research did take place to test theoretical hypotheses, it often failed to confirm the theory's predictions.

Wortman & Silver (1989) compared theoretical and traditional clinical assumptions about the 'normal' way to cope with loss (which are often based on grief theories) with empirical evidence. They particularly questioned the necessity of feeling distress, to 'work through' the loss, and the assumption that complete adaptation or recovery after the loss (the final phase in most of the stage- or phase models) is possible. Reviewing the empirical evidence for each of these assumptions, they conclude that there is contradictory evidence for all of them, and that they do not account for the variability in reactions to loss.

Conclusion

An important difference between the theories we discussed lies in their purpose and perspective. Some, such as cognitive stress theory, try to give a general explanation of reactions to stress, and concentrate on a state-like or situational view of the reactions and less on the explanation of individual differences. Psychoanalytic theory explains from a personal dynamical perspective: why does this individual react in this way? On the other hand, the behavioral approach tends to be more change-oriented, and primarily concerned with the question of how to bring about changes in dysfunction after bereavement, while considering intrapsychic reactions as less relevant.

In addition, the existing theories differ, of course, in the specific sources to which they ascribe the symptoms of bereavement. The psychoanalytic theories explain differences in functioning primarily from the characteristics of (early) bonding or cathectic experiences of the bereaved. For behaviorally oriented theory, the explanation is found in the (operant) conditioning by the environment. The

sociobiological approach ignores for a substantial part individual differences as well
as social mechanisms in grief, and emphasizes the role of genetic survival. Post
traumatic stress theory concentrates on a general explanation of the processes, rather
than the individual differences.

Although nowadays the modern versions of neither framework deny the
importance of the other, it shows how the focus of theories on bereavement differs,
and makes comparison difficult.

The validation of theories on bereavement has hitherto not led to the emergence of one
'most suitable' theory. The observations in empirical research typically seem not to fit
in with one single framework. As yet, the advances in theory and the empirical field
have not progressed to the point of offering one framework in which both the
dynamics and the multitude of influences on adaptation and its course are
satisfactorily accounted for.

On the other hand, we see a tendency in the grief literature to apply more general
psychological stress theories to bereavement. Loss of a loved one is more and more
considered to be a type of loss event which, although having specific characteristics,
is not fundamentally different from other life events that require adaptation, such as
loss of a job, physical impairment or divorce.

In line with this, we will look for a more global stress approach to bereavement, in
which today's theoretical and empirical knowledge are empirically tested within an
elaborate framework. The following sections will offer the outline of such a structure.

2.8   Functioning after bereavement: a model of tasks and resources

Adaptation to a stressful event, as seen before, is not only dependent on the
characteristics of that event, but also differ widely from individual to individual.
Many models have been developed which describe the relationships between coping
with stress and the resources a person can draw from[9].

In the earlier models of psychological stress, the accent was on the stressful event
(cf. Section 2.6). In recent times, more attention has been given to the factors which
make up the resource side of the equation. One example is the *model of conservation
of resources* (Hobfoll; 1988, 1989). The basic tenet of this model is that in all
circumstances "..people strive to retain, protect, and build resources and that what is
is threatening to them is the potential or actual loss of these valued resources."
(Hobfoll, 1989). Although setting another goal for coping with stress, the model can
be seen as an elaboration on the one developed by Lazarus et al. in the sense that it is
consistent with their mechanisms of appraisal. Types of resources, proposed by

---

9   For a comprehensive review of stress models see Hobfoll, 1989.

Hobfoll, are *object resources*, valued because of their physical nature, rarity and eventual gain of status they imply (e.g. a mansion, a sports car); *conditions*, resources to the extent that they may provide roles and (social) functions that are sought after (like marriage); *personal characteristics*, which may aid stress resistance, and *energies*, which include resources such as time, money, and information, which serve as facilitators for the acquisition of other resources.

Another categorization that seems helpful in describing the relationships between a person's resources and reactions after bereavement is given by Diekstra (1990). His categorization is a condensation of several stress-models, and based on the 'life span developmental' approach, which considers our life as consisting of a large number of tasks. Some are innately developmental in nature, such as learning to walk or speak. Others are individually chosen tasks, whether or not on the base of social expectations, such as artistic achievement or career development. A third class of tasks is the consequence of situations and events which are often not chosen, but 'happen' to an individual. In the demand-resource model, the stress resulting from these tasks is a function of five components or sets of factors (listed in Table 2.2).

Table 2.2
Components of the demand-resource model

---

(1) *Task-demands* The type, pattern and number of the tasks a person is involved in[10].
(2) *Social support* This comprises affective or emotional support, practical or instrumental support, and informational support.
(3) *Available material resources* Financial, socioeconomic and technical resources.
(4) *Attitudes with regard to task-demands* Self confidence and image, belief in one's own competence, perception of the meaningfulness of a task, among other things influenced by personality traits.
(5) *The environment or context in which the tasks are carried out* such as the neighborhood or area in which one lives.

When a large discrepancy exists between task-demands (1) on the one hand and available support, material resources, attitudes and environment (2 through 5) on the other, this leads to debilitating stress and an increased risk of health deteriorating. In this respect, the model can be seen as belonging to the category of balance models of stress. Although this type of model has recently been under criticism for the likely

---

[10] Note that 'task' in this context has a somewhat different meaning from the one outlined in Section 2.5. There, the tasks were formulated in terms of *goals* to be attained by the bereaved. In the task-resource model, tasks are formulated as *demands* on the bereaved.

overlap between independent and dependent aspects (see Hobfoll, 1989), it seems suited as a framework for bereavement since loss by death is somewhat less likely than other tasks to be a mere *consequence* of the characteristics of the resources. Bereavement thus constitutes a task more or less independent from the resources of the bereaved.

2.8.1   The task-demands of bereavement

Bereavement can be seen as imposing important task-demands on a bereaved, but it is also clear that not every loss imposes the same demands.

It is important to have some indication of the components which make up the *type* of task the bereaved has to cope with. The type of the task-demands is largely defined by the characteristics of the loss, centering on two subjects: the way in which the loss took place, and the characteristics of the person (and therewith the relationship) that was lost.

The loss event

The cause and the circumstances of death define the characteristics of the loss event. The cause of death may encompass a number of (psychologically) relevant aspects: the death may be violent or peaceful, expected or unexpected, natural or unnatural. Also other elements of the loss event may be salient to the bereaved, like his presence or absence at the moment of death, and (partial) responsibility for the death[11].

The age of the deceased can be considered as a characteristic with regard to the timeliness of death. The death of a young person will be regarded as untimely in most societies.

The lost person and relationship

The position the deceased had in the life of the bereaved also defines the type of task the bereaved has to cope with. We can distinguish formal and informal characteristics of this position.

By *formal characteristics* we mean the socio-biological and cultural positions of deceased and bereaved. The most important reflection of formal position is the family relationship (or kinship) between bereaved and deceased. The relationship between spouses is different from that between siblings, or the parent-child relationship. The position of these dyads is not only biologically distinct, but also differs on a cultural and social level. The parent-child combination as a dyad has a different social role than the marital dyad, often with corresponding material and social resources allotted to them.

---

[11] For a more elaborate description see Section 3.3.

Most of the so called 'sociodemographic' characteristics can also be counted among the factors determining the type of task-demands.

The gender of deceased and bereaved not only stands for a biological difference. Also more or less stable psychological and psycho-biological differences exist, e.g. in the area of (psycho)hormonal or immunological differences. Gender also is a denominator for the socio-cultural position of the individual in our society. Often, different qualities are valued in women and men. Women more frequently are (or are expected to be) the principal caregivers to their children. Women also often have different support networks than men. Likewise, the type of support provided by the environment may systematically differ between men and women.

The age of the bereaved determines the place of bereavement in the *pattern* of task-demands an individual has to cope with. The meaning of bereavement may differ with the life phase of the bereaved individual, of which the age of the bereaved can be seen as an indicator. To a young child, who has not yet fully developed his cognitive abilities, it may be difficult or impossible to conceive the permanent loss of his mother. Bereavement during adolescence may be different in nature, since many other developmental (competing) task-demands exist at the same time. The loss of one's spouse in early adulthood during child-rearing may imply a heavier load of demands than losing a spouse at an older age.

Among the *informal characteristics* of the dyad we can count the psychological aspects of the relationship between bereaved and deceased, like the closeness of the relationship, intimacy, and other qualities like dependency and dominance.

Bereavement also has characteristics which make it different in nature from other task-demands. An important aspect of bereavement is that the structure and strength of the resources (2 through 5 in Table 2.2) may profoundly and directly be influenced by the task-demand bereavement (1) itself. The deceased may have been a principal source of social support for the bereaved which is lost permanently, or a major link to other sources of support (2). The deceased may also have been a breadwinner to the bereaved, and there may be a drop in income (3). Whether or not a consequence of the foregoing, a change in the environment and displacement of the bereaved may occur (5). For instance, a bereaved spouse may have to move to a smaller home or a home for the aged.

Bereavement may also *lessen* the task-demands for an individual. Suicide may bring relief from worrying for those close to the victim and death after a long-term illness may mean an end to burdensome care.

Bereavement theories from the demand-resource perspective

When we contrast the theories on bereavement processes discussed in Sections 2.1 to 2.3 with the model of task-demands and resources some hiatuses appear. In most theories, attention to the character and magnitude of the task-demands in bereavement is given to only one aspect.

In psychoanalytically oriented and attachment theory, the main definers of the task demand are the qualities of the relationship with the deceased, while characteristics of the mode of death are largely neglected. In most of the theories on bereavement, the process of adaptation is described as more or less structurally independent from the position the lost person had to the bereaved in a multitude of areas of functioning. However, if we want to study adaptation to bereavement, we cannot treat this as a *ceteris paribus* condition.

With regard to the resources side, there is also the problem of one-sidedness. Typically, in each theory only some resources are considered of importance. In psychoanalysis and attachment theory, individual resources are seen as primarily responsible for (mal)adaptation. In behaviorally oriented theories, the resources of interest are only environmental in nature, such as social reinforcement and social support. The role of material resources is even totally absent in all theories.

To conclude, we can state that the model of task-demands and resources offers a structure which allows us to study the factors that play a role in the adaptation after bereavement in a more comprehensive way. In the next chapter we will give a more precise operationalization of the task-demands of bereavement.

2.8.2   Dimensions of functioning

There is an aspect which has remained undiscussed in the preceding section. Given the demands on a person and his or her resources, in what terms should we define the results of the balance: i.e. the functioning of the person after the loss? In other words: which criteria should we use to describe adaptation after bereavement?

Three dimensions of functioning

The touchstones for functioning after a loss can be derived from the task-models of grief mentioned in Section 2.5. Accomplishment of a task can be seen as the goal of the process of adaptation in a specific area of functioning, and thus be a criterion for functioning. Since in setting the norms for adaptation to loss we do not wish to make assumptions on how it is achieved, intermediary tasks like 'experiencing and expressing painful effects' will be excluded as goals. Each task must also be empirically verifiable.

Since in our study we prefer to examine the *level* of functioning in the bereaved in different areas of functioning, instead of speaking of 'tasks' that have to be fulfilled in the adaptation to bereavement, we will prefer to speak of *dimensions of functioning*.

Following the above criteria and drawing from the tasks mentioned in this section, we can formulate three dimensions[12] of functioning (see Table 2.3). These dimensions comprise the specific reactions to the loss event, as well as the general functioning of the individual in terms of health and social adaptation.

Dimension (a), the level of adaptation to the loss, concentrates on the cognitive and emotional adaptation to the new situation arising from the loss, and thus can be seen as a dimension specific to bereavement. As part of this dimension we may consider both adaptation to the absence of the deceased and adaptation to the trauma of the loss event as such. Dimension (b), the level of psychological and physical health, refers to general functioning of the individual in the new situation which may or may not be a result of the loss. The dimension concerning the level of social functioning (c) can be seen as an indication of the degree to which the bereaved has resources available to respond to current and future task-demands.

Table 2.3
Dimensions of functioning after bereavement

(a)	*The level of adaptation to the loss,* comprising the recognition of the reality of the loss, the development of an image of the circumstances of death, post traumatic stress, and the degree of detachment from the deceased.
(b)	*The level of psychological and physical health,* including the level of physical complaints, depression, and the perception of self-efficacy.
(c)	*The level of social functioning,* comprising the availability of meaningful and supportive relationships with others, and sufficient material and informational resources.

When we look at these dimensions against the background of the demands-resources model presented in the preceding section, we can position them on the result side. Thus, in addition to 'reducing the direct consequences of prolonged stress', which was already on the outcome side of the demands-resources model (corresponding to dimension (b) in Table 2.3), we will also assess functioning in terms of loss-reactions, and the condition of the bereaved's resources (dimensions (a) and (c) in Table 2.3).

---

[12] It must be noted that while employing the term 'dimensions' we do not suggest any level of independence between them. It is very likely that they are related to each other and this has of course to be checked in empirical findings.

2.8.3   A model for the present study

Drawing in this way both from the demands-resource model and the task models of bereavement, we can assemble a model which seems suited to be employed in empirical research. This combination is graphically represented in Fig. 2.1. The characteristics of the demands on the bereaved and the state of his or her resources are listed on the left side of the model. On the right, we find the dimensions of functioning, which are considered to give an indication of the resulting psychosocial situation of the bereaved. Note that in the model, functioning is considered to be a function of both the availability of resources and the need for these resources (as dictated by the task-demands).

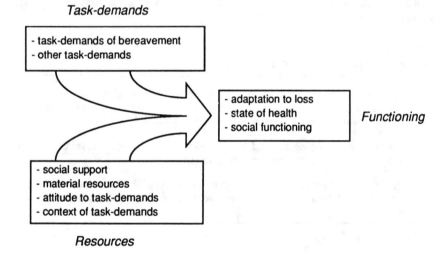

Task-demands

- task-demands of bereavement
- other task-demands

- adaptation to loss
- state of health
- social functioning

Functioning

- social support
- material resources
- attitude to task-demands
- context of task-demands

Resources

Fig. 2.1   *A comprehensive model for the study of the consequences of bereavement.*

The above model will serve as a framework for classifying and describing the phenomena associated with bereavement, without making assumptions on the way in which adaptation is achieved. On the other hand, we can empirically verify which task-demands and characteristics of the resources are most strongly related to adaptation. Theoretically, we assume that different processes may lead to the same desired outcome[13]. A satisfactory level of functioning on a dimension can be looked upon as a part of the adaptation after the loss.

---

13   This complies with Bertalanffy's (1968) notion of 'equifinality' for open (living) systems.

In fact it is dimension (a), the level of adaptation to the loss, that makes the present model a specific model for bereavement. By replacing this 'target' dimension by another, we can make it a more or less universal framework for coping with life events.

Conclusion

In this chapter we discussed a number of theories on grief and bereavement. As we concluded in Section 2.7, the diversity of the viewpoints of most grief-specific theories combined with the lack of systematic empirical evidence for their assertions, makes it necessary to apply a more general framework to study the consequences of bereavement. In the preceding section, we have tried to outline such a framework on the basis of a model of task-demands and resources. We have also defined the type and positions of the variables within that framework. Many aspects of functioning after bereavement may be looked upon as both dependent and independent. When we want to assess functioning after bereavement, we saw that coping with the task-demands of bereavement cannot be the only measure involved. The state of the individual has to be assessed in terms of dealing with the loss (which constitutes the primary task-demand of bereavement), his functioning in terms of psychological and physical health, and social functioning. This is why, rather than selecting only one, we have defined a set of dimensions of functioning.

In the subsequent chapters, we will apply this framework to discuss the findings of empirical research, and use it as a basis for our own empirical study.

Chapter 3

Empirical Research on Bereavement

In general, the field of the empirical investigation into human grief has developed relatively independently from grief or stress theory. Only a few theorists have founded their views on the basis of systematic empirical research. Most researchers in turn do not explicitly put theories to the test, and employ explorative correlational methods.

Different methods have been used to obtain insight in the various aspects of bereavement. One line of study concentrates on epidemiological aspects and tries to link up sociodemographic, morbidity and mortality data in using existing sources of information such as health status, population or death registers, and data from national census institutes. Epidemiological studies typically give insight into morbidity and mortality risk among the bereaved, they are however limited in their scope when it comes to the psychological, emotional and behavioral aspects of bereavement. Although this line of study has specific methodological problems we shall not consider these here (for a discussion, see Bowling, 1987).

Another line of research tries to get a closer look at the situation of he bereaved individual and the processes involved. It typically uses at least partially structured survey methods such as interviews or questionnaires, using self-report as the most important source of information. The design of these studies is either cross-sectional or longitudinal. In cross-sectional studies the situation is assessed at one point in time, and often the time between the loss and the study differs considerably between participants. In longitudinal studies, a group of bereaved individuals is followed over time, and multiple interviews or questionnaires are held. In this way, it is possible to monitor individual change over time, and to find factors that contribute to change. Typically, the time since bereavement at the successive measurements is more or less equal for each respondent.

In this chapter we will take a closer look at what is known about adaptation after bereavement from an empirical point of view. In that aim, in Section 3.1 we will first discuss the commonly employed measures of adaptation. In Section 3.2 the findings on the prevalence of poor adaptation after bereavement are discussed.

In looking at the many factors which influence adaptation after loss, we have to employ a rationale by which to arrange them. A template which is suited for this is the classification of task-demands, resources and functioning, as was presented in Section 2.8.

In Section 3.3 we will look at the role of task-demands in adaptation after bereavement. Aspects of the task-demands that will be discussed are the mode of death, the formal family relationship (or kinship) to the deceased, and the qualitative aspects of the relationship with the deceased. Also other aspects, related to the *pattern* of task-demands, will be discussed here such as the influence of concurrent and antecedent stressors, and age and sex of the bereaved on adaptation.

In Sections 3.4 through 3.6 the relationship between resources and adaptation will be discussed. First the effect of social support for the completion of the task-demands on adaptation will be examined (Section 3.4). Then, the role of available material resources will be questioned in terms of socioeconomic status (Section 3.5). Finally, the role of attitude with regard to the task-demands of bereavement will be considered in terms of the characteristics of personality and coping style (Section 3.6).

In Section 3.7 we will look at the results of multivariate studies into the relative contributions of task-demands and resources in adaptation. At the end of the chapter some general conclusions will be drawn.

3.1   Indicators of functioning after bereavement

Empirical studies have concentrated on the assessment of different aspects of bereavement outcome, or just in terms of well-being. In order to map the type, incidence, prevalence and seriousness of problems during a given period after bereavement, most studies measure functioning in one or more of the following areas:

- *Mortality*
- *Physical health* in terms of (self-reported) complaints or immunologic and physiological (stress) measures.
- *Psychological health* mostly in terms of depression, anxiety, neuroticism, and suicidal ideation.
- *Social functioning* reflected by involvement with others or social support
- *Detachment from the deceased* in terms of the degree to which the bereaved has accepted, or adapted to the new situation, and can reengage in the demands of daily life.

In most of the studies, not all these indicators of functioning are assessed. Epidemiological studies often focus on mortality, and sometimes health measures, while observational studies employing interviews or questionnaires also look at social functioning, psychological health and detachment.

In recent years, more biopsychosocial studies have appeared that include objective measures of physical (e.g. immunological and endocrinological) functioning along with self-reported physical and psychological complaints, and social functioning (e.g. Zisook, 1987; Calabrese et al. 1987; Baron et al., 1990).

3.2 Prevalence of ill-health and poor functioning after bereavement

One of the important goals of empirical research on bereavement is to learn more about *poor* functioning after the loss. An initial step in many population studies is often to estimate the percentage of the bereaved population that evidences problems after loss.

However, there are a number of serious methodological problems in comparing data on adaptation as collected in bereavement outcome studies. One major difficulty resides in the different ways of assessing adaptation. Some studies use the respondent's own judgement about adjustment (Zisook et al., 1987). Others employ bereavement specific scales (Zisook & Lyons, 1988). Yet others use expert judgements of the level of well-being of the survivor (e.g. Parkes & Weiss, 1983). A related problem is the diversity and obscurity of the criteria for judging functioning as 'poor' or 'bad'. Thus the percentages of maladaptation reported in studies may reflect different and incomparable criteria. Fortunately, in the last decade, the use of validated general depression criteria as outcome measures has increased (e.g. Lund et al. 1986; Stroebe et al., 1988; van der Wal, 1988).

In a number of studies efforts have been made to determine the number of people who do not or who only partially recover after bereavement. Once again, as explained above, they are difficult to compare, which has to be taken into account while interpreting findings of several (recent) studies, shown in Table 3.1.

The percentage of persons having severe difficulties in adjustment one to four years after bereavement, range from 18% to 34% in general population studies. Zisook & Lyons' (1988) study gives much higher percentages. The latter is, however, not comparable with the majority since it was conducted in a clinical population applying for mental health treatment.

Interestingly, the length of time passed since bereavement seems not to be associated with a lower poor-outcome percentage. In longitudinal studies this has been confirmed, especially for the period after the first year.

Zisook & Schuchter (1986) found, after an initial decrease in symptoms, virtually no change in depression, anxiety, and other distress symptoms over a period of 49 months after the loss. Work, social functioning and relationships with others, however, continued to improve slowly after the first year of bereavement. Lehman, Wortman & Williams (1987), who investigated the long-term effects of losing a spouse or child in a motor vehicle crash, found no differences in adaptation between those who lost child or spouse 4-5 years ago and those 6-7 years ago. They also

Table 3.1
Prevalence of poor functioning after bereavement in some outcome studies.

Study	Population	Age	Source of sample	N	Respons	Time since loss	Poor functioning	Criterion
Lund, Caserta & Dimond (1986)	Widowed (M+F)	>50	Obituaries	161	39%	3-4 Weeks	15% (M) 19% (F)	At least mild depression (Zung depression scale)
Zisook, Schuchter & Lyons (1987a)	Widows	26-83	Department of Health Services	189	13%	2 Months	28%	Clinical depression (DSM III criterion)
Stroebe, Stroebe & Domittner (1988)	Widowed (M+F)	M=53.8	Death registers	60**	39%	6 Months	42%	At least mild depression (BDI-criterion Beck)
Maddison & Walker (1967)	Widows	45-60*	Death registers	132	48%	13 Months	21%	Severe health deterioration (authors judgment)
Stroebe, Stroebe & Domittner (1988)	Follow-up earlier sample			49**	32%	2 Years	27%	At least mild depression (BDI-criterion Beck)
Lund, Caserta & Dimond (1986)	Follow-up earlier sample			138	39%	2 Years	20% (M) 14% (F)	At least mild depression (Zung depression scale)
Parkes & Weiss (1983)	Widowed (M+F)	<64	Obituaries	68	25%	4 Years	34%	'Bad outcome': combination of coders overall assessment
Zisook, Schuchter & Lyons (1987b)	Widows	24-66	Department of Public Health	70	30%	4 Years	20%	Respondent's rating of being fairly or poorly adjusted
Zisook & Lyons (1988)	Bereaved family members	18-94	Mental hospital intakes	430	100%	0-64 Years	63% (Parents) 56% (Spouses) 48% (Siblings) 46%(Ad.chldrn)	Patient feeling that dealing with the loss was still difficult

Note: * = Age of the deceased spouse, ** = Excluding the matched controlgroup (n=60) found smaller change in adaptation between later points in time after loss. Furthermore, it seems that initially effective copers with the loss remain effective throughout the first year (Johnson, Lund & Dimond, 1986).

Bereavement may be related to serious mental health problems, as is shown in the study of Zisook & Lyons (1988). They found unresolved grief in 210 (21%) of a sample of 1,000 patients who completed an intake questionnaire at the Gifford Mental Health Clinic. Of 430 patients who had lost at least one relative, 53% evidenced unresolved grief. Loss of mother resulted more often in unresolved grief (among 46%) than loss of father (among 39%). No differences between relationships was found for other variables such as depression, health or psychosocial impairment. This is not surprising since the sample consisted of people applying for psychological or psychiatric treatment. Furthermore it is likely that in such a clinical population often a premorbid personality structure existed, giving rise to more difficulties in coping with life stresses.

Conclusion

A valid comparison of outcome studies of bereavement is difficult and sometimes impossible. Criteria for poor adaptation often differ widely, and are sometimes unclear or even not explicitly mentioned. Despite this, there is evidence that the impact of the loss may play a role in severe mental health problems.

The general picture is that, several years after the loss, between one-fifth and one-third of the bereaved still show moderate to severe problems in adaptation. To what extent the loss-event forms a luxation point for latent problems is unclear. Due to typically low response percentages, it is furthermore not certain whether these percentages adequately reflect population figures. The direction of this bias might be different for male and female samples, leading to an underestimation for men and an overestimation for women (see Section 3.3.3).

From this point, it appears important to find factors that *differentiate* outcome variability, in order to discover characteristics that distinguish between those bereaved who evidence problems and those who appear to adapt successfully to the loss. In the following sections, the findings of observational (epidemiological and survey) studies in this area will be reviewed and discussed.

3.3 The task-demands of bereavement

The relationship between the characteristics of bereavement and adaptation will be discussed here. First, factors related to the type of the task-demands such as mode of death, sex and relationship to the deceased will be highlighted, followed by a discussion on factors related to the patterning and number of task-demands such as age of the bereaved and other task-demands.

3.3.1   Mode of death and adaptation

Mode of death may determine to a certain extent the problems the bereaved have to deal with. In bereavement terms, each mode of death can be seen as a combination of aspects which may play a relatively independent role in adaptation to loss. The different modes of death can be classified according to different dimensions:

- Expectedness (expected versus unexpected)
- Naturalness (natural versus unnatural)
- Responsibility or actor (self versus other killing the deceased)
- Timeliness (timely versus untimely)

Each cause of death can be ranged along each of these dimensions. In Table 3.2, the left column lists a number of modes of death. The subsequent columns indicate the global position of each of these on the three dimensions related to mode of death. The fourth dimension is not directly or uniquely related to the mode of death, but also to age of the deceased, individual aspects and mode of death. For instance: the death of a young child will virtually always be considered as untimely. On the other hand, the death of a severely handicapped, suffering baby may sometimes be experienced as timely. The death of an old man who has suffered a long-term illness may be felt as timely, but so may be in some cases the suicide-death of a younger person with a long history of severe mental problems and depression.

While different combinations of expectedness, naturalness and responsibility are essential elements in the profile of each death, we will look at them in more detail before concentrating on mode of death. Attention will be given to some qualitative and adaptational differences between suicide death, traffic-fatality death and long-term illness death in their consequences.

Expectedness of death

Most of the studies including forewarning of death as a variable are those conducted among bereaved from sudden natural death causes and long-term and short-term illness death. The results are unequivocal. In the majority of the studies, it appears that forewarning of death has no (e.g. Roach & Kitson, 1989) or very little impact (Cleiren, van der Wal & Diekstra, 1988) on the adaptation after bereavement, in others it seems to be the major predictor of outcome (Carey, 1977). The research that finds a worse outcome after unexpected death is often conducted among a younger age group (see Table 3.3). Ball (1977-1978) and Parkes & Weiss (1983) found this association in a (sub)sample aged under 46. Parkes (1975b) stated that in older samples death, even sudden death, will not be entirely unexpected. For the effect of sudden-loss to be detrimental to the survivor, the loss has to be untimely as well. This may indeed be an indication that the study of forewarning has to be controlled for untimeliness (or for age of the deceased, being its indicator).

Table 3.2
Dimensions of the cause of death

Mode of death	Expectedness	Naturalness	Actor
Suicide	Low/high	Unnatural	Deceased
Traffic-fatality	Low	Unnatural	Deceased/other
Homicide	Low	Unnatural	Other
Sudden illness	Low	Natural	Unclear
Prolonged illness	High	Natural	Unclear

Parkes (1975a), in comparing sudden and short-term illness death with long-term illness death, found that short forewarning of the spouse's death was predictive of bad outcome. Poor outcome was associated with cause of death not being cancer, short terminal illness, and lack of opportunity to discuss death with partner. However, since Parkes did not control for mode of death and both accidents and short-term illness are included in the 'short preparation group', it is not clear whether it is 'preparation time' or 'mode of death' which account for the effect.

Attempting to distinguish between these effects, Sanders (1983) in her study of 86 bereaved close family members, spouses and parents, divided the sample into a sudden death group, a short-term chronic illness (less than 6 months) group and a long-term chronic illness (more than 6 months) group. Shortly after bereavement, she found similar levels of grief for all three groups, but at 18 months the short-term chronic illness group was better off than the other two. The sudden death group showed higher depression scores at 18 months than at 2 months, elevation on somatization and physical symptom scales, more anger, and feelings of loss of control. Unfortunately, a very important not controlled factor may have confounded these results. There were more parent deaths in the short-term illness death group (58% vs. 7% and 18%), and more children deaths in the sudden-death group (30% vs. 8% and 7%). Since loss of a child is estimated to have the most serious consequences (see also Section 3.3.5), and adult children who lose a parent are known to be the least affected kinship group in bereavement it may be kinship that is responsible for this result (cf. Sanders, 1980; Zisook & Lyons, 1988; van der Wal, 1988).

Table 3.3
Overview of studies on the influence of forewarning on functioning.

Study	Sample	Age (years)	Time since bereavement	Beneficial effect of forewarning on functioning ?
Cleiren et al. (1988)	Family members	M = 46	4 Months	No
Gerber et al. (1975)	Widowed	M= 67	6 Months	No
Ball (1977-1978)	Widows	18-75	6 Months	Under 46: slight Over 46 : no
Bornstein et al. (1973)	Widowed	M= 61	13 Months	No
Parkes & Weiss (1983)	Widowed	< 45	3 Weeks 13 Months 2-4 Years	Yes Yes Yes
Hill et al. (1988)	Widows	> 55	2 Months 6 Months 12 Months	No No No
Maddison & Walker (1967)	Widows	45-60	13 Months	No
Carey (1979-1980)	Widows	Med.57	13-16 Months	Yes

There is some indication that forewarning of the impending death may elicit specific coping mechanisms in the bereaved. Remondet et.al. (1987) conducted a retrospective study of the influence of rehearsal before widowhood to adaptation afterward. 'Behavioral' rehearsal, such as social comparison with the widowed, and making plans for their future, appeared to be adaptive, and associated with higher well-being after the loss. Bereaved who reported they had been ruminating about the death and its implications (cognitive rehearsal) evidenced more problems in adapting to the loss. Along the same lines Hill et.al. (1988) constructed a scale to measure, what they called, 'spontaneous rehearsal' during the time before bereavement. This was operationalized as discussions on the subjects of funeral arrangements, financial security, fears of being left behind, and what the future would be when the spouse died before them. They found that widows who before bereavement had spontaneously rehearsed for the time after bereavement were *worse* of in depression terms than those who had not rehearsed. This finding is not very surprising, since their concept of 'spontaneous rehearsal' strongly resembles worrying or ruminating about the time after the loss. These activities may reflect fear of being unable to cope rather than adaptive preparation.

Cleiren et al. (1988) found that the length of time that the bereaved had been aware of the impending death did only feebly predict outcome in terms of health and post-traumatic stress. A much better predictor appeared to be the extent to which the bereaved had given up hope for recovery of the patient during the last month of his life. When this predictor was partialled out, it appeared that the duration of forewarning did not predict adaptation to the loss at all. Giving up hope may be seen as a cognitive preparation for the loss. Although forewarning in principle *enables* the bereaved to cognitively prepare, preparation is not given with forewarning itself.

Natural versus unnatural death

Unnatural causes of death are more often unexpected and untimely than natural deaths. A human actor is usually involved in bringing about the death, purposely or accidently.

An unnatural death is often a violent death. The body of the deceased may be severely damaged or mutilated. Identification by family members may be necessary, and this may in itself be a traumatic experience. The unexpected confrontation of the finder of the body, especially if this is a family member, may constitute an even greater shock (Van der Wal & Cleiren, 1990).

One of the differences with a natural death is that the police is involved. The investigation, especially in the case of murder, and uncertainty about suicide or murder may be lengthy. When not conducted carefully with regard to the survivors this may be a source of intense additional stress (Barraclough & Shepherd, 1976, 1977; Van der Wal & Cleiren, 1990).

Kitson et al. (1989) in their review of the literature state that initial responses are the same for both unnatural and natural death causes, but that some of the particular characteristics correlated to suicide and homicide may debilitate longer-term adjustment.

Vargas, Loya & Vargas (1984) investigated the differences between natural, accident, suicide and homicide deaths. They found that accidents and homicides elicited the most intense grief reactions. Bereaved from natural causes and suicide had less intense reactions. However, the study was not controlled for kinship: the accident and homicide group consisted for the larger part of parents, the natural death group were mostly spouses, while the bereaved from suicide were mostly siblings. It might well be that the differences found are entirely attributable to kinship.

Responsibility for the death

We can distinguish two types of responsibility for the death of the deceased: one is the *proximate* responsibility, which pertains to the action of the death itself, the other can be seen as *ultimate* responsibility: the array of reasons which led to the death. Proximate responsibility is closely related to the mode of death: in the case of a murder, a human being other than the deceased was the actor. In the case of suicide it is the deceased him or herself.

Coming to terms with the loss may be more complicated when it is brought about by someone else. Often anger towards the person responsible is long-lasting and distressing. In those cases where a natural person is responsible, along with the police inquiry, there may be a wearisome juridical (criminal) procedure. Dissatisfaction with a verdict, and the question whether or not to start an appeal procedure may prolong the distress (van der Wal & Cleiren, 1990).

The ultimate responsibility is often much harder, or even impossible to retrace and may be attributable to entirely different sources. For instance, the murder victim may have started the fight in which he was killed, or a suicide victim may have been pushed to his act by people in the environment, by the community, or by extreme misfortune. Preoccupation with the question of who or what was ultimately responsible for the death is common, especially among bereaved after suicide (van der Wal, 1988).

Conclusion

The effect of forewarning of death on adaptation in bereavement is not clear-cut. When effects are found, they indicate the longer the time of forewarning, the better the adaptation. This has mostly been found in younger (widowed) samples. In forewarning, preparation or rehearsal for a life without the deceased may be an intervening variable which determines whether outcome is positively influenced. The type of rehearsal seems important however. A positive attitude with regard to ones ability to cope with a life without the spouse seems to improve adaptation afterwards, while ideations in terms of ruminations and fears for the time after the loss forebode difficulties.

Of unnatural death causes, it is presumed that adaptation may pose greater problems. This may also depend on juridical and other procedures which are specific for unnatural death causes.

As shown in 2.4.1, each mode of death is a combination of different dimensions. In studying the influence of naturalness of the mode of death for instance, it may be difficult to distinguish this from the expectedness of death. By the same token, to what extent the difference on outcome measures can be ascribed to forewarning itself, remains questionable. In many studies, forewarning is entangled and confounded with mode of death and untimeliness of death. It might very well be that those two variables account for a major part for the effect now attributed to forewarning (cf. Carey, 1979-1980, Parkes & Weiss, 1983).

There are also a number of methodological differences which make the available studies difficult to compare. The definition of 'long-term illness', 'sudden death' and 'unexpected death' on one hand, and 'short-term illness', 'prolonged death' and 'expected death' on the other hand differ considerably with the authors. Another problem is the often retrospective assessment of forewarning, which may be colored by the present (psychological) health situation.

3.3.2 Qualitative differences between modes of death

In this section, some qualitative differences between three modes of death: i.e. suicide, traffic-fatality and long-term illness death will be discussed. The reason for the selection of these modes of death is that they are the causes of death under study in the subsequent empirical study.

3.3.2.1 Suicide

In 1986, in the Netherlands 1604 people died by suicide (CBS, 1988). This amounts to 1.3% of the total number of death in that year. Herewith, the number of suicide victims outnumbered the number of deaths in traffic-fatalities (1491). Like for most other modes of death, suicide occurs more frequently among men (in 62% of the cases) than among women.

Van der Wal (1988, 1989-1990) reviewing the literature on suicide-loss lists a number of qualitative differences with other causes of death. The bereaved may engage in a lengthy search for the motives of the deceased to commit suicide. Also religious questions regarding the fate of the deceased may arise. Envisaging the fact that suicide is the death cause may be so painful that this is denied. In contacts with others, the bereaved may conceal the cause of death, for fear of stigmatization. The bereaved are more prone to feelings of being rejected by the deceased (Barrett & Scott; 1987). The survivor may also fear being hereditarily susceptible to the same problems, and may be afraid of committing suicide as well.

Van der Wal (1988) stresses that the aforementioned characteristics do not generally occur, and that the extent of their impact on adaptation to the loss is not clear.

In some countries, a public inquiry is held to establish the death as a suicide, and the results of these inquests are sometimes published. Shephard & Barraclough

(1976) found these to be a particularly stressful aspects for the suicide bereaved. Newspaper publication of the inquiry was often a cause of further grief.

There are also some characteristics that are not unique to suicide bereavement, but which are believed to play a more prominent role in comparison to other causes.There may be feelings of guilt for not having prevented or intervened at an earlier stage. Henslin (1970), Wallace (1973) and Van der Wal (1988) found more guilt and suicide amongst bereaved from suicide. The bereaved may be angry with the deceased for leaving him/her behind, and ashamed for what has happened (Barrett & Scott, 1987; Van der Wal, 1988). Social support may be less, because of the unacceptable character of suicide in society.

The extent to which suicide is an 'unexpected' death may differ from case to case. It does not always come as a complete surprise. The suicide is often preceded by a history of severe mental health problems and depression. Earlier attempt(s) may have taken place, and the deceased may have threatened to kill him- or herself before.

3.3.2.2   Death by traffic-accident

In 1984, 1,615 people died in a traffic-fatality (CBS, 1985). A large part (36%) of them were between 15 and 29 years old. Traffic accidents are the principle cause of death for younger age groups. Most of the victims died immediately (50%) or within four days after the accident (42%). Most of them were men (73%). The number of traffic-deaths appears to be slowly decreasing over the last 20 years.

The loss of someone close in a traffic accident is virtually always unexpected, and comes as a great shock. Since traffic accidents furthermore are the principle cause of death for younger age groups, they are generally felt as untimely. Often, a second party is involved which caused the accident and more or less clearly 'killed' the deceased. In those cases elements of manslaughter or murder are present. In others, it remains unclear what or who caused the accident, leaving open explanations such as heart attack, suicide, or an unknown second party. Sometimes several people are killed in the same accident, and the bereaved suffer a multiple loss.

It seems that bereavement from traffic-fatalities encompasses a number of risk factors for developing health problems. There has been very little systematic research on this form of bereavement however. One study was performed by Lehman, Wortman & Williams (1987). They interviewed 39 spouses and parents of people who died in motor vehicle crashes 4 to 7 years after bereavement and compared them to matched non-bereaved controls. Notwithstanding the long time since bereavement, they found marked differences in general functioning, depression and psychiatric symptoms, especially in spouses. Many of the respondents (up to 85%) continued to ruminate about the accident, what might have been done to prevent it, and it seemed the larger part was unable to accept the loss or find any meaning in it (68% of the spouses, 59% of the parents). About 38% of the sample still reported that the death sometimes felt unreal and that they sometimes felt they would wake up and it would prove not to be true. On the whole the bereaved sample still showed severe signs of distress. The scores on 7 out of 9 mental health scales were at the same level as those for psychiatric outpatients.

3.3.2.3   Death after long-term illness

Death after an illness is the most common type of death in Western industrialized countries. In 1986, in the Netherlands, 87,177 people died from the consequences of malignant neoplasms (cancer) or diseases of the circulatory system, together accounting for 70% of all deaths in that year.

There are several aspects which distinguish bereavement after a fatal chronic disease from other modes of death. Taking care of the patient, especially when exercised during a protracted period of time, may be an exhausting and traumatic experience (Silverman, 1974). The intensive and lengthy care may lead to social withdrawal and social isolation. This in turn may lead to a lack of social support in the time after bereavement (Fulton & Gottesman, 1980; Sanders 1982-1983). On the other hand, this mode of death generally offers a possibility of anticipating and preparing for the loss (see also Section 3.3.1), and bidding the dying person farewell.
   A number of authors have investigated the influence of duration of illness on bereavement outcome. Gerber, et al. (1975) found no difference in medical consumption and health between widowed from a sudden illness death and those who had experienced a forewarned death. They found, however, that an extended illness period (more than 6 months) lead to an increase in medical complaints and psychotropic medicine intake. Sanders (1983) also found that long-term chronic illness (longer than 6 months) resulted in relatively more feelings of isolation, alienation and emotional upset. It is probable that those problems are related to exhaustion, due to excessive and intensive long-term care (Cleiren et al., 1989). Death may thus also lead to a sense of relief, often bringing an end to unbearable suffering of the deceased and burdensome care by the bereaved.
   Some proof that long-term illness death is related to an earlier (pre-bereavement) onset of health problems was found by Lundin (1984a). He compared unexpected and expected deaths with a population control group, and found that there was a difference in onset of psychological and health problems for the bereaved in the expected death group. Their state of health was already worse than in the population and the sudden-death group before bereavement, but did not show a decline after the death of spouse or child. The health status of the sudden death group was comparable

with general population before bereavement, but worsened considerably afterwards. In an eight-year follow up study, Lundin (1984b) found no significant differences between sudden and unexpected bereavement groups on several outcome measures.

3.3.2.4   Comparative studies into mode of death

As mentioned in Section 3.3.1, differences in mode of death imply differences on a number of psychologically relevant dimensions. Suicide, in this respect, is unique. Of the unnatural causes, it is the only one in which actor (killer) and victim are always the same person. This is possibly one of the main reasons why many of the comparative studies into mode of death contrast suicide bereavement with other (natural and/or unnatural) modes of death.

Suicide versus other modes of death

Barrett & Scott (1987, 1990) studied 57 widowed from suicide, accidental death, sudden natural death and long-term illness death, 2 to 4 years after bereavement. They found no general differences between suicide and non-suicide bereavement outcome. Suicide bereaved showed slightly more grief reactions and more feelings of shame, felt more stigmatized and rejected, but evidenced virtually the same level of adaptation as the other groups. Shepard & Baraclough (1974) and McNiel et al. (1988) also found no overall difference between functioning after suicide and the adaptation after other modes of death. Demi (1984) compared suicide with unexpected natural death and accidental deaths in 40 widowed, between 12 and 21 months after the loss. She found no difference with regard to the level of social adaptation. There were some differences in the patterns of social adjustment. Suicide survivors evidenced more guilt and resentment. More important in determining outcome than the cause of death was the suspicion that the spouse might die (forewarning). Range & Niss (1990) conducted a small scale study among 68 students who were bereaved more then two years previously. They compared bereavement after suicide, homicide, accidents, natural anticipated and natural unanticipated death. They found no differences between any of the causes of death in terms of social support and a range of outcome measures. This result must, however, be interpreted with caution, since in the natural death groups, the deceased was more likely to be a family member than in the other groups[1].

Farberow et al. (1987), comparing suicide with natural death, interviewed 307 older widowed 2 months after the loss. The only significant difference between the two groups was a stronger anxiety reaction in bereaved by suicide.

---

[1]   As will be pointed out in Section 3.3.5, the kinship relationship to the deceased may be of major importance in adaptation to bereavement.

Suicide versus accidental death

Flesh (1977) compared death by accident with suicide. She studied 69 children, parents and siblings of the deceased one month after loss, and found that 52% of the suicide survivors showed impaired functioning but that among accident survivors this percentage was even 69%. It is unclear, however, whether or not the groups were matched with regard to kinship to the deceased. Pennebaker & O'Heeron (1984), in a small scale study of 19 widowed, 10 to 18 months after bereavement, found no appreciable differences in outcome between suicide or accidental death. Suicide survivors confided more in others. Somewhat similar results were found by Trolley (1986) in a study among 40 bereaved parents in self-help groups, 6 months after the loss. He found no differences in outcome between suicide and vehicular accidents, but there was a difference in the themes in the grief process.

Van der Wal (1988), comparing suicide and traffic-fatality bereaved four months after the loss[2] found that there was only a little difference between those groups on a series of outcome measures. Survivors of traffic-fatalities had more difficulties with missing the deceased. Feelings of relief and guilt, and negative reactions of the environment were found more often among the bereaved from suicide. The latter were also somewhat, but not much, less socially integrated, and not less satisfied with social support.

Conclusion

Sanders (1988) states that the evidence of a greater impact of suicide above other modes of death is meager. Still, she estimates that the bereaved from suicide form a higher risk group. Findings in systematic research do not confirm this view. In general, it seems that the level of adjustment is virtually the same for suicide and other kinds of bereavement, but that the themes during the process may be somewhat different. The omission to control for relationship to the deceased in much of the comparative research into mode of death undermines, to a substantial degree, its conclusions. More information about the effect of kinship might substantially alter these.

3.3.3   Sex and adaptation

As was pointed out in Section 2.8, sex of the bereaved determines to a substantial degree the type and the patterning of task-demands for an individual. Sex not only encompasses a more or less fixed general difference in physical (e.g. endocrinological) functioning. It is generally related to specific socio-cultural roles

---

[2]   Subsamples of the present study

and development. The social position, access to resources, and ways of coping may differ according to sex. Social support obeys different rules for men and women: in our society physical supportive contact, for example, is less likely to be given to men than to women, and women more often than men seem to be mediators in supportive social networks. In this perspective, the sex of the bereaved can also be considered as one of the aspects defining the situation after bereavement.

In the discussion, a distinction will be made between the findings on morbidity after bereavement in terms of (mental) health problems, and mortality.

Sex differences in morbidity among bereaved spouses

In the general population, women report higher distress and depression than men. Several authors have commented on the reasons for differences in reported complaints between the sexes. Wingard (1984) concludes in a review that there are general sex differences in illness behavior, utilization of health services, and physicians behavior. In the Dutch population, the same relationships as found by Wingard can be observed (CBS, 1984). Parkes & Brown (1972) concluded that men typically report less symptoms and affective distress than women, and that this existing difference makes widows appear more distressed than widowers. Stroebe & Stroebe (1985, 1989-1990) who share this view, state that another probable bias in interview studies is that men employ more stringent norms of self-control than women. When depressed, this makes them more afraid of showing emotion. The authors hypothesize that this may in turn lead to more men refusing participation in interview research. Written questionnaires are perhaps less sensitive to this form of drop-out. Stroebe & Stroebe (1987, 1989-1990) in their non-response study found indications for sex-specific differences in depression between those who refuse and those who participate in bereavement research. It appeared that male refusers were more depressed than cooperating males, while female refusers were *less* depressed than cooperating females.

In bereavement research, the bereavement reactions of widowers are a relatively under-researched area. Much of the research has concentrated on widows. One probable reason for this is that there are more bereaved women than bereaved men, especially in the older age groups. It seems that the available comparative research in this area comes up with inconsistent findings.

In some cases no difference is found between bereaved men and women. (Clayton, 1974; Clayton et al., 1972; Heyman et al.,1973; Gallagher et al., 1983; Lund, Caserta & Dimond, 1986).

Some researchers find that widows experience more difficulties in adjusting to the loss than widowers (Farnsworth et al., 1989; Carey, 1979-1980; Lopata, 1973; Greenblatt, 1978). In a study conducted among 114 acutely bereaved spouses, one month after bereavement, Jacobs et al. (1986) found that widows showed more numbness, disbelief and depression, but both sexes evidenced equal yearning for the deceased and a tendency to cry. Arens (1982-83) in a national probability sample found widows to be in poorer health than widowers and linked this to deprivation of financial support. The majority of studies, however, finds that widowers experience more difficulties after the loss (Berardo, 1968; Gerber et al., 1975; Gove & Shin, 1989; Helsing et al., 1981; Parkes, 1970, 1975; Parkes & Brown, 1972; Rees et al., 1967; Richards & McCallum, 1979; Stroebe et al., 1981; Stroebe & Stroebe, 1983; Young et al., 1963).

Studies which include married control groups can provide insight into the excess-risk of bereavement for male spouses. Virtually all studies of this type conclude that widowers are relatively more depressed upon bereavement (Parkes & Brown, 1972; Stroebe & Stroebe, 1985; Radloff, 1975) and show more mental illness (Gove, 1972a; Bloom et al., 1978) than their married counterparts, whereas for women this difference is much smaller or even absent.

Glick et al. (1974) concluded that widowers take longer to recover than widows, and stay significantly more depressed and have poorer physical health than married men. Widows had higher scores on depression after one year, but later on they were no more depressed than married women.

In contrast, Gallagher et al. (1983), interviewing bereaved men and women at 2 months and matching them with married controls, found no excess-risk for depression in either sex. However, their response rate was quite low (30%). It might well be that a possible interaction here is blurred by a relative underestimation of depression in widowers, and overestimation in widows, due to differences between refusers and cooperators, as mentioned above by Stroebe & Stroebe (1987, 1989-1990).

Sex differences in morbidity in other than spousal relationships

Much less is known about sex differences in other relationships. Some data are available on differences among parents who lose a child. Fish (1986) found mothers to be more strongly affected than fathers. They felt more isolated than their husbands. Zisook & Lyons (1988) also found mothers to be more seriously affected than fathers, moreover they came out as the most affected group compared to spouses, siblings, children and friends. Van der Wal (1988), in a subsample of the present study, found that among the children, siblings and parents of the deceased, the women experienced higher levels of depression than men. This contrasts with the findings for bereaved spouses, where depression was highest among men.

In their overview of the literature on sex differences Stroebe & Stroebe (1983) stated that all methodological shortcomings in empirical studies taken into account, it is clear that men suffer more. As a possible explanation they suggest that widowed men have less resources in emotional support and nursing than widows. Their access to social interaction diminishes as they loose the intermediary function of their wife. Some evidence for this role-related explanation is provided by van der Wal's (1988) study, since he found men to be less affected than women in losses other than spousal, as the latter are not accompanied by the disappearance of this type of resources.

Sex differences in mortality

Although, in the general population, women evidence more health complaints, men have higher mortality rates for all modes of death than women. The difference in mortality may be attributable to differences in lifestyle and biological factors.

In the area of epidemiological studies into mortality there is no consensus either. Most of the studies report more serious illness and higher mortality in widowers (Helsing & Szklo, 1981; Kaprio, Koskenvuo & Rita, 1987; Reissman et al. ,1985). They generally find a higher long-term risk for widowers, possibly connected to social isolation when they do not remarry. Jones (1987) investigated a 1% sample of population England and Wales in the period 1971-1981. He found no excess post-bereavement mortality from heart disease in either sex, but for all death causes there was a peak over the first six months for widows, while for widowers the excess-risk was less sharp but nonetheless marked over a longer period of time following bereavement. Kraus & Lilienfeld (1959) and Stroebe et al. (1981) found that widowers have more excessive mortality rates from all causes than do widows compared with married controls.

In contrast, a 10-year follow-up study of an American national sample (N=13,380) by McCrae & Costa (1988) found that the widowed were no more likely to die in between surveys than married, and were no more affected on measures of self-rated health, psychological well-being and depression. However, in their study the exact period of time between bereavement and interview was not known, and for most participants this should be seen in terms of decades rather than months or years. Since many other life-events may have occurred in the meanwhile for both bereaved and non-bereaved, and a possible initial loss effect may have played a relatively small role in this result.

In a recent 20-year prospective study in an American nationally representative sample, Smith (1990) compared mortality among a group of 147 widowers and 380 widows with a matched group of 1108 married couples. He found no excess-risk for either men or women above the age of 64. He found an interesting differential excess-risk for men and women between 40 through 64 years old. While both evidenced a clear excess mortality risk, for widowers the greatest excess-risk exists when their wives die relatively suddenly (with less than six months between death and onset of the conditions which led to the death). For widows, the excess-risk was most marked when their husbands died after a chronic medical condition (more than six months between death and onset of the conditions which led to the death).

Reviewing the literature on mortality among the widowed, Stroebe & Stroebe (1987) conclude, as does Bowling (1987), that there are some indications that widowers are most at risk during the first half year of bereavement, and that for widows the peak in risk occurs during the second year.

In the excess mortality after bereavement, suicide takes an important place. Kaprio, Koskenvuo & Rita (1987) in a prospective study of a large sample (N=95,647) found a considerable excess-risk of suicide (2.42 times the general population rate over a 5 year period). Suicide risk was greatest during the first weeks after bereavement. Bojanovsky & Bojanovsky (1976) and MacMahon & Pugh (1965) found that widowed men were more at risk for committing suicide in the first months, while the risk for widows was spread over a longer period. This is in line with the findings for other causes of death. Suicide risk may, however, not be solely a loss-effect. Bunch (1972) found that among the bereaved who committed suicide, previous psychiatric breakdown was more frequently found than among the other bereaved.

Gove (1972b) in a study of the American national statistics 1959-1961 compared suicide ratios among married and bereaved for both sexes. He found a greater excess suicide risk for widowers compared to married men than widows compared to married women. He found more attempted suicides among women but it appeared that there was a greater excess-risk of attempts among widowers compared to married men than widows compared to married women.

Conclusion

What is known about sex differences in morbidity upon bereavement is largely based on studies conducted among spouses. In general, most writers agree on the possibility of more serious problems for widowers than for widows. Bereavement appears to have more extreme effects on the mental health of widowers than of widows. This is established most firmly for depression, and repeatedly shown in studies with married controls. There are some indications that the difference may be related to loss of social relationships and (financial) support. A more elaborate discussion on this subject is given in Sections 3.4 and 3.5.

The sex difference among parents having been found to be the opposite of that among spouses, one must be wary of generalizing the finding of sex differences between spouses to other relationships. Perhaps what is termed as a sex difference may, in fact, be highly connected to sex-characteristic changes in marital or other roles.

The studies on excess mortality risk after bereavement produce somewhat equivocal results. Excess mortality may be different depending on age (see next section) and chronicity of the condition leading to the death. Following Morgan's (1990) explanation, higher excess mortality may occur in chronic-death widows as they may tend to be more involved in burdensome care for their dying spouse, while neglecting their own health. Men coping with sudden death of their wife may be less able to prepare themselves for the loss both psychologically and in terms of resources of emotional and practical care.

3.3.4   Age and adaptation

Like sex, age is another sociodemographic variable that can be considered as defining the task-demands of bereavement. Age is more or less fixedly related to a range of physical, developmental and psychosocial characteristics. Physically, in younger years there is a development which is marked by growth, physical maturation, and physical mobility and flexibility, while old age may be accompanied by decreased mobility, increased vulnerability and dysfunction. This process is also accompanied by neurological and endocrinological changes, which determine part of the developmental tasks a person faces. Psychologically, age is linked to increasing cognitive development and psychosocial transitions. If a person is confronted with a loss at a time when his or her cognitive development is not yet fully mature, bereavement may be incomprehensible to the person, and might pose problems. In addition, the nature of other tasks is closely related to age such as adolescence, and family and career building, while the characteristics and pattern of social support also covaries with age. Bereavement at each age thus has its own set of developmental tasks and psychosocial transitions, which form the background or pattern against which the loss must be placed.

Age differences in morbidity

In the general population it is known that with increasing age goes an increased risk of deteriorating health. This is true both for men and for women. There is also an increase in the recourse to medical services and medical consumption with age (CBS, 1984). This association is, however, more clear-cut for physical than for psychological health. No consistent relationship has, for instance, been found between age and depression. There is a positive correlation between age and moderate depression in men, but for women there is a peak around the age of 35-45 years and an increase after the age of 55.

Although one would expect that negative health impact of bereavement consists in exacerbating or accelerating existing health problems, the major part of the empirical research gives rise to the opposite conclusion: younger bereaved appear to suffer more severe health deterioration, especially on psychological health measures.

Maddison & Walker (1967), Carey (1979-1980), Kitson (1987), and Sheldon et al. (1981) found younger widows to have higher mental and physical illness scores than older ones. Ball (1977-1978) found that the youngest widows showed more health symptomatology. Suffering a sudden loss had an additional negative effect. She concluded that age is a more important factor than mode of death with regard to intensity of the grief reaction. Stein & Susser (1969) found in a controlled study that excess of mental illness in widowed as compared to nonbereaved controls was largest at younger ages. Gove & Shin (1989) in a study including widowed as well as divorced spouses, found the older widowed and divorced to be in better psychological health than the younger.

The results of empirical studies are not entirely unambiguous though. Stroebe & Stroebe (1987) failed to find an effect of age on any of their health measures. However, the age range of their sample was limited and did not include bereaved in the older age groups (over 60). Jacobs, Kasl et al. (1986) interviewed 114 acutely bereaved spouses one month after bereavement. They found the older spouses as much affected as middle-aged group in terms of health complaints, disbelief and emotional numbness. Sanders (1981) interviewed bereaved spouses at 2 and at 18-24 months. At two months, the younger widows showed greater grief intensity and higher levels of guilt. Older spouses scored higher on denial. At 18-24 months she found the younger widows were doing better in terms of depression and hope for the future. The older bereaved showed more grief reactions, high scores on social isolation, depersonalization, and death anxiety. She interprets this result as an initial denial defense mechanism against anxiety. In her view, age itself is not responsible for the severe reactions among the aged, but rather the isolation and loneliness of the older women. These assertions remain speculative, since the study did not include control groups. However, it draws attention to the possibility that the differing situations of younger and older widowed may lead to different courses in the bereavement process. It is also in line with the idea that age is strongly related to the structure of task-demands.

Parkes (1975a, 1983) found that the younger widows suffered more from psychological problems, while the older reported more physical complaints. It is not clear, here, whether these physical health problems are bereavement specific reactions or rather a common problem of old age, since matched controls were not included. The latter explanation seems more likely in view of the existing positive association between age and illness.

Age differences in mortality

As concerns mortality, there is a general increase with both sexes after adolescence for all causes of death (cf. Stroebe et al., 1987).

Under the age of 35, in the United States, accidents are the principal cause of death. In the age group of 35 and over, heart disease and cancers become the principal causes, in old-age along with strokes (Mechanic, 1978 in Stroebe & Stroebe, 1987).

In the Netherlands, this pattern is not very different. In the 5 to 19 years age group, accidents are the most important mode of death, accounting for 79% of male, and 63% of female deaths. Motor vehicle accidents are the most important cause of death in this age group, especially for men. In 1986, 33% of the deceased men, and 27% of the deceased women in this age range died from the consequences of traffic accidents. With increasing age, the importance of illness deaths increases, with diseases of the circulatory system (e.g.heart disease) and malignant neoplasms (cancer) becoming the most important modes of death, accounting for 44% resp. 29% of the deaths of males over 19 years old, and for 48% resp. 22% of the deaths of females over 19 years old (CBS, 1989).

Not much is known about the relationship between age and differences in post-bereavement excess mortality risk. Most of the prospective mortality studies (e.g. Helsing & Szklo, 1981; Kaprio et al., 1987) may be confounded with expectedness of death, which is likely to be far smaller in the younger age groups. A positive exception is the study of Smith (1990). He too shows that, controlled for expectedness of death, younger age groups (under 65) are likely to have excess mortality risk after bereavement, whereas in older age groups he did not find excess mortality in comparison with a matched group of married men and women.

Conclusion

There is some evidence that, in the widowed, younger age is related to increased health problems after bereavement. It is probable, however, that, rather age itself, the corresponding task-demands like the social and developmental situation, play an important role in bringing about this difference. It seems that younger widows are at a higher risk of developing psychological problems, as well as increased mortality in comparison to older widows. On physical health problems the data are less conclusive, but tend to point in the same direction. The absence of differences between younger and older age groups or their smaller magnitude in empirical studies may be due to the phenomenon that the increased health deterioration in the younger widows brings them to the same, relatively lower, level of health of older age groups. It is not clear whether bereavement constitutes an excess-risk at old age.

3.3.5   Kinship to the deceased and adaptation

A task demand often neglected in the study of bereavement is the kinship to the deceased. The kinship relationship defines to a substantial degree the character of the loss. Depending on kinship, there may be, among other aspects, a difference of frequency in contact, reciprocal dependency, intimacy and mutual support. For example, in the case of partner loss, there may be a larger loss of material and support resources than in other kinship groups. Parents, in general feeling very responsible for the well-being of their child, may be (more) prone to suffer from feelings of guilt after the loss of their child. It is possible that siblings, being more often in the same age range as the deceased, may be more strongly confronted with their own mortality, while adult children may have acquired a large degree of independence from their parents. Their reaction may differ yet again. For them, there is often the accompanying fact that with the death, a reversal of the caretaker role may take place with regard to the surviving parent. The fact that they are now the oldest generation of the family and so 'bear the family rule' may also have an effect.

Bereavement research has usually concentrated on partner loss. The position of other first-degree relatives is vastly neglected. Some research has focused on loss of a child, but very little attention has been given to the systematic study of adult children loosing a parent, and virtually none to bereaved siblings. In this section, the available studies on other than spousal bereavement will be discussed.

Death of a child

Loss of a child is almost universally regarded as untimely and extremely difficult to overcome. Fish (1986, in Sanders 1988) found that mothers were more strongly affected than fathers, with loss of younger as well as older children. Mothers experienced greater levels of guilt and anger, even two years after the loss. They felt greater social isolation, and they tended to feel that they were the only mourners for their child.

Miles & Demi (1984) examined different sources of parental guilt (cultural role, death causation, moral, survivor, and recovery guilt) with 28 bereaved parents who responded to an open-ended questionnaire while attending a seminar at a national meeting for bereaved parents. The most common types of guilt were death-causation and cultural-role guilt. They found rationalizing and sharing to be the most adequate guilt-reducing strategies used.

Rando (1983) found, among parents of 54 children who died from cancer, that during the third year grief actually worsened. Videka-Sherman (1982) found that among bereaved parents, the best coping styles were active and externally directed. These comprised replacement of the child and altruism. The least adaptive styles were escape and preoccupation with the lost child. The death of a child may put the relationship between the parents under severe pressure (Osterweis et.al., 1984). In a literature overview they state that between 50 and 70 percent of the bereaved parents suffer more or less severe problems in their marriage. Lehman, Wortman and Williams (1987) found that during the 4 to 7 years following bereavement, significantly more bereaved parents had divorced than in their matched control group during the same period: 20% of the bereaved parents divorced against 2% of the controls.

Klass (1986-1987), reporting on his experiences in self-help groups under his lead, found two central themes among parents after death of a child. One was the paradox of a newly established tie between them and at the same time a great deal of estrangement in their separate grief experience. The second theme was a strong sense of reordered priorities and sense of self as a center of strength to cope with the new situation. The second theme in particular is probably related to the support and work in the self-help group and specific to this sample.

Death of a parent

The impact of parental loss seems to be more important in younger than in adult children. Elizur & Kaffman (1983) followed a sample of young kibbutz children who lost their father during the war. There was a gradual decrease in adaptational problems, nevertheless at 4 years 39% still experienced emotional disturbance. The consequences of this type of loss on mental well-being and depression in later life is not clear (cf. Osterweis et.al., 1984).

Loss of a parent at an older age is generally not regarded as giving rise to serious problems. In many cases the adult child has built up a relatively independent world of his or her own, with his/her own house, family and children. Often the loss is not untimely and considered to be in the normal course of nature. That adult children seem to suffer much less from the loss of a parent has been found in the scarce comparative research conducted in this area. Sanders (1979-1980) found adult children to be the least affected group in comparison to widowed and parents. Owen et.al. (1982-1983) found them to be the least affected among family survivors.

Death of a sibling

On the impact of sibling death the data are fragmentary and mainly of a descriptive nature. Bank & Kahn (1982) stated that consequences are largely dependent on the kind of relationship they had. If the surviving sibling identified closely with the deceased or if the relationship was strongly polarized or rejected, this may result in bereavement problems and survivor guilt. This assertion may, however, also hold true for any other (family) relationship. There is an indication, drawn from systematic study, that some siblings at least may be vulnerable to serious problems after bereavement. Zisook & Lyons (1988) found in their aforementioned study that when only the most recent death was considered, the prevalence of unresolved grief was almost identical for siblings and spouses applying for psychiatrical care.

Other deaths

Equally scarce as data on sibling bereavement are those on loss of a close friend. In one study, Murphy (1986) compared loss of a family member to loss of a friend. Among 31 relatives and 18 friends of deceased disaster victims he found that relatives' scores on mental health and depression were significantly higher than those of friends. Both decreased however considerably between 11 months and 35 months after bereavement.

Comparative studies

The few available comparative studies all indicate that loss of a child is the most devastating of bereavements. Sanders (1979-1980), Levav (1982), Miles & Demi (1984) and Osterweis et al. (1984) found that intensity of grief was greatest in parental bereavement. Parents showed more depression, anger, guilt, and despair than those who lost a spouse or older parent. They experienced an overwhelming feeling of loss of control over the world and their lives.

Zisook & Lyons (1988) asked people at 1,000 consecutive intakes for an outpatient-facility of a mental health clinic to fill in a questionnaire, including questions about dealing with past first-degree bereavement losses. Forty-three percent (430) had experienced the death of at least one first-degree relative. 37% of the sample had lost at least one parent, 10% at least one brother or sister, 5% had lost a spouse to death and 3% had lost at least one child. Grief resolution was measured by the patients feeling that dealing with the loss was still difficult. The highest 'unresolved grief' rate was found among parents who lost a child (63%) followed by spouses (56%), siblings (48%) and children who lost a parent (46%). It appeared that mothers were more strongly affected than fathers. They formed the most affected group of all.

Loss of a mother resulted more often in unresolved grief (among 46%) than loss of a father (among 39%). No differences were found between relationships for other variables such as depression, health or psychosocial impairment. This is not surprising, since it concerns a population applying for psychosocial treatment. This study offers important insights into the relative importance of bereavement problems in the different relationships and their relationship to mental health problems. The magnitude of the effect, however, may be somewhat overestimated. One of the problems is that the authors' definition of 'unresolved grief' is not clear. Furthermore, the unresolved grief percentages may be biased by the fact that depressive problems were prominent in the sample: 29% of the sample obtained a diagnosis of clinical depression. Since it is known that depressed persons tend to have a generalized negative view of their past and present coping abilities, it is probable that their one-question assessment of grief resolution is not entirely valid, and may lead to overestimation of the problems. Nevertheless, this study is one of the few that consider different relationship-groups. The result of the comparison between these groups is valid in its own right, and furnishes an indication of important differences between them.

Conclusion

Despite the lack of systematic research in the area, the available literature is quite unequivocal in stating that loss of a child is probably the most difficult type of bereavement to cope with, followed by spousal bereavement. Sibling death and death of a parent during adulthood, on the other hand, seem to have a lesser impact. However, very little research in this area has been undertaken and no reliable conclusions can be drawn concerning the magnitude of the problems among siblings and adult children.

3.3.6   Quality of the relationship and adaptation

In this section, a closer look will be taken at the different aspects of the relationship that existed between the deceased and the bereaved before the loss and their role in subsequent adaptation. We will focus on three characteristics: dependency on the deceased, ambivalence about the deceased, and intimacy of the relationship.

Dependency

Dependency in the relationship with the deceased have been noted to make adaptation to the loss more difficult. Parkes (1975a) and Parkes & Weiss (1983) found in their Boston study that widowed who were overly dependent were prone to function poorly. The dependent spouses clung to their partner after his/her death in order to maintain their accustomed role of helplessness and inability to cope. Lopata (1973b, 1979) also found that disorganization in widowhood was related to marital roles. Widows intensely involved with their husband's life, and who were psychologically and socially dependent on him had more problems adapting than autonomous widows.

Parkes & Weiss (1983) draw attention to the interlocking of dependency and dominant needs of the spouse in marital relationships: dependence during a marriage may have mainly been the result of the need for dominance from the side of the spouse. Thus the bereaved of a dominant partner may instead or next to feeling helpless, feel a certain degree of relief of the dependent role, and experience little problems in taking control of his/her life

Ambivalence

Lindemann (1944) already reported ambivalence as being an important factor in adapting to the loss. Parkes & Weiss (1983) found the most severe grief reactions when the relationship had been ambivalent. In their sample, shortly after the loss, the ambivalent spouses seemed to do better, but after two years they showed signs of poor recovery and maladjustment. Stroebe & Stroebe (1987), reviewing the evidence on this subject, state that it is possible that ambivalent and dependent spouses were already psychologically unstable during their marital relationship. Thus, it would be the individual disposition itself, rather than bereavement, which leads to a diminished psychological well-being.

Intimacy

The role of intimacy of the relationship in the grief process is less documented. In the case of partner or parent loss we may view the loss of an intimate relationship as loss of a major source of emotional support. It seems however that the 'after image' of the deceased may form an internalized source of support. Moss & Moss (1984-1985) explored the ways in which the elderly widowed experienced, recalled, and were affected by the image of the deceased spouse. They argued that the tie persists through and beyond the period of grief. Positive themes of the marital tie continued throughout widowhood: caring, intimacy, family feeling, and commitment often persisted in providing continuing comfort and support to the widow(er).

In the case of loss of a young child or an adult sibling, the loss of intimacy may have another quality. It is not necessarily associated with a massive loss of emotional and service support, and the confidant role may be more a matter of choice.

Conclusion

Looking over the literature on bereavement, a large discrepancy appears between the role claimed for qualitative aspects of the relationship in many grief theories, and the small amount of systematic research conducted into this subject. From the above studies, the evidence for the influence of qualitative aspects of the relationship on the adaptation after bereavement appears to be inconclusive. Partly responsible for this is the often close intertwining of intimacy, dependency, dominance and ambivalence. Generally, the extremes of each of those concepts have been found to be related to poor outcome. Since it is likely that strongly unbalanced relationships sprout from unbalanced individuals, it remains unclear whether poor functioning in highly ambivalent or dependent relationships must be seen as solely a result of the loss.

3.3.7   Other task-demands and adaptation

Next to the loss itself, there may be other task-demands that concur with the loss. These may be of a developmental nature or other stressful situations themselves. In this section, we will look firstly at the available evidence for the influence of loss of a family member during childhood. Then, the influence of other situational stresses occurring before or alongside the (target) loss will be discussed.

Concurrent developmental tasks: childhood loss

Each period in life is marked by a specific set of developmental tasks. While old age is sometimes characterized as the period where 'coping with loss and death' is the most important task, this period is marked by no other concurring developmental tasks, although of course voluntarily exercised developmental tasks may occupy an important place. Childhood on the contrary is probably the period with the largest number of developmental tasks.

Although some studies have studied the impact of loss in early childhood, the consequences of this type of loss mental functioning in later life are not clear. Empirical results are contradictory.

Some authors argue that bereavement early in life is not associated with well-being in adult life. Brown & Harris (1978), however, empirically found support for a link between childhood loss and depression in individuals at a later age. Brown et al. (1982), in a large scale study among women who had lost their mothers in childhood (N=3000), found that the most important factor contributing to adult depression was lack of care in childhood. Since no non-bereaved control group was included, it is not clear whether this association is unique to bereavement reactions or applicable to the population at large.

In their study conducted among 79 women whose mothers had died and fathers had remarried, Parker & Manicavasagar (1986) found that the father belonging to a lower social class was the most important predictor for depression in adulthood (r=.34). The next important predictor (a long time lag between mother's death and the stepmother adopting her role) explained a lower percentage of the variance. Depression in the bereavement phase was in no way predictive for state or trait depression in adulthood. These studies suggest that other factors on a micro-level may play a more important role than bereavement itself. The influence of childhood bereavement on adult life health may be mediated by other factors. Silverman (1987) states that the problem may not lie in the fact of death itself, but how the significant others in the child's world react to it.

Antecedent stressors

In a number of studies it has been found that stress before bereavement plays a role in the outcome of the bereavement process.

Parkes (1975a) found that multiple life crises were predictors for poorer outcome, in particular: infidelity, loss of job, pregnancy, and previous divorce. Elizur & Kaffman (1983) interviewed 25 bereaved Israeli children whose father had died in the October War. They found that pre-bereavement factors such as long-term separation from their father before the loss were influential in early months after loss, whereas concurrent post- bereavement circumstances exacerbated the reactions over the years of measurement.

In the study of response to stressful life events, however, the mechanisms are not clear. Existing general dysfunctional coping styles and depression may lead to multiple chronic and acute life stresses such as marital problems, financial problems, job loss, and divorce. Life events may also be connected to loss of social support. This natural intertwining of stressful life events with aspects of personal functioning makes a causal inference difficult. Whatever the case may be, we may state that the presence of antecedent stressful events is connected to increased risk for impaired functioning after bereavement.

Concurrent stressors

Stress and stressful life events during the period after bereavement may make the weight harder to bear. Parkes (1975), Raphael & Maddison (1976) and Elizur & Kaffman (1983) found that concurrent crises formed an increased risk factor for negative bereavement outcome.

Cowan & Murphy (1985), in a controlled study among 69 bereaved and 69 matched non-bereaved, found that concurrent life stress was the most important predictor for all outcome measures, for bereaved as well as non-bereaved. This is not surprising, since looking at it from another perspective, bereavement is only a high ranking major stressor among others. That other loss-events may have at least the same impact as bereavement loss, is confirmed by the findings of Murrell, Himmelfarb & Phifer (1988). They compared attachment and non-attachment bereavement with other losses such as loss of job and home in their influence on subsequent health. To their surprise, they found only a significant (but modest) effect on health in the other-loss group.

Parkes (1975a) found that the secondary effects of bereavement (problems with children, jobs, and financial difficulties) were mentioned most frequently by poor outcome subjects. As with to what was said about antecedent stress, the causal inference here is unclear. A number of authors consider problems on the economic level as secondary loss effects, and believe that poor adjustment to bereavement can be largely attributed to financial and economic hardship (Atchley, 1975; Harvey & Bahr, 1974; Bahr & Harvey, 1980; Morgan, 1976).

Health before bereavement

There are indications that poor health prior to bereavement may have a negative effect on adaptation after bereavement (Parkes, 1975a; Parkes & Weiss, 1983). Bunch (1972) discovered that previous psychiatric breakdown is more frequently found among bereaved who committed suicide than in those who did not. Mor, McHorney & Sherwood (1986) found that persons who used health services before the loss were more susceptible to poor bereavement outcomes. These findings are, however, to be expected and do not corroborate the case for ill-health as a risk factor, since those who use services are already in poor health before bereavement, and there is no reason why their health should improve after the loss.

In general, we have to be careful in interpreting the results of studies without control groups in this area, since it is probable that there are high correlations between pre- and post-bereavement measures of physical and psychological health.

In establishing the influence of deteriorated health before bereavement on adaptation afterwards, also other problems are involved. Deteriorated health and age are positively correlated variables in the general population, but of the bereaved, the younger widows seem to sustain more health problems (see Section 3.3.4). A possible confounding factor, suggested by Stroebe & Stroebe (1987), is the fact that death at a young age is usually unexpected or untimely, leading to more severe reactions. Thus age could be confounded with expectedness of death.

But is expectedness related to adaptation in this way? Some light on this is shed by Lundin (1984a), who compared the health status of bereaved from sudden death, expected death with the population at large, in a well-controlled and matched prospective study. He found that the somatic and psychiatrical health status of the sudden-death group was comparable with the general population before bereavement, but worsened considerably afterwards. The health status of the expected death group was already worse than that of the matched non-bereaved control group before bereavement but did not show a decline after the death of the spouse or child. In an 8 year follow up of this study, Lundin (1984b) found that the differences between these groups on the outcome measures had disappeared. Lundin's (1984b) findings suggest that there are no long-term differences between expected and unexpected deaths. It may thus be that, in the long run at least , expectedness of death does not contribute to the explanation of the health difference between younger and older widows.

Another important inference from these results is that expected and unexpected death may also differ in the onset of the health problems and that this onset in many cases lies before death. Norris & Murrel (1987), in a prospective study conducted among bereaved and non-bereaved, found that stress levels in the bereaved were already higher before loss than among non-bereaved, although here depression only differed significantly after the loss.

Conclusion

The data available on the influence of antecedent and concurrent stresses in bereavement indicate that more stress is related to poorer adaptation. It is questionable, however, to what extent stress and stressful life-events for an individual occur independently from individual characteristics known to be (closely) related to adaptation, such as social status, coping style, and personality. It is possible that concurrent stresses in bereavement occur, at least partly, as a consequence of the loss.

The findings for pre-loss health, especially those of controlled and comparative studies, suggest that pre and post bereavement health are thoroughly intertwined and hard to unravel. With Sanders (1988) can be stated that the evidence for the influence of prior health variables on the adaptation after bereavement is still meager. Establishing conclusive evidence in this area is difficult.

3.4 Social support and adaptation

Social support can take several forms. It may comprise emotional or affective support, practical support and informational support. As outlined in Section 2.8, we should evaluate social support from two different points of view. One is the relationship between the social support of the environment in the task of coping with the death. Another perspective is the possibility that the death also means the loss of the principal social supportive person. This perspective implies that there are additional task-demands in mobilizing new resources, i.e. setting up a new supportive network.

The loss of social support

In the case of spouses, in particular, one of the consequences of bereavement may be a decrease in social support. Marriage can also be seen as a primary support relationship: loss of a partner thus results in a major loss of support. Lund, Caserta & Dimond (1988) found bereaved spouses scoring lower on social anchorage (measured with the Twenty Statements Test) than a married control group. This difference was already apparent three to four weeks after the loss, and persisted through the first two years after bereavement.

It has been assumed that social support has a protective or buffering effect in the reaction to severe stress. In case of a stressful event, the support network should cushion the shock, resulting in less severe reactions and dysfunction in well-supported individuals. Some studies involving bereaved and control groups have searched for this effect. In Stroebe & Stroebe's (1987) study it appeared that widowed with children were better off than those without, but this was also true for the married control group. There were main effects of social support, sex and marital status on depression (BDI), but no interactions between them. Thus, no buffering effect of social support for bereavement outcome was found. This was true for each subscale of support, as well as for the summation of these. The number of social contacts made no difference in depression, suggesting again that it was not the number, but the quality of the relationships which was helpful. Greene & Feld (1989) also found no buffering function in social support. The connection between support and well-being was the same in married and in widowed women.

Sanders (1988) states that some modes of death may lead to extensive loss of support, e.g. death from AIDS may lead to social stigma, and negative social support. Barrett & Scott (1987), in a study among survivors from suicide, sudden natural death, long-term illness, and accidental death, found no significant differences between these groups in loss of social support. Bereaved who were intensively involved in caring for a dying family-member have been found to isolate themselves more from their former social contacts (Cleiren et al., 1988).

There are also sex-differences involved in social support. Sarason et al. (1987) found that support measures themselves are often biased towards the relationships that women tend to find supportive, and that men possibly value more contacts which take their minds off troubles, whilst women search more confiding relationships. Stroebe & Stroebe (1987) found that men were less motivated than women to use social support in coping with traumatic life events. In the study of a sample of 242 older widows Caserta et al. (1989) found that social support to be hardly related to adaptation.

Emotional and practical support after the loss

The role of social support in adaptation after stressful life-events is considered important, but how supports operate in relation to health is not clear. This may partly be due to the above mentioned intertwined aspects. Raphael & Nunn (1988) state that support after a loss is partially specified by cultural prescriptions and the support situation before death, and on the other hand dependent on characteristics of interpersonal style such as the ability to mobilize people and openness. In addition, Vachon & Stylianos (1988) mention that the 'goodness of fit' of the support, as well as perception of the environment as 'helpful' or 'unhelpful' is determined by the impact of the loss on other network members and other, concurrent stressors.

The multitude of aspects which make up social support is reflected in empirical studies, where the concept is operationalized in many different ways.

One line of research uses only the number of social ties. These studies usually show a fairly weak connection between social support and health status (Bankoff, 1985). Vachon et al. (1980) found that the number of friends had no relationship to health for widows. In contrast, Lopata (1972) found in an older widowed sample that the number of friends had a positive relationship to health. McCrae & Costa (1988) found that long-term widowed women's social networks were a little smaller than those of matched married women, but no differences were found in general health, openness to experience, extraversion, and self rated health.

That the 'number of friends' is not solely a property of the social environment was shown by Lopata (1988). In a large scale study of 82,078 American widows, he found that the widows with the least number of friends were those who had moved to a new neighborhood or lacked skills in making friends (a clear personal style-factor). Those who suffered health or financial problems had less friends as well.

Other studies concentrate on the availability of support after the loss. Greene & Feld (1989) measured different forms of social support in terms of availability. In a controlled study among 151 (first) married women and 144 widows, they found that in subgroups exposed to much bereavement stress, social support was negatively correlated with well-being. Recent widows with more social support available were less happy, longer-term widows with more social support available were happier. A possible explanation is that with the recent widows, the kind of social support provided did not meet their needs.

On the other hand, one can look at the utilization of support. Coyne, Aldwin & Lazarus (1981) found that depressed persons searched more for emotional and informational support than non-depressed. It may thus be that increased actual use of the available social support is indicative of decreased well-being, and that the causal relationship might be the reverse here.

Yet another way of looking at social support after the loss is to measure to what extent the offered support meets the needs of the receiver. Maddison & Walker (1967) found that more unmet needs in interpersonal relationships among widows were associated with poor outcome. Kitson, Babri, Roach & Placidi (1989), reviewing the effects of widowhood and divorce, conclude that in predicting adjustment, subjective evaluation of the aid received seems more important than the frequency of help. Related to this is the quality of support. Holahan & Moos (1986) found that a better quality of social relations in the family protected from negative consequences of life stress. Brown & Harris (1978), in a sample of London widows, found that the presence of only one confidence figure was already sufficient in providing adequate support.

Sarason, Shearin, Pierce & Sarason (1987) extensively studied the interrelations between social support measures. They found that it was the perception of support, rather than the actual receipt of support, that was most indicative for good adjustment. Furthermore, they found that measures of perceived support, no matter how the construct is broken down into specific areas of instrumental and emotional support, generally assess the extent to which an individual is accepted, loved and involved in relationships in which communication is open. Measuring these aspects might thus provide the most accurate assessment of social support.

Informational support after the loss

The influence of informational support on adaptation is vastly understudied. Informational support considers provision of availability of sources of instrumental and emotional support, as well as provision of information and knowledge on what consequences bereavement may have in different areas of life. In many cases, informational support will be provided along with other forms of social support, but little is known about the adequacy of this information.

Informational support in the form of advice may be provided verbally, or consist of written information, such as books or brochures. It may also be less explicit, e.g. modelling in the form of seeing other bereaved cope with the loss, which is a potentially powerful aspect of the support in self-help groups. To what degree the bereaved is provided with adequate models of adaptation, formed by other bereaved, is not clear (De Boer & van der Wal, 1987).

One thing that can be said about informational support is that the need for information among the bereaved is considerable. In a subsample of the present study (Cleiren, 1989) it was found that more than 50% of the bereaved after a long-term illness would have appreciated practical information in the form of a brochure shortly after the death. At the same time, it appeared that such information was not available at that time.

Conclusion

Social support is multifaceted. Looked upon as an outcome of bereavement, it seems that bereavement of a spouse may constitute a loss of instrumental and emotional support in coping with the demands of life.

Considered as a resource for adaptation to bereavement, the strongest associations with well-being are found when the bereaved's perception of (availability of) support is measured, rather than 'objective' enumerations of supportive people and behaviors. Most of the research shows that the presence of others and a confidential interaction with others appears to ameliorate the negative effects of bereavement.

To what extent this reflects objective actions from the environment and to what extent this depends on the general functioning of the bereaved him/herself, remains unanswered. Social support cannot be seen as a purely environmental or circumstantial influence. Individual factors such as extraversion, and depressive coping styles may influence both the presence and the perception of social support. There may also be a relationship with socioeconomic status, which may dictate the characteristics and quality of support. This will be further examined in the next section.

3.5 Available material resources and adaptation

Most of the empirical studies on bereavement include measures of socioeconomic status, commonly abbreviated as SES. Socioeconomic status is usually viewed as a conglomerate of income level, educational and professional level. The term social class generally refers to the same concept.

Like other resources, SES may be considered as an independent variable and a resource for adaptation to the death, e.g. determining the degree to which someone has financial means to adapt his situation. SES can, however, also be seen as an outcome variable of the death: a widow may suffer an accompanying loss of income or housing. Additional task-demands may be placed on her to restore financial resources.

The literature on the role of SES in bereavement, in contrast to that on social support, has concentrated more often on entanglement with other resources and has considered SES both from the dependent and the independent point of view. In this section, the role of this sociodemographic aspect will be discussed in more detail.

Socioeconomic status and health

In the general population, social class and income seem to be inversely related to mental illness and mortality. Schwab & Schwab (1978) found that people in socially disadvantaged situations showed more psychiatric disorder and more depression than those in a relatively advantaged position. The same results have been found in treatment statistics and community surveys (cf. Kessler et al., 1985).

This finding has been ascribed to different causes. One line of interpretation presumes that the association is due to stressful life-events. Some suppose that low-

SES individuals are exposed to more stressful life events (Dill et al., 1980). Others claim that stressful life events have a greater impact on low-SES individuals. The reason for this difference in impact has in turn been ascribed to a reduced availability of social support. There is evidence that supportive social contact is less available to low-SES individuals (see Liem & Liem, 1978 for an overview).

Another explanation is that incompetent copers 'drift' to the lower classes, while they cannot reach a high level of high socioeconomic achievement. This seems only to be true however for extreme severe disorders, such as schizophrenia (Turner & Gartrell, 1978). Status-related differences in patterns of living, such as poor nutrition, housing, restricted access to health care, and unhealthy jobs, may also lead to poorer health in low-SES individuals. Again, this is only likely to hold true for extreme cases.

The impact of bereavement on SES

That socioeconomic status may be influenced by bereavement was found by several authors. Babri & Kitson (1988), Balkwell (1981), Berardo (1970), Hyman (1983), Morgan (1989), Weiss (1984) and McCrae & Costa (1988) found that widowhood in men as well as women was associated with a drop in family income, although for widowers this loss is smaller than for widows. Morgan (1989) found, in a comparative longitudinal survey in the United States, that 40% of widows and 26% of the divorced fell in the 'poverty' category within 5 years.

In line with this, Harvey & Bahr (1974) and Atchley (1975) hold that the negative impact of widowhood results more from a change in socioeconomic status than a change in marital status: the lowered income leads to lowered morale and reduced social involvement. This in turn leads to greater anxiety. Harvey & Bahr (1974) even state that socioeconomic factors can account for much or even all the variance in the adaptation after widowhood. This however is improbable. Parkes & Weiss (1983) found that widows in initial period after the loss were unable to use their social resources, regardless of social class and income. Interestingly, Kitson et al. (1987) found that greater grief in widows was associated with lower SES, education and lower anticipated income but no such association was found between these variables among divorcees, although the changes in SES are, to a certain extent, comparable for both groups.

There is no consensus about the way how SES and adaptation are related. Sanders (1980, 1989) and Morgan (1976) state that low income does not contribute directly to poor bereavement outcome, but rather operates as a preexisting factor that would contribute negatively to any stressful situation. Morgan (1981) later states that the difference in income between married and widowed women may also be a consequence of inverse relationship between social class and mortality. Poor widows may be overrepresented in the bereaved samples, while their husbands, being in a disadvantaged social position, die at a relatively younger age.

SES and adaptation after bereavement

The association between low SES and lower well-being in the general population has been found within bereaved samples as well. Many authors estimate that income, education and employment status have direct and indirect effects on adjustment, e.g. via social support (Atchley, 1975; Bahr & Harvey, 1980; Coysh et al., 1989; Lopata, 1973, 1979; Parry, 1986; Pierce, 1982). On the other hand, Caserta et al. (1989) found in a sample of older bereaved widows (N=242) that working outside the home, although positively related to a number of outcome measures, was *not* related to a higher level of social support. As for education, it seems that higher educated widows are better adjusted (Carey, 1979-1980), more likely to restructure their identity (Lopata, 1973) and engage more in social interactions (Kivett, 1978).

Parkes (1975a) found lower class respondents more likely to be in the bad outcome group. Sanders (1988) states that functioning in widowhood is strongly associated with the financial situation of the widowed person. The question remains whether these differences reflect only the general population effect mentioned above, or that low socioeconomic status constitutes a specific risk factor to the bereaved.

Studies including non-bereaved control groups (Morgan, 1976; Gallagher et al., 1983; Sanders, 1980) typically find that low income and low-SES are associated with more sadness and depressed mood, boredom and loneliness in both bereaved and controls. They fail to find an excessive risk for the widowed.

One study that indicated an excessive risk is Bahr & Harvey's (1980) study, carried out among young widows after a mining disaster. They found that education explained more variance in morale scores (happiness, perceived quality of life) in the widows, compared to non-bereaved matches.

The relative importance of socioeconomic status in reactions to the loss seems small. Many studies find that the relationship between bereavement and health measures is only slightly reduced by introducing a social class covariate. (Glick et al.., 1974; Stroebe et al., 1985; Gove & Shin, 1989). Sheldon et al. (1981) found a somewhat stronger relationship: in their study, a combination of age and socioeconomic status accounted for 22% of the score variance on the General Health Questionnaire in widows.

Conclusion

It appears that there is a relationship between socioeconomic variables and well-being in the general population as well as in the bereaved. However, from the above we can conclude that a causal relationship is far from clear. Socioeconomic status can be seen as a typical 'high order' variable: it is thoroughly intertwined with many social, behavioral and personality characteristics, which may be both cause and effect of a certain socioeconomic level. In view of the findings discussed above, a simple univariate relationship between well-being and socioeconomic status is unlikely.

Controlled comparative studies rarely find an exacerbating effect of social status on bereavement outcome. The magnitude of the influences of SES-aspects in bereavement appears to be small in comparison to other factors.

Changes in SES after bereavement such as loss of income or job may pose additional task-demands. Still, these changes do not happen to all the bereaved, and financial stress cannot be seen as a general explanation of the loss-effect (cf. Stroebe & Stroebe, 1987). Apart from that, we must also be aware that inferences about the relationships between SES, income, and social support rest mainly on research among widows. Thus, although certain relationships may apply to the specific situation of most widows, they may operate much differently with widowers, and may not apply at all to other bereaved family members.

Last but not least, considerable cross-cultural differences may exist in the impact of bereavement on SES. Countries differ vastly in the level of social security and social services: factors which may largely influence the financial consequences of bereavement. The absence or presence of guaranteed widows' and orphans' pensions, with related independence or dependence on voluntary help of others may be an additional reason for differences in the role of SES.

3.6   Attitude to adaptation after bereavement

In the following sections, a closer look will be taken at the role of intrapersonal aspects which may influence adaptation after a loss. The beliefs a person holds about himself may influence the way in which he copes with the adaptation to the death of someone close. Experience with earlier losses may influence the way a person sees his ability to cope with bereavement.

An individual's personal style in coping with stressful situations will also most probably determine the efficacy in dealing with the loss. Beliefs about one's ability to cope may also be influenced by prior loss experiences and the knowledge of one's own reactions to them.

Prior losses

With regard to the influence of prior bereavements on later life health, there is a difference between the findings for previous childhood losses and loss during adulthood. In Section 3.3.7 it was shown there are some indications for debilitating effects of childhood loss in later life. In this section, where the accent lies on attitudes towards (coping with) the loss, we will look at prior losses taking place during adulthood in their effect on adaptation.

For losses during adulthood Bornstein et al. (1973) found in a depressed subsample of bereaved that in 25% of the cases it was their first loss of a relative, in comparison with 4% in the non-depressed group. They concluded that earlier experience facilitates good adaptation. Huston (1971) and Vachon (1976) suggested the same association. On the other hand Kastenbaum (1969) points out that a quick succession of losses, such as in war or in a disaster, might constitute a high risk for a loss of feeling of control, hopelessness and depression. Sanders (1980) found that depressed respondents had more often experienced multiple family losses in the past than non-depressed bereaved.

Personality and coping style and adaptation after bereavement

Hansson & Remondet (1988) stated that personal control is the integrating theme in the factors that influence adaptation after a loss. This aspect can be found in bereavement research under associated terms such as helplessness, ego-strength, self-efficacy, shyness, locus of control, and attribution of control. In this section some of the findings in this area will be presented.

Stroebe et al. (1988) found that low-control individuals were more depressed than those in the high-control group. This was true of the bereaved, as well as of a matched sample of married controls. Bereavement was associated with an increased belief that events are controlled by chance. Low-internal control individuals reacted with more depression to the loss than those with high-internal control. Furthermore, individuals who suffered an unexpected loss and had lower internal control beliefs reacted with much greater depression than those who had expected the loss. The authors state that this might be due to differential effort in regaining control after a sudden loss. An expected loss might provide the low-control survivor with the possibility of regaining control over the situation by other means.

In several studies it has been found that the amount of experienced distress is closely related to the perception of oneself. Holahan & Moos (1986) found in a community sample (N=493) that, among other things, self-confidence and an easy-going disposition formed a protection from the negative consequences of life stress. Stroebe & Stroebe (1987) found that emotionally stable individuals showed less depression than unstable individuals. This was true in their bereaved sample, as well as in the controls. Johnson, Lund & Dimond (1986) obtained data from 192 older bereaved spouses, aged 50-93. They found that low self-esteem was related to poor coping, and that early bereavement stress was reduced by positive self-evaluations. Initially effective copers remained effective throughout the first year. In a study of a subgroup of this sample Burks et al. (1988) found a strong association between positive self-evaluations and remarriage.

Other personality characteristics may also be related to the effectiveness in dealing with life crises. In a general study of an adult sample, McCrae & Costa (1986) found that neuroticism, extraversion and openness to experience were related to coping effectiveness. Vachon et al. (1982) administered the General Health Questionnaire and a 16 factor personality questionnaire to a sample of conjugally bereaved. In the low-distress group they found the people who were emotionally stable and mature, conservative, conscientious, and socially precise. In the high-distress group they found more anxiousness, worrying, and low emotional stability.

Sanders (1980), in her longitudinal study, discovered four discernable groups in which there was a relationship between certain styles of coping and experienced stress. The first was a 'disturbed group' of bereaved. They had few defenses that might offer relief from distress, suffered feelings of inadequacy, inferiority, insecurity, and felt a long-lasting desolation. A second group was depressed: they evidenced tensions, inordinate sensitivity and intense emotionality in response to stresses, and trait anxiety. A third pattern was found in the 'denial group'. They showed optimism and used strong defense mechanisms to cope with crises. They also used physical symptoms to avoid responsibilities or to resolve conflicts, and were not aware this defense was being used. This group kept a 'stiff upper lip', and was reluctant to admit common human weaknesses. They did not deny death itself but only their overt emotions surrounding it. The fourth, Sanders termed the 'normal grief-contained group'. They were found to have the best adjustment to bereavement, having good emotional control and ego strength, and little expression of confusion. They were in touch with reality, able to share feelings with others and not likely to seek help. Typically, they saw grief as not lasting forever and managed to get through bereavement by focussing on a better future.

Gass & Chang (1989), drawing from Lazarus & Folkman's (1984) stress-coping framework, found that better psychosocial functioning was associated with low threat appraisal (little fear for other bereavement-related losses and problems that exceed one's power), more problem-focused coping (engagement in managing or altering the situation that causes distress) and less use of emotion-focused coping (engagement in regulating the emotional response to the problem).

Conclusion

In many studies, personality aspects such as perceived control, neuroticism and self-evaluation have been linked to adaptation to life crises in general, and also specifically to bereavement.

Although most of the research seems to point in the same direction, one must be cautious in interpreting these results. It is noteworthy that the aforementioned personality aspects are known to be related to well-being in the general population as well (cf. K. Parkes, 1986; McCrea & Costa; 1986). Furthermore, 'personality' aspects such as the feeling of being in control, being able to handle the situation, being happy with oneself and open to others may be seen as aspects of well-being in general. It may thus be that part of the associations between personality and well-being are due to spurious correlations since the operationalizations show conceptual overlap.

Since studies into the relationship between bereavement and personal style employing a population control group are rare (with the noted exception of Stroebe & Stroebe, 1987), it is unknown to what extend bereavement itself, or other stressful events for that matter, play a role in this association. In addition, since personality has virtually always been retrospectively assessed, the cause-effect relationship is not clear. Only research including pre-bereavement personality measurement could make clear whether post-bereavement personality and coping measures reflect stable traits or, rather, reaction patterns to the loss.

3.7 Multivariate relationships between resources and adaptation

In the preceding sections, the relationship between resources and adaptation to bereavement was treated in a bivariate way. Although this may serve as a convenient way to categorize and describe the relationships, the entanglement of resources and the task-demands in bereavement makes it almost impossible to draw conclusions about the role of each individual variable.

The entanglement of sociodemographic aspects

From the preceding sections it is clear that the role of sociodemographic characteristics in adaptation after bereavement is not always unequivocal. Although they are generally considered to play a small but significant role in adaptation, it is very hard to determine their exact relationship to well-being, even in controlled studies.

As already shown to some extent above, an important problem is the fact that sociodemographic variables such as sex, age, social status and marital status are related to each other, often in a more or less 'natural' way. In the older age groups, women are more likely to be bereaved than men, and perhaps more likely to be poor.

In addition, life-phase specific relationships between sociodemographic variables may occur. There may be a curvilinear intra-individual relationship between age and SES. Young people may start out with a low initial income and socioeconomic status, climb to a higher SES at middle-age (because of job development), and suffer a drop in status again after retirement or bereavement.

There may also be time-cohort related differences in income for specific age groups. One example is the increase of women working outside the home and providing their own income over the last decades in many western countries. Related to this may be the increase in cardiovascular illness in women, and increased stress in women of the younger age groups (CBS, 1984). These interactions may be to a large degree culturally defined, and differ subtly between the American and the different European cultures, forming a possible ground for the inconclusive findings in this area.

Prediction of adaptation

In the preceding sections we discussed the relationship of a number of aspects in a primarily bivariate way: each variable was considered with respect to its possible unique bearing to criteria of adaptation. A logical step would then be to consider what is known about the *relative* importance of those aspects in adaptation to the loss. Is it possible to distinguish clusters of variables which, together, make up a profile of bereaved at risk for developing serious problems? In some studies efforts have been made to find a multivariate constellation of variables that indicate the level of adaptation after the loss (see Table 3.4).

Typically, data gathered shortly after the loss are used to predict the situation at a later point in time. In most of the cases this is done by means of multiple linear regression techniques. Here will be looked at some of the results in this area. As is clear from Table 3.4, not every study assesses systematically the same concepts.

In general, socioeconomic variables do not seem to contribute in a substantial way to the adaptation after bereavement in the different studies. This is in line with what was said in Section 3.5.

The gender of the bereaved seems to play a more important role. Interestingly, however, in the only study to our knowledge controlling for pre-bereavement health (Norris & Murrell, 1987), the sex of the respondent fails to show a significant effect on outcome. This supports the view that the difference in health between men and women is due to pre-existing differences rather than to differential reactions to the loss (cf. Section 3.3.3).

Situational pre-bereavement aspects of stress, health, and quality of the relationship to the deceased, as well as loss-aspects such as suddenness and expectedness of death are only sporadically measured or entered for regression analyses. When entered, they appear to be important predictors for outcome. However, since interrelations of these concepts are probable, it is difficult to draw general conclusions about their relative importance in the adaptation to the loss.

Table 3.4

Predictor strength of independent variables for health status after bereavement in some regression designs

	Dimond et al. (1987)	Farnsworth et al. (1989)*	Norris et al. (1987)	Parkes (1976)
Time since death:	2,6,12 and 24 months	0 to 24 months	6 months	13 months
Dependent variables:	depression, coping, health	well-being, loss managem.	health, distress	overall outcome
Independent variables:				
Age	*	n.s.	n.s.	--••
Sex	* *	* * *	n.s.	--••
Income	--	n.s.	--	--••
SES (incl. education)	n.s.	--	n.s.	* *
Pre-bereavement health	--	--	* * *	--
Pre-bereavement stress	--	--	n.s.	--
Quality of relationship	--	* * *	--	--
Anticipation, suddenness of death	--	--	--	* * *
Social network aspects	*	--	--	--
Early low self esteem, guilt, anger	--	* * *	--	* * *
Early level of grieving	--	--	--	* * *
Early level of well-being	* * *	* * *	* * *	--
Concurrent stress	* *	--	n.s.	--
Time since loss	--	* * *	--	--

Note: Magnitude of the contribution of the potential predictor variables: n.s. = none, * = small, ** = moderate, *** = large, -- = not entered for analysis. Quotation marks: • = prediction within one measurement, •• = non-significant correlations eliminated at an earlier stage.

Interestingly, in all of the four studies in Table 3.4, early post-bereavement measures of psychological functioning are highly indicative for the level of functioning measured at a later point in time.

3.8 Methodological issues in the study of bereavement

In this section we will focus on some general methodological issues of importance to a systematic empirical inquiry into the field of bereavement, and some specific problems in conducting survey research in this area.

3.8.1   General limits of statistical studies of bereavement

Aggregation level of observation

One of the more general problems in large scale observational studies is the difference in aggregation level between scientific observations and reality. This means that we employ uni-dimensional measures in studying a given phenomenon, which in fact is determined by multiple or multidimensional characteristics. In the statistical sense this implies that two variables may not correlate when we calculate them over all our cases, but may appear to be strongly related in some subgroups or on the individual level. Thus the researcher should also look within his data for local effects arising from uncontrolled conditions and responses which are given alongside the goal variables (Edwards and Cronbach, 1952).

The simplest cause for differences in aggregation level is a mediating or suppressor variable, but it might very well be a larger number of characteristics. Even when we are aware of these characteristics and able to quantify them, we are faced with major problems in putting our assumptions statistically to the test: the number of interaction effects which can be taken into account in factorial designs is always limited. According to Cronbach (1975), concealed interactions may even wipe out a real main effect of the variable that chiefly concerns the investigator.

Very large samples would provide the researcher with the possibility of taking into account more variables at the same time. The costs and amount of time invested in observational studies are, however, almost linearly proportional to the number of respondents involved, making research projects of these proportions hard to carry out.

Intra-individual causation

Harré (1978) draws attention to the fact that statistical generalizations can lead to different conclusions, each of which can give rise to a different causal interpretation. If, for instance it is known that 70% of a certain population develops depression after bereavement and 30% does not, this is open to two distinct interpretations on the individual level. Either every individual is 0.7 likely to develop depressive symptoms; or every individual of a certain domain determinatively develops depression and every individual in another domain does not, while 70% of the individuals belongs to the first, and 30% to the second domain.

The first interpretation may only hold true if (along with a number of statistical requirements) each individual has the possibility of developing depression. The second interpretation adopts a more deterministic viewpoint and focuses on individually differing backgrounds.

While searching for causal explanations by examining isolated variables in a between-subject manner, the researcher may easily overlook the fact that mechanisms of causation are always located in the individual. Even when there are collective influences or consequences for everyone, the individual history of each respondent more or less predestines him to evidence or not depression in the study (freely adapted from Harré, 1978).

The failure to establish empirical evidence for the assertions in bereavement theories might be due to the fact that on a macro level they fail to reach significance, blurred as they are by specific (hidden) individual differences which are often not under study. In other words, it may be essential to take into account the unique characteristics of the bereaved person and his/her background in order to properly put grief theories to a test.

What should be matched for ?

In comparative studies of bereavement, another problem emerges. Although, as shown in the preceding section, it is difficult to match or control for all the relevant variables, there may be some we cannot ignore. The most common procedure is to control or match for sociodemographic variables. This may not be sufficient, especially when studying bereavement with a focus on mode of death. When we simply collect (or split) a sample of bereaved on the basis of mode of death, in order to compare for instance suicide with accidental death, even when controlling for basic variables such as age, sex and social status, the subsamples may still differ in a number of relevant characteristics which, without proper control, may devalue the conclusions of a study. A short look will be taken at some of these additional control variables

One problem in drawing conclusions is that the mode of death and the adaptation of the survivors may be related to preexisting aspects: suicide may occur after years of psychiatrical illness and family systems may already have been severely disrupted before the suicide occurred. In that way, it is all but certain that we can ascribe differences between them to mode of death itself. To determine this, assessment and (statistical) control for the pre-bereavement relationships and situation is necessary.

An important variable too often neglected in the study of bereavement is the 'formal' relationship to the deceased. In some studies (e.g. Vargas, Loya & Vargas, 1984; Wagner & Calhoun, in press), friends, parents, spouses, children, cousins, and family-in-law relationships are treated as a homogeneous group, and unevenly divided over modes of death. Even when one controls for quality of the relationship, a relationship rated as 'intimate' by a spouse who lived together with the deceased may have a much different meaning than the same qualification given by a sister-in-law, who saw the deceased once a month. The kinship-relationship to the deceased thus forms a conceptually important *qualitative* variable in the character of the loss, which should be controlled for in any study of bereavement.

Assessment of excess-risk

In bereavement research, non-bereaved control groups may be included to determine whether bereavement has an exacerbating effect on the psychological health of certain subgroups (e.g. men versus women) in view of already existing differences in the general population. Bereavement studies including a matched control group are generally regarded as being the most appropriate for assessing this. They may, however, also be subject to problems, which are related to the choice of an outcome criterion. This is perhaps best illustrated by an example.

Suppose we want to study whether parental bereavement has a differential effect on the well-being of fathers of the deceased child as compared to mothers. We decide to include a matched non-bereaved sample of parents in our study to assess whether there is an excess-risk for fathers or mothers. Both groups complete a depression questionnaire. A higher score indicates greater depression. The ideal-typical results are shown in Fig. 3.1a. When we conduct an analysis of variance on these data, we will find a main effect for bereavement and a main effect for sex (father vs. mother), but no interaction. We may thus conclude that there is no differential excess-risk for the sexes after bereavement.

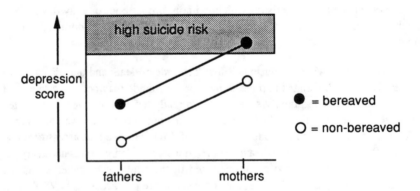

Fig. 3.1a *Imaginary depression scores of bereaved and non-bereaved parents with the norm-score for high suicide risk*

Another researcher, thinking in diagnostic terms may, however, argue that we have to look at the absence or presence of severe depression since, in contrast to lower levels, this is related to a high suicide risk. To this goal he employs a certain cut-off score. For the ease of illustration we will assume a within-group variance of the depression scores of zero. Looking at the partial contingency table (see Fig. 3.1b), it appears that none of the non-bereaved parents, and none of the bereaved fathers fall in the risk group, but that all the bereaved mothers run a heightened suicide risk. This results in a highly significant partial-chi-square for the table in Fig. 3.1b, and suggests the conclusion that for mothers there is a large excess-risk of evidencing severe problems upon bereavement, while for fathers there is none.

	fathers	mothers
non-bereaved	0%	0 %
bereaved	0%	100 %

Fig. 3.1b *Imaginary partial contingency table of bereaved and non-bereaved parents against absence or presence of high suicide risk, with in-cells percentage of subjects evidencing high suicide risk.*

This shows that, depending on the choice of the use of discrete diagnostic classes (norm groups) or continuous scale scores, the same data may lead to different conclusions. The result and conclusion thus depend to a large extent on nuances in the formulation of the question. The approach to be chosen is not always clear, since both types of questions are legitimate. The example shows, however, that great caution must be taken in drawing conclusions.

3.8.2   Specific problems in survey studies of bereavement

Empirical research of the survey type in the field of bereavement poses its own problems. Loosing someone close is not an easy subject to report freely about to a non-involved researcher. In the bereaved, recounting the circumstances of death and one's behavior and feelings about it is likely to elicit strong emotions.

It seems to be particularly difficult for the bereaved to cooperate during the time shortly before and after the loss, . This is perhaps best reflected in the relatively low participation rates in this type of research. On the whole, acceptance rates appear to be lowest in those studies conducted shortly after the loss, when the emotional disturbance seems to be the most intense (cf. Van der Wal, 1989-1990; Stroebe & Stroebe, 1989-1990).

A major question is thus whether or not the participants in bereavement research are representative of the bereaved population. Studies recruiting respondents from self-help groups (e.g. Trolley, 1986) or volunteer samples (e.g. Heyman & Gianturco; 1973) are vulnerable to systematic (self-) selection, and only lend themselves to limited generalizing (cf. Sanders, 1988).

There are also indications that refusers form a differentially affected group in terms of mental and physical well-being. Stroebe & Stroebe (1989-1990) elaborately examined the reasons for participation in their study. They compared total refusers with interview participants and questionnaire participants (the latter being interview refusers). They concluded that depression affects the willingness to cooperate, but that it acts differently for widows and widowers. Widowers who were less depressed agreed to be interviewed, whereas the cooperating widows were more depressed than their refusing counterparts. There were no overall differences between refusers and cooperators. Reviewing the literature, they state that acceptance rates for interview-studies are typically lower than those of mailed studies, unless special effort is undertaken to obtain samples. Some caution must be taken in generalizing those results however, since the group which refused the interview but was willing to fill in a questionnaire was only 15% of the total number of refusers: again a small subsample.

Another possible source of disturbance might be the method of data-gathering. There is, however, some indication that this might be of smaller importance. Caserta, Lund & Dimond (1985) assigned 192 bereaved elderly adults (aged 50+ yrs) randomly to a home interview (n=104) or a mailed questionnaire (n=88). Response rates for both groups were virtually equal (40%). Comparison on measures of depression, life satisfaction and a number of bereavement-related feelings and behaviors, revealed no effect due to group assignment. Although significant changes over time were observed on most measures, these changes were independent of whether the respondents were interviewed or not. The presence of interviewers was, however, associated with higher and more consistent completion rates at each measurement. Their results suggest that there are probably no important (assessment-dependent) interview-effects in bereavement research. Personal interviews are, however, preferable to mailed questionnaires because of the higher completion rate.

Finally, there still is a certain limitation in our scope on bereavement which results from the selective focus of the main stream of empirical research. Much of the research on the effects of bereavement, so far, has concentrated on people loosing a spouse, and has been mainly conducted among widows (e.g. Parkes, 1975; Ball

1976-1977; Lopata, 1972; Greene & Feld, 1989; Vachon, Lyall e.a., 1982; cf. Stroebe & Stroebe, 1989-1990). This is partly due to the fact that more women than men become widowed, since women have a considerably longer life expectancy. The situation of other family members such as bereaved children, parents and especially siblings, has been largely neglected in bereavement research. This means that we only have a limited image of the general impact of a loss for the family. As mentioned before, virtually all the claims for sex differences in the bereavement process and bereavement outcome stem from studies of widowed samples. In this light, those differences might not be generalizable to other types of kinship, and may be primarily attributable to marital role differences.

3.9   Conclusion

In this chapter, an inventory was made of factors that may possibly play a role in the adaptation after the loss. First, this was done in a univariate way and, in the last section, in a multivariate way. In general, there are only few factors on which consensus exists on their role in adaptation after bereavement. Studies frequently come up with contradictory results. The reasons for this may be found in low response percentages, methodological flaws, cross-cultural differences, but also simply in the large number of situational and personal aspects involved in the process. Since it is often necessary to make a choice between them, it is not surprising that different researchers set off with different sets of variables, thereby giving rise to difficulties in comparing results.

It is relatively rare for the influence of resources on adaptation after the loss to be studied in a multivariate way. Since many of these are interrelated, we must be careful about drawing conclusions on the relative importance of these factors from bivariate correlational studies. It is, however, hardly possible to give a combined evaluation of the results of multivariate studies.

Although some studies are available, multiple problems arise for adequately comparing their results. One problem is the difference of the outcome measures which are predicted. Another is the difference in design, time and elaborateness of measurement between the different studies. It is apparent from Table 3.4 that every study incorporates its own specific set of independent variables. Adding up these problems, it is also hardly surprising that the clusters of variables found to be related to outcome differ for each study. One important conclusion, however, which can be drawn from multivariate studies, is that problems in adaptation to the loss might already appear in the early period after the loss.

As noted throughout this chapter, when studying bereavement we have to be aware that bereavement itself may imply profound changes in the pattern and availability of resources. This also means that bereavement creates additional task-demands and stresses. In view of the methodological positioning of our variables, it implies that strength and characteristics of resources can be seen from two different, but equally valid, perspectives on the relationship between event and consequences.

Resources may be seen as as *independent* variables, forming the background or combined cause of the (health) situation after the loss (a position often taken in bereavement research). One step further in this direction also suggests that the loss itself may (partly) be a consequence of the pre-existing situation. From another point of view, resources may be considered as *dependent* variables, with debility and loss of resources resulting directly from the death.

Some tentative conclusions on adaptation after bereavement

In this survey of the literature, we saw that empirical evidence is thin for many of the causal relationships between resources and adaptation after bereavement. Conclusions must thus be given bearing in mind the reservations listed above. Of course, these conclusions do not account for the relationships between the demands and resources, since relationships could not be reliably assessed in a multivariate way. Partly as a result from that, no causal inferences can be drawn from them.

One clear conclusion is that there is a substantial group of bereaved people who, several years after the loss, still evidence problems in adaptation in terms of physical and mental health. Also mortality in bereaved spouses is higher in comparison to the married.

Forewarning of death may have a favorable effect on adaptation, especially among the younger widowed. Subjective cognitive preparation is probably more strongly related to adaptation than length of illness. Unnatural or violent deaths entail different problems for the bereaved, and it is presumed that adaptation poses greater problems. Strong empirical evidence for this is, however, not available.

The role of the mode of death in adjustment seems small, and although the themes may differ, the level of adaptation appears virtually the same for suicide and other kinds of bereavement.

Widowers probably experience more problems than widows in terms of adaptation. The sex difference in parents seems to be the reverse, and little is known about sex differences in other relationships. In general, younger widowed are at a higher risk for developing psychological problems, as well as for increased mortality in comparison to older widows.

Kinship relationship to the deceased may constitute an important factor in adaptation. Loss of a child is probably the most difficult type of bereavement to cope with, followed by spousal bereavement and, at some distance, by sibling death and death of a parent (during adulthood). Of the latter two groups, however, no reliable position can be given.

There is a little, but inconclusive, evidence that heavy dependency on the deceased, dominance by the deceased and ambivalence in the relationship may predispose for less favorable outcome. Concurrent and antecedent task-demands (stressors), including pre-loss health appear to be indicative for poorer adaptation after bereavement. The bereaved's perception of social support is related to adaptation. On other (objective) measures of support, the data are less clear.

Bereaved with a (extremely) low socioeconomic status seem to have more difficulties after bereavement. The influence of socioeconomic status on bereavement adaptation appears to be small, however, in comparison to other factors, and its mechanisms are not clear.

In many studies, personality aspects such as perceived control, neuroticism and self-evaluation have proven to be linked to adaptation to life crises in general, and also specifically to bereavement.

Insufficiently studied topics

When comparing the available data on adaptation to bereavement to the model, we find a number of blank, or virtually blank, spaces in the field of bereavement research.

Looking at the task-demands of bereavement, very little systematic research has been undertaken into an important aspect of the type of bereavement: the formal or kinship relationship to the deceased. Most studies are either only concerned with spousal bereavement, or indiscriminately include different types of relationship in their samples without adequate control.

With regard to the pattern of tasks that concur at the moment of bereavement, little is known either. Of interest would be the way in which adaptation to bereavement disturbs other tasks such as maturation, life transitions, and personal development, or to what degree bereavement adaptation itself is favored or debilitated by them.

At the resource side, there are also some empty areas. The influence of informational social support on adaptation is largely unknown, and systematic assessment of the context in which adaptation has to take place is rare.

Methodological aspects

With regard to research-methodology, we indicated a number of general and specific problems. Concluding on this aspect, we may state that our knowledge about bereavement would benefit from more representative samples of bereaved, an elaborate systematic measurement of the situation and history of the bereaved combined with qualitative information, and a more systematic comparison between different kinships and modes of death. In the next chapter, a research project which attempts to incorporate these aspects will be presented.

Chapter 4

The Leiden Bereavement Study:
Objectives, Method and Response

Drawing from the discussion in the foregoing chapters, the objectives and setup of the Leiden Bereavement Study will now be discussed. We will also present a model for the assessment of our objectives. The instrument of the study, response, non-response and drop-out for the second measurement will be discussed in detail.

4.1   The design of the present study

Given the problems mentioned in the preceding chapters, we chose to study bereavement by exploring elaborately and systematically the known phenomena which accompany the bereavement process, without employing an a priori explanatory model as to how they are related. As we saw, systematic research may profit from taking a modest theoretical standpoint, making few assumptions about the precise dynamics of bereavement processes, leaving them open to investigation.

In order to study functioning after bereavement empirically, we will make a conceptual distinction between those aspects that we consider to reflect the adaptation to bereavement, and those that we see as factors potentially influencing this adaptation. A framework combining the model of task-demands and resources (Section 2.8) with the dimensions of adaptation (proposed in Section 2.9), will be used as the basis for this distinction .

Adaptation after bereavement: the dimensions of functioning

Functioning of the bereaved after the loss will be defined in terms of the three dimensions of functioning, proposed in Section 2.9. Functioning will be examined in terms of loss-reactions, health, and social functioning.

In terms of empirical research, each dimension can be seen as a bipolar construct. The three adaptational dimensions, listed in 2.2, will thus be operationalized in the measures of the present study. It is likely that these dimensions are not independent of each other, and that the interrelationships between them vary over time. Thus, the interrelationships between them will also be examined closely.

Each dimension in itself is multifaceted. Loss-reactions comprise multiple aspects such as shock-reactions to the event and detachment from the deceased. Health comprises physical and psychological health, as well as medicine and other substance use, while social functioning can be seen in terms of outgoingness, social integration, and experience of emotional support. Each of these facets will be assessed independently before combining and evaluating them in terms of the three dimensions.

Factors potentially influencing adaptation: task-demands and resources

The survey of the literature provided in the preceding chapters has given us some insight into the aspects which may play a role in functioning after bereavement. Most of these aspects, forwarded both in grief theories and empirical studies, were operationalized in the Leiden Bereavement Study. We will classify these aspects in terms of the demand-resource model (Section 2.8). Demands and resources will be evaluated with regard to their relationship to functioning after bereavement. We will not employ an a priori model of the relationship between the task-demands and resources.

As shown in Chapter 2, the factors claimed to be related to adaptation after a loss are legion. In the Leiden Bereavement Study, we tried to elaborately operationalize the task-demands of bereavement as well as the resources of the bereaved. With this aim in mind, we selected those resources and demands that were found, in the empirical literature, to be related to outcome (see Chapter 3). Some empirically translatable elements of grief theories were also investigated, especially concerning the attitude to the loss in terms of guilt, anger, and relief.

A recursive model

As shown in Section 3.8, in a groupwise study we have to take care that, in considering the general effects, we do not lose the view on the mechanisms within the individual. Because we wish to assess both the individual situation of a bereaved, and how this situation articulates with other bereaved, a number of requirements have to be met.

In the first place, task-demands, resources and dimensions of functioning had to be unambiguously translated into observable variables.

Secondly, in order to avoid some of the problems associated with too high an aggregation level of our observations, the quantitative character had to be complemented by a more qualitative approach to the field. Large-scale studies can benefit from a detailed account on the context in which each case was studied.

It is desirable to combine the possibilities offered by advanced statistical methods, while not losing track of the position of the individual. The Leiden Bereavement Study was designed in such a way that it was possible to conduct a thorough statistical analysis (a focus on group characteristics), as well as in-depth case analyses (a focus on individual characteristics). To this goal, we used a structured interview instrument, assessing all variables for all subjects. A number of open questions allowed for highly personal accounts and experiences on the part of the bereaved, and a short case report was written up by the interviewer directly after the interview.

The combination of a quantitative and a qualitative approach can be described in the recursive model that is graphically presented in Fig. 4.1.

Task-demands, resources and aspects of functioning are operationalized in a large number of items and scales. The data were consequently measured by means of an interview. This interview resulted in statistically analyzable data[1], and in a case report for each bereaved.

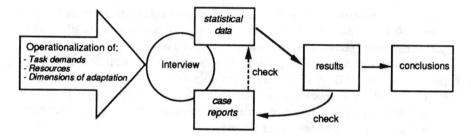

Fig. 4.1 *Model for research into adaptation after bereavement with quantitative and qualitative data.*

The findings of the statistical assessment are then checked against the findings on the individual level in several ways.

In the first place, qualitative case information will be used to elucidate and illustrate statistical conclusions (the 'check' arrow from results to case reports in Fig. 4.1).

In the second place, we can select individuals with specific outcome characteristics (e.g. high, middle or low scoring on a measure of adaptation) and look into the case reports for eventually shared characteristics in those subsamples.

---

1   The first step in analyzing the statistical data will, of course, be the analysis of internal validity of our data (not shown in the model). Only when the measure appears to be reliable and valid, is the scale applied in further analysis.

In addition, combinations of variables will serve to select subsamples which may be explored for specific dynamics (e.g. subgroups scoring high on depression but low on grief reactions).

In this way, to a certain extent, we are able to check whether or not the overall findings can be retraced in the individual. If not, we may suspect other factors to be involved.

If necessary, this may in turn lead to a re-analysis of associations within specific subgroups of the sample (the 'check' arrow from case reports to statistical data in Fig. 4.1.). By checking the statistical results in this way, a feedback loop is constructed, where feedback on the adequacy of statistical conclusions is provided by the contents of the case reports. This constitutes the recursive aspect of the model. By opting for this combined technique an attempt is made to get more insight into, and control over possible problems with a uniquely between-subject design.

4.2   The Leiden Bereavement Study

The present publication reflects the results[2] of the Leiden Bereavement Study, a controlled longitudinal study of 309 family-members (parents, spouses, siblings and adult children) of people who died from three different modes of death: bereaved after suicide (n=91), a traffic-fatality (n=93) and bereaved of people who died after a long-term illness (n=125). A standardized and elaborate interview was administered approximately four months after the death occurred. A follow-up interview, principally screening the events and changes in functioning since the first, took place approximately fourteen months after the loss.

The original aim of the study was to examine the effects of suicide as a cause of death. The primary focus was on the role of expectancy of the death. In order to make a reliable assessment of the role of expectancy of the loss, two comparison groups were chosen: death after a traffic accident, in which the loss was likely to be totally unexpected, and death after a long-term illness, in which case the death was likely to be expected.

The scope of the study has since been broadened and, although the comparison between the modes of death remains important, the focus is not uniquely on suicide anymore. Also other questions can be answered, given the elaborateness of the interviews, with the systematical measurement of a large number of variables (more than 1000 variables per bereaved were measured). The detailed assessment of the

---

2   The Leiden Bereavement Study contained a number of variables which will not be considered here. Variables which were not measured for all modes of death and a number of personality variables were, and will be, dealt with in other publications.

characteristics of the situation before the loss, the circumstances of death itself and the post-loss situation made it possible to examine the role of a multitude of effects.

In a number of publications, parts of the findings of the Leiden Bereavement Study have been presented. Some publications have concentrated on the first measurement in the suicide subsample (Van der Wal & Moritz 1986, Van der Wal, 1987), others on the first measurement among both suicide and traffic-fatality bereaved (Van der Wal, 1988; Van der Wal, Cleiren, Han, & Diekstra, 1988; Van der Wal, Cleiren & Diekstra, 1988; Van der Wal, Cleiren, Diekstra, & Moritz, 1988; Van der Wal & Cleiren, 1990), and some on the first measurement among the bereaved after a long term illness (Cleiren, 1988; Cleiren, Van der Wal, & Diekstra, 1988a,b).

The present publication is the first to comprise both first and second measurement and to offer a comparison between all three modes of death.

4.3   Method

In the following sections, the procedures used to identify, locate and approach our sample will be described in some detail.

4.3.1   Registration of the sample

To obtain a representative sample of the population bereaved from the designated modes of death, the time-sample method was used. The objective was to approach all families who suffered a loss from the given causes of death in a certain area during a given period of time. This outreaching approach avoids self-selection in the sample[3]. The details of the methods employed will be discussed in Sections 4.3.2 and 4.3.3.

Systematical inclusion and exclusion criteria for the study were:

(1)   The bereaved had to be at least 18 years of age, since the interview was designed for adult respondents.

(2)   In approaching the bereaved we approached family members in the first remove: parents, partner, children and siblings of the deceased.

(3)   Preferably we invited people who had shared a household with the deceased.

(4)   Bereaved who had sustained the loss of another close person in the time period between the target loss and our approach were excluded from the study.

(5)   Those who had lost someone in a traffic accident were not invited to participate if they were severely injured themselves in that accident.

---

3   For an elaborate discussion on the subject of privacy and ethical aspects of the method, see Van der Wal (1986, 1988).

When it was possible to interview more people in one family, the maximum number of respondents per deceased was five, and a mean number of 2.1 family members per deceased. Although interviewing more than one bereaved family member per deceased leads to a certain dependence within the sample, it is inevitable if we wish to obtain both a representative and a sizeable sample of bereaved family members.

Criteria (4) and (5) were employed to avoid too large an influence of those events on our data. The reactions to these other losses, such as other deaths or loss of one's own physical ability, are likely to be entangled with the reactions to the target loss. It then becomes difficult to compare them with those who sustained single losses.

4.3.2   Approach of the subjects

In order to obtain an optimal coverage we used different ways of tracing the members of our goal-populations for each cause of death.

To obtain the names and addresses of the survivors of suicide we worked together with the police forces of 7 towns in the western part of the Netherlands. The police makes a report on every death from unnatural causes. Suicides are thus registered by the police. This juridical registration is considered to be more accurate than other sources. Because of an assumed incomplete reporting in this registration (van Egmond, Diekstra, & De Graaf, 1983), we also examined other unnatural causes of death in some of the bigger towns. During the testing-period of our procedure we found one case in which 'drowning' was given as a cause of death, while from the description of the event it became clear that it was a matter of suicide. During the effective registration period (July - November 1985), we found no such cases. For the duration of this period, members of the research team were posted at the police forces. In the smaller towns, where the occurrence of suicide was rare, there was only a periodic telephone contact. The addresses and names we received were given and treated under strict conditions of confidentiality. Thus we registered 59 suicides. Looking at the number of deceased, it appears that of 48 out of 59 suicides (81%), at least one family member could be interviewed.

The registration of traffic-fatalities was originally performed in cooperation with the basic health services and the municipal health service (G.G.& G.D.). Later on, it appeared that this procedure did not work out well. We then changed to a registration on the basis of newspaper reports (not to be confounded with obituaries) in a number of regional and national newspapers. This registration period lasted from January to July 1986. In total we registered 75 fatal traffic accidents. In 37 cases (49%), at least one bereaved was prepared to cooperate in our study.

Given the problems we had with the registration procedure involving the health services, we chose to register the long-term illness deaths from obituaries in three national and two regional newspapers, in which the formulation pointed towards a death after a long-term illness. In the traffic-fatalities sample, we found that in approximately 85% of the cases there had been a death announcement in the newspaper. We suspected no systematic selectivity by this means of registration. In a series of t-tests we checked if there were indeed no differences between the groups which did and did not put an obituary in the newspaper. It appeared that the group which did not put an obituary had a somewhat lower mean income and were members of a lower professional group. The educational level did not differ for the two groups. This suggests that not putting an obituary might be related to financial reasons in the first place. There were no significant differences in other background variables. We registered 124 obituaries matching the criteria. From 60 of these bereaved families (48%), we interviewed at least one respondent.

The lower percentage of cooperation on a family level in the traffic-fatality and illness samples is largely due to the fact that for these groups, only one address was available, while in the registration of the suicide group often several names and addresses per deceased were accessible. When the approached person did not want to take part in the study, he or she often acted as a 'gatekeeper' to other family members and often was not prepared to provide us with other names or addresses within the family. Since contact with a family in the suicide group was not entirely dependent on the cooperation of one person, the coverage of the families was higher in these cases.

4.3.3   Contacting the bereaved

For all three of the death-causes, we used about the same manner of contacting the respondents.

First, a letter was sent to each address obtained. In this letter we informed the subjects about the backgrounds, objective and means of our investigation, and formulated our request. After that, we got in touch by phone to obtain their reaction to the request for cooperation. When, after several attempts, we could not reach them by phone, we wrote a second letter with a request to return the attached response form on which they could give their consent and a suggestion for date and time of the interview.

One exception to this procedure formed the subgroup of traffic-fatalities which was registered in cooperation with the health services. In these cases, we could not get in touch directly with the respondents. The health service sent a letter to the bereaved family, and only if they did return an attached answering form was the address given to the investigators. Because of the lower response rate and the lack of insight into the causes of non-response, we changed to the procedure using newspaper reports, as mentioned above.

4.4   Response

Table 4.1 lists the distribution of the bereaved over the modes of death and the kinship groups. In our case-finding procedure, there was no explicit goal to have an equal number of respondents for each combination of kinship and mode of death. This lead to some inequality between the cells. However, since it is possible to apply adequate statistical correction for this, it was not considered a problem.

Table 4.1

Composition of the sample (first interview in absolute numbers) by mode of death and kinship relationship to the deceased

	Spouses		Parents		Siblings		Children		Total
	M	F	M	F	M	F	M	F	
Suicide	5	9	7	11	19	16	15	9	91
Traffic-fatality	6	12	14	14	13	15	6	13	93
Long-term illness	18	23	9	12	12	11	16	24	125
Total	29	44	30	37	44	42	37	46	309

Notes: M= Male, F= Female

4.4.1   Characteristics of the non-response

In Table 4.2 the response and reasons for non-response for the three causes of death at the first interview are given. The response percentage was satisfactory. For all three modes of death the percentages were the same: 66%.

Looking at the percentage of the families that responded, a clear difference occurs: whereas we interviewed at least one family member of 81% of the deceased after suicide, this percentage was much lower for both other modes of death. The reason for this difference is that in the case of suicide, due to the procedure that was followed, the investigators often disposed of the addresses and phone numbers of more than one family member. For the other modes of death only one address was available. In the latter case, this meant that, when there was no contact with the identified bereaved, or when he or she did not wish to cooperate, access to the entire family was lost, while in the suicide group we were still able to contact other members.

Table 4.2

Response and reasons for non-response for the bereaved from three causes of death

	Suicide	Traffic-fatality	Illness	Total
Bereaved approached:	137 (100%)	140 (100%)	189 (100%)	466 (100%)
of how many deceased :	59 (100%)	75 (100%)	124 (100%)	258 (100%)
Response:				
Bereaved interviewed :	91 (66%)	93 (66%)*	125 (66%)	309 (66%)
of how many deceased :	48 (81%)	37 (49%)	60 (48%)	145 (56%)
Non-response				
-No personal contact	9 (7%)	18 (13%)	10 (5%)**	37 (8%)
-Interview broken off	-	-	2 (1%)***	2 (0.5%)
-Refused interview:				
Not up to it, too difficult	15	11	14	40
Don't want to go over it again.	5	5	13	19
Don't see the sense of it/not interested.	3	1	6	10
Don't want to talk about it with strangers.	-	1	3	4
Have talked about it too much already	-	-	2	2
No time for it	2	-	4	6
Angry	3	1	2	6
Denial cause of death	2	-	-	2
Fear for reaction partner	1	-	-	1
No reason given	6	11	8	25
Total refused:	37 (27%)	29 (21%)	52 (28%)	115 (25%)
Outside population**:**				
Cause of death outside criteria	-	-	3	
Other loss in meantime	-	1	1	
Seriously ill	1	-	1	
Address unknown	2	1	1	

*	51 respondents via G.G.& G.D. registration and 42 via newspaper registration procedure.
**	In two cases the person was hospitalized in a psychiatrical clinic
***	In one case there were signs of psychic decompensation during the interview, other respondent saw no sense in finishing the interview.
****	Not included in response-percentage

The percentage that refused cooperation -the most important factor liable to systematic selectivity- was relatively small: 25%. While we had no possibility of studying the refusers' health and general state of well-being, we could not determine whether they had characteristics different from those of the respondents. The reasons for non-cooperation, however, were often related to difficulty with the loss (see Table 4.2). This suggests that at least part of the refusers shows a severe reaction to the loss, forming possibly a more seriously affected subgroup. This will be taken into consideration when interpreting the results.

For the follow-up interview, conducted approximately 10 months after the first one, we managed to interview 90% of our original sample (see Table 4.3). Five percent of the drop-out actually refused a second interview. Four percent of the sample was unreachable. In 2 cases, this was due to serious illness: respondents were staying in a hospital (according to family members). In one case a respondent had died.

4.4.2   Non-response at follow-up

For the second interview it was possible to make a more thorough analysis of the non-response. The people who dropped out of our sample at the second interview (the T-2 drop-out) were compared with those who cooperated at T-2 on the measures obtained from both groups at T-1. In this section we will discuss in some detail the characteristics of the drop-out. This was done firstly by comparing the background variables, death-antecedent variables and well-being scores on the first interview between the entire group of respondents at the follow-up and the drop-out (31 cases) on follow-up. Secondly, subsamples were checked for eventual specific mechanisms.

There appeared to be no major differences between response and drop-out groups on the main background variables of age, gender, social status, religion and size of residence. The drop-outs, however, had somewhat more ambivalent feelings towards the deceased person during the first interview (t=2.40, df= 305, p=.017). At the follow-up interview, in general, respondents did not differ from the drop-out in terms of psychological health at the first interview. An exception formed the (VOEG) general health scores, which were significantly higher for the drop-outs (t=2.33, df= 305, p=.021). They also showed a trend for more frequent use of medication.

A possible explanation for these last differences is that, while some of the non-response was due to death or serious illness, these respondents presumably already had a deteriorating health during the first interview. To test this hypothesis, we excluded the non-response from serious-illness or death, and compared only those subjects who refused the second interview for different reasons (category 'refused interview' in Table 4.3) with the respondents who cooperated (category 'response' in Table 4.3). Here, as expected, the difference on general health scores disappeared.

Other comparisons between the refusers and the respondents on T-2 showed a significant difference on the Social Integration Scale (SIS): refusers felt somewhat more isolated than cooperators (t=1.42, df=303, p=.02), and here a slight trend persisted for refusers to feel more ambivalent about the deceased (t=-1.70, df=305, p=.09).

Table 4.3

Response and reasons for non-response for the bereaved from the three causes of death at the second interview

	Suicide	Traffic-fatality	Illness	Total
Total population first interview:	91 (100%)	93 (100%)	125 (100%)	309 (100%)
Response				
Bereaved interviewed:	78 (86%)	88 (95%)	112 (90%)	278 (90%)
% of original population	(57%)	(63%)	(59%)	(60%)
Non-response				
- Unreachable	4 (4%)	3 (3%)	2 (2%)	8 (3%)
- Interview lost	-	-	2 (1%)	2 (1%)
- Seriously ill/died	1 (1%)	-	2 (2%)	3 (1%)
- Refused interview:				
Not up to it, too difficult	1	2	1	4
Don't want to go over it again	-	-	3	3
Don't see sense of 2nd interview	-	-	1	1
Don't want to think/talk about it	3	-	-	3
No time for it	-	-	1	1
Personal problems/confused	2	-	-	2
No reason given	2	-	2	2
Total refused:	8 (9%)	2 (2%)	6 (5%)	16 (5%)

On closer inspection in an ANOVA with ambivalence as a dependent variable and refusal, sex, and mode of death as independent variables, an interaction effect of sex x refusal was found ($F=6.18$, $p=.014$). It appeared that the female refusers evidenced much more ambivalent feelings towards the deceased during the first interview than the female cooperators ($t=-3.53$, $df=153$, $p=.001$). The male refusers did not differ systematically from male and female respondents on ambivalence.

Response rates by kinship and mode of death

In an analysis of variance, it appeared that the drop-out proportion did not differ systematically between the sexes, the kinship groups, or the modes of death. Among parents, however, the drop-out was smaller than among the other kinship-groups: only one out of 66 parents did not participate in the second interview. From Table 4.4 it appears that the drop-out is largest among the spouses bereaved after suicide.

Table 4.4

Drop-out for the second interview in absolute numbers and percentages, by mode of death and kinship relationship to the deceased

	Spouses	Parents	Siblings	Children	Total
Suicide	5 (36%)	0 (0%)	5 (14%)	3 (12%)	13 (14%)
Traffic-fatality	2 (11%)	1 (4%)	1 (4%)	1 (5%)	5 (5%)
Long-term illness	5 (12%)	0 (0%)	4 (17%)	4 (10%)	13 (10%)
Total	12 (16%)	1 (1%)	10 (12%)	8 (10%)	31 (10%)

When refusal was examined by means of an analysis of variance, no systematic differences between sexes, kinships and modes of death were found.

The refusal rate was slightly, but not significantly, higher among men (7%) in comparison to women (3%). A further check on background variables revealed, however, that a significantly larger proportion of the people living alone refused a follow-up interview (10%), as compared to those who shared their home with at least one other person (3%).

Background of drop-out and refusal per kinship group

To detect possible differential reasons for drop-out in each kinship group, the latter were examined separately. As in the preceding section, the drop-out at T-2 was compared with the response at T-2 on the sociodemographic, death-antecedent and well-being scores on T-1.

In the spouses group, next to the already mentioned general difference in general health and medical consumption, the drop-out (11 of the 73 spouses) evidenced a heightened shock reaction at T1. The only parent who dropped out, refusing the second interview, was a 57 year old father of a boy who died in a traffic accident. He had a relatively high medical consumption at T1 and, at the time, was involved in psychiatrical care. The drop-out among siblings (10 out of 86) was not distinguishable from the responding siblings on any of the variables. Among the children, in addition to having lower well-being scores, the drop-out (8 of the 83 children) felt emotionally somewhat less supported ($t=-2.38$, $df=81$, $p=.02$).

A similar comparison was made within each kinship-group between the group that refused the second interview and those who cooperated. Among the spouses, the refusers (4 cases) were in an older age group. Four months after the loss, they felt more isolated ($t=2.33$, $df=63$, $p=.02$) and evidenced relatively more negative reactions from the environment ($t=2.71$, $df=62$, $p=.009$). No difference was found in the sibling group between respondents and refusers (6 cases). Among the children, the ones who refused (3 cases) evidenced a very low level of social activity during the first interview (t=2.62, df=76, p=.011), and little confidence in their ability to cope with the loss in the future (t=2.75, df=75, p=.008).

Looking at the separate modes of death, it appeared that within the group of traffic-fatalities, the drop-out was worse-off in terms of physical and psychological health. A remarkable interaction effect (F=4.77, p=.009) was found with regard to relationship satisfaction. In the suicide group, the refusers felt significantly *less* satisfied with the relationship they had shared with the deceased, while the refusing survivors of death from a long-term illness had been significantly *more* satisfied.

Conclusion

From the above, we can conclude that there is a difference in general health between response and non-response on follow-up. The segment of the drop-out that refused cooperation differed at four months from the cooperators in social integration. Health at four months seems not to be related to personal refusal at fourteen months.

It is unclear whether the severe morbidity (2 cases) and mortality (in one case) in our sample were related to the loss, but there were indications that severe health problems in those cases already existed before death. There may be differential backgrounds for non-cooperation in specific subgroups of our sample. Ambivalence towards the deceased seems to play a role in the refusal of cooperation in women, but this is not found in men. When looking at the different kinship-groups, it appears that the backgrounds for non-cooperation may also differ. The general tendency seems to be that the subjects who dropped out at the second interview were physically (but not psychologically) less healthy during the first one, relatively more ambivalent or dissatisfied about the relationship with the deceased, and were socially less integrated than the subsample which continued to cooperate.

4.5   Sociodemographic characteristics of the sample

In order to give an idea of the background of the sample, and to put it in perspective with the general Dutch population, some sociodemographic characteristics will be discussed here. The frequencies and percentages pertaining to most of the characteristics are listed in Table 4.5.

Educational level

The educational level did not differ significantly between the modes of death. There was, however, a significant difference between the the sexes (F=23.5, p=.000), where women had reached a significantly lower level than men, and between the kinship-groups (F=5.5, p=.001), where spouses and parents had a relatively lower level of education than siblings and children of the deceased. Since educational level is negatively correlated with age (r = -.30), and the older respondents are mainly found in the spouse and parents groups, this last difference is most probably related to age.

Table 4.5
Some sociodemographic characteristics of the sample

Social occupation	Frequency	Percentage	Occupational group (of those currently working, n=145)	Frequency	Percentage
Working	145	46.9 %	Unskilled labour	11	7.6 %
Housewife	79	25.6 %	Skilled labour	25	17.2 %
Study/schoolgoing	34	11.0 %	Lower employee	34	23.4 %
Retired	25	8.1 %	Self-employed	19	13.1 %
Unemployed	13	4.2 %	Medium employee	24	16.6 %
Incapacitated	13	4.2 %	Higher profession	32	22.1 %

Religion	Frequency	Percentage	Household Living with:	Frequency	Percentage
None	137	44.3 %			
Roman Catholic	87	28.2 %	Family members	228	73.8 %
Protestant	69	22.3 %	Alone	68	22.0 %
Other	16	5.2 %	Other house-mate(s)	12	3.9 %

Educational level	Frequency	Percentage	Net family income (p. month, Dutch guilders)	Frequency	Percentage
Primary school	56	18.2 %	Less than 1,000	36	12.2 %
Lower vocational training	58	18.9 %	1,000 < 1,500	56	19.0 %
Lower general second. education	44	14.3 %	1,500 < 2,000	47	15.9 %
Intermediate vocational training	42	13.7 %	2,000 < 2,500	51	17.3 %
High school/grammar school	44	14.3 %	2,500 < 3,000	35	11.9 %
Higher vocational training	41	13.4 %	3,500 < 4,000	35	11.9 %
University	22	7.2 %	More than 4,000	35	11.9 %

Social occupation

A major part of the respondents works (46%). The second most frequent occupation is housewife. In the sample, 47% of the women are housewives, while 33% work outside the home. Of the men, the percentage working is 63% work.

The children in the sample differ clearly in occupation from the other groups: not surprisingly, because of their overall younger age, none of them is pensioned, and joblessness is somewhat more frequent among them.

Occupational level

In an ANOVA with kinship, sex and mode of death as independent variables, no systematic differences appeared between the modes of death or the kinship groups. The occupational level of men was significantly higher than that of women ($F=27.2$, $df=1$, $p=.002$), although the absolute difference is small.

Income

The income level of the sample in general lay around Dfl. 2,000.=. In an ANOVA with kinship, sex and mode of death as independent variables, some systematic differences appeared. Men reported higher income than women ($F=45.7$, $df=1$, $p=.000$). A significant difference also exists between the kinship groups ($F=70.3$, $df=3$, $p=.000$): siblings of the deceased reported lower income than bereaved children and parents. The spouses took an intermediate position here. There was a marked difference between widows and widowers in income level which is reflected in a significant interaction between kinship and sex ($F=44.3$, $df=3$, $p=.003$): the income of widows was much lower compared to that of widowers. This effect can be explained from the fact that in most cases, the deceased was the breadwinner. For the widows, it thus appears that there is a drop in income due to the loss. There was no significant income difference between the modes of death.

Household

Not surprisingly, the type of household differed considerably with the kinship group. Bereaved spouses most often lived alone (in 53% of the cases) as compared to the other kinship groups. Bereaved children, in most of the cases, lived together with the remaining parent and/or other family members (in 90% of the cases).

Religion

A relatively large part (more than 44%) of the sample is not member of a church. There are no differences between kinship groups or the sexes in the distribution over the religions. When looking at church membership, there is some difference between the modes of death: the bereaved after a traffic-fatality, when religious, are more often members of a Protestant church, while the suicide bereaved in this case are more often members of the Roman Catholic church.

Age of the respondent

Age, in the context of the present study, is a variable which is not likely to be equally distributed over the different kinship groups. Parents are, for instance, more likely to be in the older age groups than children of the deceased. The term 'children', in this study, must be understood in terms of kinship and not as an age criterion. Table 4.6 lists the mean ages for each kinship group. As can be seen, the mean age also differs considerably and significantly ($F=8.1$, $df=2$, $p=.000$) between the different modes of death.

Table 4.6
Mean ages (with standard deviations) of the respondents by mode of death and kinship relationship to the deceased.

	Spouses		Parents		Siblings		Children		Total	
	M	SD	M	SD	M	SD	M	SD	M	SD
Suicide	43.4	18.4	57.1	12.3	39.4	16.1	40.5	9.3	43.8	15.6
Traffic-fatality	43.7	18.6	51.9	10.5	32.1	17.2	30.0	5.9	39.9	16.6
Illness	54.7	13.7	54.5	17.2	47.1	16.6	31.7	9.9	45.9	17.1
Total	49.8	16.7	54.1	13.4	39.1	17.4	33.8	9.8	43.5	16.6

The children in our sample were mostly somewhat older (m= 33.8) and often had households of their own, functioning quite independently from their parents. The children who lose a parent by suicide are furthermore markedly older than those in the other modes of death. A large percentage of variance in age of the respondent is explained by kinship (25%, $F=36.3$, $df=3$, $p=.000$).

Age of the deceased

In Table 4.7, the age of the deceased is broken down by the kinship relationship of the respondent to the deceased and mode of death. The age of the deceased covaries even stronger with kinship ($F=95.0$, $df=2$, $p=.000$). The kinship relationship explains 44% of the variance in the age of the deceased. In the long-term illness group, for spouses and siblings, the deceased was relatively older than in the other modes of death, while with the parents and children, the deceased died at a relatively younger age than in the other modes of death. This accounts for a small but significant interaction between mode of death and kinship ($F=3.1$, $df=6$, $p=.006$).

Table 4.7

Mean ages (with standard deviations) of the corresponding deceased, split up by mode of death and kinship relationship to the deceased

	Spouses		Parents		Siblings		Children		Total	
	M	SD	M	SD	M	SD	M	SD	M	SD
Suicide	44.4	18.2	28.7	9.3	39.7	16.6	67.9	12.4	45.7	20.3
Traffic-fatality	43.9	17.8	21.8	9.0	30.6	16.3	64.9	8.2	37.5	20.7
Illness	54.9	15.0	24.0	14.4	45.8	19.1	62.6	13.8	50.5	20.2
Total	50.2	17.0	24.3	11.3	38.4	18.0	64.7	12.4	45.2	21.0

Representativity for the Dutch population

Comparing the socio-demographic characteristics of our sample with the Dutch population at large (CBS, 1984, 1988), the sample seems not to differ significantly. The distributions over the types of social occupation, income level and the educational level are virtually the same. In our sample, the occupational level of those currently working (Table 4.5, 'Occupational group') is somewhat higher. This difference is most marked in the 'unskilled labour' category: 8% in our sample against 24% in the Dutch population. Also, the distribution over the religions is somewhat different, with a relatively larger percentage professing no religion than in the general population (44.3% versus 32.6%). This higher percentage may be due to frequent omission of people to pass their change to a non-religious denomination on to the census registration offices, from which the population figures are drawn. This is more often the case among former Catholics, and may also be reflected in the lower percentage of Catholics in our sample (28%) in comparison with the general population (36%).

Conclusion

Although a number of significant differences exists in sociodemographic variables in the sample, between the modes of death and the different kinship groups, most of these are not very large. To the extent that differences exist between men and women, they are in the expected direction for the Dutch population, with men on the whole having slightly higher levels of education, occupation and income.

The differences in age between the groups are due to the fact that the groups are natural groups and we did not seek to match for this variable. The findings for the strong relationship between kinship and age, and to a lesser extent, that between mode of death and age, may be qualified as natural differences. Nonetheless, they make it necessary to statistically control for those variables (especially for kinship) when the role of age in adaptation is to be examined.

Except for the relatively high occupational level, there is no reason to assume that the present sample in sociodemographic background differs considerably from the Dutch population.

4.6   The interview

In order to obtain a more or less complete and structured image of each respondent in his/her present situation, we used structured personal interviews, consisting of a combination of categorical and open questions.

The interview method has a number of advantages. The response rate is positively influenced and the number of missing values can be limited. Furthermore, not only can the relationship between variables be traced, but also their meaning. In addition, more justice can be done to the individual situation of the bereaved, especially since many of the questions are of a very personal and intimate nature. The questions were arranged in a chronological order, passing from demographic variables and questions about the time before and around death to the situation at the time of the interview.

Most of the interview consisted of items with pre-coded answering categories. The method of field-coding was used. The interviewer posed a question and asked the respondent which answering alternative reflected most properly his or her opinion. The interviewer wrote the answer down in the chosen scoring category. The interviewers were instructed to note the respondent's elaborations and to stimulate elucidations on an answer if necessary. These comments were written down along with the pre-coded answer.

After the interview, the interviewer gave ratings on the conversation and the respondent's situation, and wrote a short case-report. Thus each interview formed a sort of instantaneous photograph of the individual's situation, providing a systematic screening of the concepts involved, as well as an more impressionistic view.

4.7   Questions addressed in the present publication

The present publication will mainly focus on answering the following three questions:

1) *What is the role of mode of death and kinship relationship to the deceased[4] in the adaptation of the bereaved in the short and longer term after the loss?*

As concerns this question, the objective is to give a description and comparative analysis of the role of mode of death and kinship relationship in loss-reactions, physical and and psychological health, and social functioning, at four and fourteen months after the loss.

2) *How do the different aspects of functioning after bereavement relate to each other?*

We will address this question by describing and analyzing the relationship between the different aspects of functioning: loss-reactions, physical and psychological health of the bereaved, and social functioning at four and fourteen months after the loss.

3) *In what way is functioning after bereavement related to the characteristics of the loss, the situation in which it occurred, and the resources available to the bereaved?*

For this question, we will look at the predictive power of loss characteristics and individual characteristics for functioning of the bereaved four and fourteen months after the loss. Once again, this will be done in terms of loss-reactions, health and social functioning.

Answering the questions

We will now give a crude indication as to which steps will be taken in answering the principal questions of the present study.

To answer the first question, the scores on each of a range of measures of functioning will be discussed to obtain a more detailed view on the prevalence of problems in different areas of functioning. A systematic comparison will be made between sexes, different kinship groups, and causes of death. Changes which occur between four months and fourteen months will be highlighted. We will deal with this in Chapter 5.

For our second question, we will combine the measures of functioning into the three dimensions of functioning. On a combined conceptual and statistical basis, three

---

4   The terms 'kinship relationship' and 'kinship' will be employed here to indicate the type of first-degree family relationship between bereaved and deceased.

general dimensions will be formed: one reflecting loss-reactions, one reflecting health, and a third one indicating social functioning. Using an explorative approach, we will describe the relationship between the dimensions, and the positions of the modes of death and kinship groups in relation to them. To this goal, nonlinear principal components analysis (PRINCALS, see Gifi, 1985) will be used exploratively. Checks will also be performed for differences between the structure of adaptation at four months and at fourteen months. Chapter 6 will deal with the answer to this second question.

With our third question, we will search for early indications of later problems after bereavement. The general dimensions of adaptation, which were constructed for our second question, along with a measure for change in functioning, will serve as criteria. Data from the first interview will be projected on the situation as measured during the follow-up study. Multiple regression analysis will be performed with the earlier constructed dimensions as dependent variables, and the task-demands and resources of the bereaved (comprising sociodemographic variables, loss and pre-loss characteristics) will be entered as predictor variables. This will be done in Chapter 7.

As can be seen in this section, in answering the subsequent questions we move from a more or less univariate evaluation to a multivariate approach. To some extent, the second and third question build on the answers to the foregoing questions.

4.8   Measurement variables

Many of the variables discussed in chapter two were operationalized in the Leiden Bereavement Study. The variables which are involved in this dissertation are, however, a selection from the data gathered in both the first and the second interview. This selection excludes all variables which were specifically related to a certain cause of death, because of the comparative character of the present study.

Examples of such specific variables are questions about hope for recovery of the patient in the long-term illness group, details about insurance for the traffic-fatality group, and (dis)satisfaction regarding contacts with the police in the suicide group. Also, some questions are omitted which were likely to have a totally different connotation for each of the causes of death. The above variables are dealt with in other publications (Cleiren, 1988; Van der Wal, Cleiren, Han, & Diekstra, 1988; Van der Wal, Cleiren & Diekstra, 1989).

Another group of variables -a number of personality traits measured with a personality questionnaire- will not be considered here. The reason for this is that they cannot be placed in the present design, since they were only assessed at follow up.

The variables involved in the present dissertation can be divided into three groups on the basis of the model outlined earlier. We will distinguish variables defining the task demand, variables pertaining to the resources of a person, and those defining functioning of the bereaved after the loss.

In the following sections, the contents of all the variables involved in answering the three central questions in this publication will be briefly presented[5]. Often scales were constructed or adopted to provide a more valid measurement of the concepts involved. A more detailed account of the choice of the scales, as well as a complete presentation of the scales involved can be found in Van der Wal, Cleiren, Han, & Diekstra (1988).

Task-demands

Each of the following, more or less formal, aspects of the task demand were measured with single questions:

* *sex* of the deceased and the respondent
* *age* of the deceased and the respondent
* *mode of death* : suicide, traffic-fatality or long term illness.
* *kinship to the deceased* bereaved either being spouse, parent, sibling or child of the deceased.

To assess the, what we shall call, 'informal' task-demands, scales and variables of our own design were employed which concentrated on the following aspects:

* *Quality of the relationship with the deceased* was measured by use of a number of scales:
  * *Intimacy Scale:* measures the degree of intimacy between the bereaved and deceased before the loss.
  * *Dominance Scale:* measures the degree to which the bereaved felt dominated by the deceased before the loss.
  * *Independence Scale:* measures the extent to which the deceased was independent from the bereaved before the loss.
  * *Relationship Satisfaction Scale:* measures the satisfaction of the bereaved with the relationship that existed with the deceased before the loss.
  * *Ambivalence Scale:* measures the presence and intensity of ambivalent feelings toward the deceased.
  * *Frequency of contact* between bereaved and deceased during the last half year before the loss (measured with a single item).

---

5   The exact properties of variables and scales will not be discussed here. Instead, they will be
     evaluated and discussed in some detail before presenting the results.

- *Other task-demands at the time of the loss* :
  - *Cumulative Stresses* during the year before bereavement, measured with a scale of our own design.
  - *Psychological health problems* before the loss, measured with a single item.
  - *Physical health problems* before the loss, measured with a single item.
  - *Expectancy of the loss*, measured with a single item.

All of the variables listed above were measured during the first interview, four months after the loss.

Resources

The availability and state of the resources of the bereaved was generally assessed with scales and items of our own design.

- *Available material resources*
  - *educational level* of the respondent
  - *occupational level* of the deceased and the respondent
  - *income* of the respondent

Each of the above variables was measured with single questions during the first interview. Some of these were checked for possible changes during the follow-up.

- *Available social support*
  - *Sufficiency of Emotional Support*, the extent to which the offered support matches the needs of the bereaved. Measured with the Experienced Emotional Support Scale of our own design (Van der Wal, Cleiren, Han, & Diekstra, 1988).
  - *Sufficiency of Practical and Informational Support*, the extent to which the offered support matches the needs of the bereaved. Measured with the Experienced Practical and Informational Support Scale of our own design (Van der Wal, Cleiren, Han, & Diekstra, 1988).

- *Attitude to the loss*
  - *Anger* Feelings of anger during the past week. Measured with the Anger Scale, a selection of the Z.A.V., a questionnaire for self-analysis (Van der Ploeg, Defares & Spielberger; 1982).
  - *Guilt* Feelings of guilt with regard to the (circumstances of) death. Measured with the Guilt Scale of our own design (Van der Wal, Cleiren e.a. 1988).
  - *Relief* Degree of relief over the death of the deceased. Measured with the Relief Scale of our own design.

- *The environment in which the task-demands are carried out*
  - *Housing situation* of the respondent, measured with a single item.

Functioning after the loss

Multiple indicators of general functioning were measured to obtain a differentiated view of the current state of functioning of the respondent. The measures are operationalizations of the three dimensions of functioning, which were presented in Section 2.9. The respondent was asked to answer these questions with regard to a limited and defined time span, generally the situation during the week before the interview. As can be seen in the following listing, there is sometimes a degree of (inevitable) conceptual overlap between the variables within each dimension.

Loss-reactions

The dimension of reactions to the loss was assessed by two single items, one scale of our own design, and one existing scale.

- *Questions about the circumstances of death.* The extent to which the bereaved is engaged in searching for explanations and elucidations about the circumstances of the loss, measured with one item.
- *Search for meaning.* The extent to which the bereaved is absorbed in finding a meaning to what has happened, measured with one item.
- *Detachment.* The degree to which the respondent emotionally and cognitively accepts that the deceased is no longer part of the daily life environment. Measured with a scale of our own design, the Leiden Detachment Scale (Van der Wal, 1986).
- *Impact of the event.* The degree to which the bereaved evidences post-traumatic stress in the form of intrusive and evasive thoughts and behaviors with regard to the loss. Measured with our own translation of the Impact of Event Scale (Horowitz e.a.,1980; Van der Wal, Cleiren e.a., 1988).

Health

Functioning in terms of psychological and physical health was measured partly with existing and validated instruments and, if these were not available, by scales of our own design.

- *Depression.* Measured with the 13-item version of the Beck Depression Inventory (Beck and Beck, 1972).
- *Suicidal ideation.* Questions about suicidal thoughts and actions and the methods of suicide considered or applied during the time before and after the death.

- *Control.* Measured with the Sense of Control Scale of our own design. The feeling that one is in control of one's life and will be able to cope with the demands of the future, has been termed a central theme in the adaptation to a loss (Hansson and Remondet, 1988). Also, in an attribution-theoretical sense, this aspect is considered important (cf. Stroebe & Stroebe,1987).
- *Somatic complaints* Measured with the VOEG, a questionnaire about health as experienced by the respondent (Dirken 1967).
- *Medicine consumption.* Frequency and quantity of the consumption of medicines.
- *Alcohol consumption.* Frequency and quantity of the consumption of alcoholic drinks.
- *Cigarette consumption.* Frequency and quantity of cigarettes, cigars, and/or pipes smoked.
- *Drug consumption.* Frequency and quantity of the consumption of soft and/or hard drugs.

Social functioning

The dimension of social functioning was operationalized in different aspects, while all scales were designed for the present study.

- *Need for Emotional support.* The need for emotional support, for intimacy and the need to talk about the loss, measured with the Need for Emotional Support Scale (NESS, Cleiren, Van der Wal & Diekstra, 1988).
- *Social integration.* A general feeling of security, being part of a group, and involvement in intimate relationships. This is measured with the Social Integration Scale (Cleiren, Van der Wal & Diekstra, 1988).
- *Social activities.* The extent to which one engages in (diverting) social contacts, measured with the Social Activity Scale, a scale of our own design.
- *Negative reactions.* The frequency and difficulty with negative reactions of the social environment after the loss.

In the next chapter, as the first step in presenting the results, functioning will be discussed in terms of each of these measures, in relationship to the main 'formal' aspects of the task demand of bereavement: sex of the bereaved, kinship to the deceased and mode of death.

Chapter 5

Mode of Death, Kinship, and Functioning after Bereavement: Empirical Results

In this chapter, we will attempt to answer the first question of our study:

What is the role of mode of death and kinship relationship to the deceased in the adaptation of the bereaved in the short and longer term after the loss?

To this goal we will analyze and describe the scores of the sample on all aspects of functioning which were assessed by the Leiden Bereavement Study. The measures are categorized per dimension of functioning. Section 5.1 deals with functioning in terms of loss-reactions, Section 5.2 will discuss the measures of physical and psychological health, while Section 5.3 will examine different aspects of social functioning. In Section 5.4, we will discuss three aspects that reflect the attitude to the death: anger, guilt and relief. In the last section we will give a summary of the findings in this chapter, and give a differentiated answer to the above question.

Method of presentation

Presentation of the data will be carried out by taking each aspect of a dimension as a unit. For each measure, we will first discuss the properties and contents of the scale. After that, the results will be presented. Thirdly, conclusions will be drawn and a short discussion given on the findings.

This way of presenting the results has been chosen in order to avoid the reader becoming confused by the multitude of aspects discussed, and to be able to make specific comparisons between the present findings and those of other studies on grief, discussed in Chapter 2. A quick overview of the major findings can be obtained by reading the 'conclusion' paragraph presented at the end of each section.

Method of analysis

All analyses discussing the situation at four months apply to the original sample of N=309. The analyses performed with regard to the second interview at fourteen months and the differences between T1 and T2 pertain to the subsample that cooperated at both interviews (N=278).

The properties of the outcome scales involved will be evaluated with Principal components analysis and Reliability analysis (Cronbach's coefficient α). For each scale, the typical items will be presented. The properties of the scales are also listed in Appendix 1.

The analysis of differences between groups

The comparison between the classes of the main variables of interest will be mainly performed by means of analysis of (co)variance with one dependent and multiple independent variables. The scores of the sample will be systematically broken down by, and compared in relation to the principal independent variables of this study: mode of death, kinship with the deceased, and sex are entered as independent variables. Age of the respondent is checked for a possible role as a covariate[1].

The analysis of changes in outcome

An assessment of the change in scores between four and fourteen months will be made in two ways. For the change in functioning on a specific measure in the whole sample, a comparison of the mean scores will be performed with a paired t-test (cf. Hays, 1981; Visser, 1982).

For some of the outcome scales which are calibrated, a more detailed analysis of directions and magnitude of change in the sample will be presented. To this goal the model of Uniken Venema-van Uden (1990) will be used. A short explanation of this model will be given here. Although it was originally used in an intervention study of effect-sizes (with a pre and post-treatment measurement), it may also serve as an adequate framework for the study of specific directions of change in the case of grief.

Cohen (1977) proposed an effect-size measure, known as 'Cohen's d' to be used as a criterion for observable change. When T1 and T2 are the two successive measurements of outcome in time, then d is the difference between the scores at each measurement, divided by the standard deviation of the first measurement:

$$d = \frac{\text{score at T2 - score at T1}}{\text{S.d. at T1}}.$$

The more the value of d differs from zero, the larger the size of the effect. Cohen stated that, in order to speak at least of a 'medium effect-size', a value of d of less than -.5 or more than +.5 was required. Values of d closer to zero, corresponding to a smaller difference between the scores at the two measurements, may be considered to

---

[1]   Since the correlation between age of the respondent and age of the deceased was very high within each kinship group, only the age of the respondent will be discussed in the analysis. In Section 5.4 some general remarks will be made about the role of the age of the deceased.

be products of chance or measurement error. If d differs more than .5 from zero, this can be considered either as a significant improvement, or a deterioration in functioning.

Although this measure forms an indication of the magnitude of change, it does not account for the *meaning* of the change: a significant improvement in health of someone who is already reasonably healthy has quite a different meaning from the same level of improvement in a formerly unhealthy person. Uniken Venema - van Uden (1990) designed an elegant model in which the norms for a measure on the second measurement are integrated. On the basis of a combination of effect-size d and norm scores, each individual is assigned to one of five categories: unchanged poor outcome, significant deterioration, unchanged moderate outcome, significant improvement and unchanged good outcome[2].

In the present study, the procedure for assigning the respondents to a dynamic class was performed as follows.

For each bereaved who had participated at both interviews, Cohen's d was computed by subtracting the score at the outcome measure at four months from the score at fourteen months, and dividing this by the standard deviation of the sample on the measure at four months. A higher score on an outcome measure always indicates more problems. In this way, an increase of problems was indicated by a positive value of d, while a decrease in problems (an improved level of functioning) resulted in a negative value of d.

Then, in combination with the norms available for the outcome measure, the bereaved were assigned to the following five dynamic classes (see also Fig. 5.1):

Class 1: unchanged favorable outcome. Those bereaved who had a good score at both four months and fourteen months, but did not show a significant improvement ($d > -0.5$) fell into this category. Also, if they showed a significant increase in problems ($d >= 0.5$), but still could be termed as having a 'good' score, they were assigned to this dynamic class.

Class 2: significant improvement. Here, we find the bereaved who showed a significant improvement at fourteen months ($d <= -0.5$). If, however, in addition to this, their score was still within the norm-category indicating poor outcome, they were nonetheless assigned to class 5.

Class 3: unchanged moderate outcome. The bereaved who did not show a significant change between both interviews ($-.5 < d < .5$) and had a moderate score at fourteen months were assigned to this class.

---

2   A perspicuous explanation of the model is given in Uniken Venema-van Uden (1990).

Class 4: significant deterioration. Bereaved were assigned to this class if they showed a considerable increase of problems ($d >= 0.5$) and did not have a 'good' outcome score at fourteen months.

Class 5: unchanged poor outcome. If the bereaved fell into the 'poor outcome' category at the second interview, and this condition had not greatly deteriorated ($d < 0.5$), they were assigned to this dynamic class. Mirroring class 1, a significantly lower score at fourteen months ($d <= -0.5$), but still being in the 'poor functioning' norm-category lead also to assignment to this class.

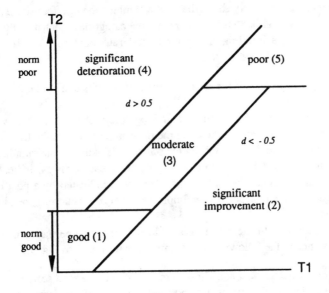

T1= score at four months, T2= score at fourteen months.
Diagonal lines: $d = -0.5$ and $d = +0.5$

Fig. 5.1   *Visual representation of the model of change and final scores (freely adapted from Uniken Venema - van Uden, 1990)*

Thus, in the classes 2 and 4 we find the bereaved who manifest a significant change in their situation: either showing an amelioration in their functioning with a moderate or good outcome at fourteen months (class 2), or a deterioration of their situation, while evidencing moderate or poor outcome at fourteen months (class 4). Membership of the classes 1, 3 and 5 indicates little change, with bereaved showing unchanged poor (class 5), unchanged moderate (class 3) or unchanged good functioning (class 1).

When no norms for a scale are available, an analysis of covariance on the scores at the second interview will be performed, with the score on the first interview as a covariate. Since this procedure, in contrast to application of the model of dynamic class, does not take into account possible ceiling or bottom effects, special attention will be given to those effects in the interpretation of the results.

5.1 Functioning in terms of loss-reactions

In this section, we will discuss the role of cognitive and emotional components of the reactions which directly pertain to the loss (as listed in Section 5.6). All questions in this section directly refer to the deceased and the loss-event itself.

5.1.1 Questions about cause and circumstances of death

Having no clear image of the circumstances or the cause of death may lead to rumination about these questions. This aspect was measured with a single item: 'How often have you been occupied with questions regarding the circumstances of death or the cause of death during the last week, including today ?'. The scoring categories ranged from 0: 'did not keep me occupied' to 3: 'occupied me continuously'.

The question was purposely worded in a general sense, since it was assumed that the type of questions might differ considerably with the individuals. The bereaved were encouraged to elaborate on the contents of eventual specific questions and uncertainties.

Results

As expected, the subjects of the questions about the cause and circumstances of death were diverse, concentrating on different aspects of the loss. The focus of the uncertainty was partly related to the mode of death.

The questions of the bereaved from suicide in this area concentrated mainly on what had been going on in the mind of the deceased before the act of suicide. Questions such as: *'Did he do it in full consciousness, or did he act in a fit of madness?'* and *'Did she really want to die, or just want to attract our attention?'* were prominent in this group.

The bereaved from a traffic-fatality were often preoccupied with the exact circumstances of the accident. A widow whose husband (age 70) died in a collision between his moped and a car asked herself why the accident had happened: *' Was it his own fault? He was often easily distracted, and I was always a little afraid when I saw him leave on his moped. On the other hand he was very careful... Did he see the car coming in his last moments? .... Did he have a stroke or a heart attack ? He had not been very well lately..'.* In some cases, information supplied by the police or witnesses gave the bereaved a better image of what had happened, but especially difficult were the 'one driver, one car' accidents. A father who lost his 22 year old son in such a fatality could not put it out of his mind: *'He drove from our home to G. where he studied. He was very cheerful, we had passed a nice weekend together. He had not drunk anything, it was a clear night... I have seen the curve where it happened: it was not sharp...there are no witnesses... I don't understand how it could have happened! I sometimes think there had to be someone else involved, he had to avoid a pedestrian, or a drunken driver.. I get very angry when I think about that...'*

The bereaved after a long time illness more often had a fairly good image of what had happened, but still, in many cases, they felt a need to be more precisely informed about what the death cause had been. In the case of cancer, the deceased often died from a complication rather than the cancer itself. In some cases the bereaved felt they had no clear image of what exactly had brought about death and felt they had not been well informed by the medical staff. This was sometimes related to suspicion of errors made by doctors or surgeons. Fourteen months after the loss, if present, questions and ruminations tended to center more on the deeper meaning of the loss.

In the sample as a whole, extensive rumination about the questions does not seem to play an important role four months after the loss. The sample in general as a whole had a mean score of .59 (s.d.= .93) at the first interview, and .43 (s.d.= .78) at the second. Nonetheless, we find 34% of the sample at least sometimes preoccupied with questions about the circumstances or the cause of death and, at fourteen months, they still make up 29% of the bereaved.

With an analysis of covariance, the main effects and interactions of mode of death, kinship and sex were tested with age as a covariate (see Table 5.1). On both interviews, there are significant but small differences between the kinship groups. Initially, the bereaved in the unnatural death groups are more occupied with questions regarding the cause of death. At fourteen months the difference has disappeared. They age of the respondent (as with the age of the deceased), introduced as a covariate, does not play a role.

At four months, there is a somewhat larger difference between the relationship groups and a small effect is found for mode of death. The combination of kinship and sex (relationship to the deceased) explains 9.3% of the variance. There is no significant difference between the sexes, and there are no significant higher order interactions.

Looking at the mean scores, it appears that parents and spouses in the unnatural death groups score highest. Most occupied are the bereaved from suicide (m=.89), followed by the bereaved from a traffic-fatality (m=.69). Bereaved of a fatal illness are less occupied (m=.30).

Table 5.1

Analysis of covariance on questions about the circumstances of death at 4 and 14 months after the loss, with mode of death, kinship and sex independent, and age of the respondent as a covariate

	Variable	Variance explained	Signific.
Questions at 4 months	Mode of death	6.9%	p=.000
	Kinship	2.9%	p=.021
	Sex	0.8%	N.S.
Covariate:	Age of respondent	0.0%	N.S.
Total variance explained	*(incl. interactions):*	17.3%	p=.000
Questions at 14 months	Mode of death	1.3%	N.S.
	Kinship	4.6%	p=.006
	Sex	1.9%	p=.023
Kinship x	sex	2.8%	p=.049
Covariate:	Age of respondent	0.0%	N.S.
Total variance explained	*(incl. interactions):*	13.6%	p=.000

In absolute figures, it appears that 50% of the parents and spouses bereaved from suicide at four months are still often engaged in questions surrounding the cause and circumstances of death (see Fig. 5.2). At fourteen months, about one fifth of all parents is still preoccupied with this, while the difference between the modes of death has disappeared.

The mean score of the sample drops significantly between four and fourteen months: from .62[3] to .43 (t=3.17, df=269, p=.002). Possible differences in change between the different (relationship and mode of death) groups were examined with an analysis of covariance. To this end, occupation with questions at fourteen months was entered as a covariate in an analysis of variance on occupation with those questions at four months. The results show no difference between the modes of death in this respect. There is, however, a significant difference between the relationship groups in the amount of change: the mothers, in particular, continue to ruminate over questions concerning the circumstances of death.

---

[3]   This mean differs slightly from the one earlier mentioned while it pertains to the group who cooperated at both interviews (N=278).

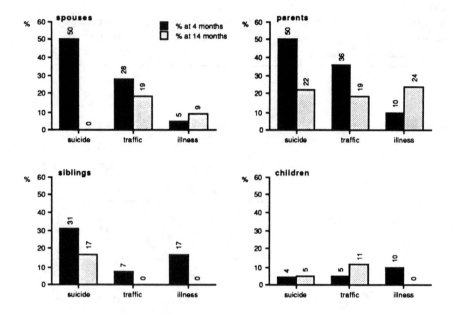

Fig. 5.2   *Bereaved often or continuously absorbed in questions about the*
circumstances or cause of death by kinship and mode of death
(percentages)

More than a year after the loss, the mean scores for all modes of death are low, and lie
within a small range. The parents remain the ones who are most occupied with
questions about the circumstances of the loss. The increase in preoccupation among
the spouses and parents in the long-term illness group is remarkable. Closer
inspection of this group reveals that the question was more often rephrased in terms
of 'What was the cause of the illness ?' rather than the cause and circumstances of
death, which were mostly known to them in detail. A mother of a 33 yr. old man who
died of AIDS: *'It is as if it was a murderer who killed him. He was not responsible*
for his illness, he was a victim.'. Another mother: *'I would like to know why the*
cancer started... what did I do wrong?' . The question about the cause of the illness
seems more related, here, to the search for meaning (discussed in the next section).

There is a considerable drop in the scores of the partners bereaved from suicide
between four months (m=1.36) and fourteen months (m=.38). Although this does not
always mean that they have a clear image of what happened, none of them seems very
occupied anymore with this particular question. Part of this decrease may,
however, be due to the drop-out in this group.

Conclusion

Most of the bereaved seem to have constructed a fairly clear image of the circumstances and cause of death at four months after the loss. A relatively large percentage of spouses and parents continues to ruminate about this, however. Parents are clearly the most concerned with questions about (the circumstances of) the loss.

An interesting finding of the present study, which has not yet been reported in previous research, is that the search for an image of the cause of death seems by no means limited to the unnatural death groups. The subject of rumination in bereaved after a long-term illness more often concerns the cause of the illness rather than the cause of death itself. Although systematic differences between the modes of death exist, they seem more clear at four months than at fourteen.

The questions that occupy the minds of the bereaved sometimes also reflect doubts about the real mode of death. In a few cases, is not entirely clear whether the death was an accident or a suicide. Some of the traffic accidents leave open the possibility of suicide (especially the one-car, one-driver accidents), while some of the suicides may also be interpreted as accidents.

Comparing these findings with the available literature, Lehman, Wortman and Williams (1987) found that four to seven years after a loss from a traffic-fatality, 28% of the parents and an equal percentage of the spouses continued to ruminate about the accident and what they might have done to prevent it. The presence of these questions is higher among the parents bereaved from a traffic-fatality in our group: at four months 46%, increasing to 66% at fourteen months, and higher as well in our spouses group where, at both interviews, 44% are occupied with the circumstances of the loss. The percentages for bereaved parents from the other modes of death are somewhat lower, but are also above those found by Lehman, Wortman and Williams (1987).

5.1.2   Search for meaning

The degree to which the bereaved is absorbed in questions about the meaning of the loss and why it had to happen was measured with a single item: 'How often are you occupied with questions such as: "Why did this have to happen to me?", or "What is the meaning of this?". As with the foregoing question, the answer categories ranged from 0: 'does not keep me occupied' to 3: 'occupies me continuously'. The respondent was asked to answer the question with regard to the past week, including the day of the interview itself.

Results

For most of the bereaved from unnatural death causes, it seemed extremely difficult to find an answer to the question "why?". Furthermore, it appeared that the inability to assert any meaning to the loss was often accompanied by a feeling of desolation or despair. Most of the bereaved from suicide and traffic-fatalities seem only capable of rephrasing the question to themselves (cf. Van der Wal, 1988): *'Why did it have to be him, when there is so much good-for-nothing scum around ?'* and *'There is no way to find an answer to it, it makes no sense.'*. A father whose 22 yr. old daughter died in a car crash: *'Every time I hear or read about an accident, all those questions about how and why pop up again.'*.

Some bereaved find comfort in talking with clergymen, but more often than not they find that their religion does not offer them an answer, like the man who lost his sister to suicide: *'I have talked about it with my parish priest, who is a friend of ours. He took away some of my fears that G. would be lost for the hereafter, but he has no answer as to the meaning of all her suffering and death...I think no one has...'* . A father who lost his son in a traffic accident found himself in a crisis with regard to his faith: *'God has ceased to exist for me. If he exists, it would be ridiculous. Why should I worship him?! Just because he needs a public..? He won't get that from me..!'*.

The bereaved generally seemed slightly more occupied with the search for the meaning of the loss than with the circumstances. However, at four months after the loss the question is not all pervading in the sample. The mean score on this question was .94 (s.d.=.98) at the first interview, and .74 (s.d.=.90) at the second: a significant but small decrease (t=3.36, df=270, p=.001).

With an analysis of covariance with age of the respondent as a covariate (see Table 5.2) the differences between groups were examined. The most significant differences were found between the kinship groups. Parents are most often preoccupied with the question, followed by spouses, siblings and children. There is more difficulty with finding a meaning among the bereaved from unnatural modes of death, with suicide posing the most problems in this respect. Ten months later, in addition to the previously discovered main effects, the sexes also differ significantly, with women being more occupied with questions about the meaning than men.

The change in score between both interviews was assessed by an analysis of covariance on the scores of the second interview, with those at the first interview entered as a covariate. This analysis revealed no significant difference in change between the modes of death but, on the other hand, a highly significant difference between the relationship groups, with mothers and fathers contrasting sharply with the other relationships. Their preoccupation with a search for meaning in general does not decrease over time: in general, it even increases.

Table 5.2
Analysis of covariance on search for meaning, 4 and 14 months after the loss, with mode of death, kinship and sex independent, and age of the respondent as a covariate

	Variable	Variance explained	Signific.
Search for meaning at 4 months	Mode of death	2.0%	p=.034
	Kinship	8.5%	p=.000
	Sex	0.7%	N.S.
Covariate:	Age of respondent	0.1%	N.S.
Total variance explained (incl. interactions):		17.6%	
Search for meaning at 14 months	Mode of death	2.8%	p=.009
	Kinship	13.6%	p=.000
	Sex	2.1%	p=.007
Covariate:	Age of respondent	0.7%	N.S.
Total variance explained (incl. interactions):		26.7%	

We will also take a closer look at the people who experience relatively more difficulty with dealing with this question. The sample was split into a 'not or hardly occupied' and an 'often or continuously occupied' group (see Fig. 5.3). Four months after the loss, 28% of the sample are often or continuously preoccupied with the search for the meaning of the death. At fourteen months, this category drops to 19%.

As shown in Fig. 5.3, the majority of the parents is preoccupied with this question. It is remarkable that, in contrast to the other kinship groups, among parents there is hardly any decrease. At fourteen months after the loss, 68% of them are at least sometimes occupied with the search for meaning. Rumination, which can be considered as being often or continuously occupied with this search, actually increases among the suicide parents.

Fathers and mothers who lost a child, regardless of the mode of death, often have a strong feeling of injustice about their child dying before they do. A mother of a 19-year old girl who died of leukemia: *'Why was it not me who died? She still had her whole life before her! If it had been possible I would have traded places with her.'* Another mother lost her daughter (40) to cancer. She had had cancer herself, but was cured: *'Why does a mother of three young children die, while an older women lives on ?'* In general, among mothers the occupation with the question 'What did I do wrong?' was not rare, irrespective of the mode of death.

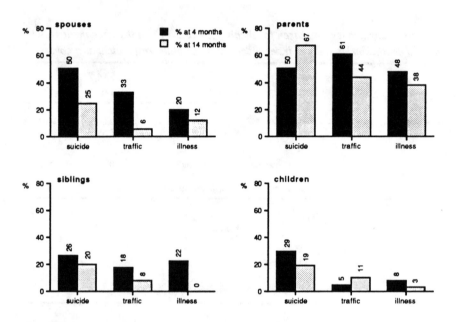

Fig. 5.3 *Bereaved often or continuously absorbed by questions about the meaning of the loss by kinship and mode of death (percentages)*

Among the widowed, questions about the meaning of the loss are relatively less prominent than among parents, while there is also a marked decrease between the two interviews. Siblings and children are much less occupied at both points in time, although, at fourteen months, a substantial part (about 20%) of those bereaved from suicide continue to ruminate about the meaning.

Among the bereaved after a long-term illness, more so than among the other groups, it made some difference whether the deceased had died at a younger or an older age: the younger the deceased had died, the more difficult it appeared to find meaning in the loss (r= -.32). Many of the older widowed in this group had more or less felt it to be 'a fact of life' that one of them had to die. When the deceased died at a younger age, however, they found themselves often left with questions similar to those in the unnatural death groups.

Conclusion

The bereaved are often preoccupied with the question of the meaning of the loss. It appears difficult for many to find an answer to this question. The absence of meaning is felt strongest among parents, of whom, at fourteen months, a substantial part is still often or continuously wondering why their child had to die. The death of a child, even if the latter is already an adult him or herself, is almost always felt as unnatural by the parents. The natural order of life is that their children survive them. Preoccupation with the question is somewhat stronger among the bereaved from suicide and traffic-fatalities. Nonetheless, it is clear that absence of meaning is also often felt among bereaved after a long-term illness, especially when the deceased was fairly young. The suicide survivors are more likely to ruminate about the meaning of the loss.

The question about the meaning also extends to the personal life of the bereaved, and as a rule, the death also evokes more existential questions. Many bereaved report that they have to find a new attitude to life in general. An answer to the meaning of the loss is rarely found, but there often seems to be a general conclusion the bereaved reaches about (his or her own) life being meaningful or meaningless at some point in time. In this respect, it appears that preoccupation with the loss is a trigger for evaluation of one's own existence.

Part of these results we can compare with the study of Lehman, Wortman & Williams (1987) among bereaved from a traffic-fatality. If we translate their criterion of 'not finding any meaning in it' into our 'at least sometimes being absorbed in questions about the meaning of the loss', it appears the percentages are somewhat lower among our spouses bereaved after a traffic-fatality: 56% (at fourteen months) in the present study against 68% in theirs. The percentage among parents bereaved after a traffic accident is, however, higher in our study: here, after fourteen months, 74% could not find a meaning in the loss against 59% in their study. In the present study, the most occupied are the parents, regardless of the mode of death. Some of the difference may be due to the difference in time since the loss which in Lehman, Wortman & Williams' (1987) study is 4 to 7 years.

5.1.3 Detachment from the deceased

Leiden Detachment Scale

Letting go of the deceased can be seen as the central theme in the time after the loss. Continued longing for the deceased and preoccupation with thoughts about him or her, can be looked upon in terms of the continued (ideated) presence of the deceased in the life of the bereaved. When ideation remains centered around the deceased as a living person, we can state that detachment has not taken place. It is commonly assumed that continued attachment in this sense is related to health and psychological problems.

The Leiden Detachment Scale (Van der Wal, Cleiren et al., 1986) is a 7-item scale designed to measure the level of detachment from the deceased, operationalized as the degree to which the respondent emotionally and cognitively accepts that the deceased is no longer part of the daily life-environment and the extent to which the respondent misses the deceased.Six items were presented as statements. Each statement comprised an open space in which the name of the deceased was filled in by the interviewer. The respondent was asked to indicate how often certain thoughts or impressions had occupied him or her during the past week, including the day of the interview. The scoring categories were 0= never; 1= rarely; 2= sometimes; 3= often. One question dealt with the difficulty the bereaved had to disengage from thoughts about the deceased, and to re-engage in the demands of daily life. The answers are scored as 0= not difficult; 1= somewhat difficult; 2= rather difficult; and 3= very difficult.

The score for the Leiden Detachment Scale was formed by the unweighted summation of the item-scores. A low sore indicates little difficulty with detachment from the deceased, while a high score indicates much difficulty.

The Leiden Detachment Scale (LDS) appeared to be a reliable and uni-dimensional instrument. On both interviews Cronbach's α was .82. The correlation between the scales at four and fourteen months (RT1.T2) was .71[*]. The item-total correlations ranged from .51 to .64 at four months, and from .47 to .64 at fourteen months. Typical items (having the highest item-total correlation) for the scale were:

'I long for ..[*name of deceased*].. '   (T1: r=.64, T2: r=.62)
'Accepting the loss of ..[*name of deceased*].. is very difficult for me'.
                                                (T1: r=.60, T2: r=.61)
'How difficult is it for you to detach yourself from thoughts and grief about ..[*name of deceased*].. and to turn your mind to other, perhaps new obligations ?
                                                (T1: r=.58, T2: r=.64)

The psychometric evaluation indicates that the scale score gives a good indication of the degree of detachment.

The scale was calibrated by Van der Wal (1988) with scores 0 through 4 indicating little or no difficulty with detachment from the deceased, 4 through 8 seen as having

---

[*]   Since the two measurements are far apart, it is questionable whether or not this correlation can be interpreted as test-retest reliability. In Appendix 2, RT1.T2 is listed for all the scales.

some difficulty, 8 through 13 experiencing moderate difficulty and 13 through 21 having much difficulty.

Results

Many respondents retain a strong feeling of the 'presence' of the deceased. A women bereaved after a traffic-fatality: *'Sitting in the living room, I often feel him standing in the kitchen. I then say: "Do come in, darling....", but of course he is not there'*.

Those who intensively took care of the deceased during a long-term illness not exceptionally suffer from strong delusions about the deceased 'needing them'. Four months after the loss, a mother often used to wake up in the middle of the night, hearing her son calling from his room for help. Most of the time, the bereaved were firmly aware that 'their mind played tricks on them'. Sometimes, however, this was not the case. One mother, living near the sea, often hears her deceased son calling her: *'At night he calls me from the water, I have to go and help him, he needs me, he wants me to be with him... my husband then has to stop me from going to him...'*. These experiences sometimes also have a more positive content. A father whose son committed suicide said that the boy had visited him. *'He came to assure me that it was not my fault that he had ended his life. That really came as a relief to me.'*. Such compelling hallucinatory experiences were rare, however, in our sample, and mostly limited to the parents and spouses groups.

At four months after the loss, in the sample as a whole, there is moderate difficulty with detachment from the deceased. The mean score for our sample on the Leiden Detachment Scale at four months is 8.9 (S.d.=5.6). Not surprisingly, at fourteen months, there is a large drop in the mean (now 6.7, s.d.=5.2) of the sample, which, according to the norm categories, indicates 'some difficulty'. In a paired t-test, this difference appears highly significant (t=8.64, df=270, p=.000).

Feelings of strong attachment to the deceased are common. Many of the bereaved at four months still had the feeling the deceased could step into the house any moment. More than half of the sample still has the feeling that the deceased is present. At fourteen months, more than 30% at least sometimes talks to the deceased in their mind or aloud, and more than 35% has sometimes at least, the feeling that the deceased can hear or see them. This appeared not to be related to religious convictions.

In an analysis of covariance, we tried to find the combined and relative importance of sex, kinship and mode of death in the problems with detachment. Possible intermediary effects of age were controlled for by adding the age of the respondent as a covariate[4].

Four months after the loss, it appears that each of these variables explains for a significant part the variance on the LDS (see Table 5.3). The largest part of the variance was accounted for by kinship to the deceased, which explained 15.4% of the variance on the LDS at 4 months, followed, at a considerable distance, by mode of death (6.4%) and sex (2.6%). The interaction effects contribute relatively little. Age of the respondent yielded a small but significant contribution. Younger age was related to greater difficulty with detachment.

There are considerable differences between the kinship groups in difficulty with detachment from the deceased. At four months, the reactions are strongest among spouses and parents (see Fig. 5.4). Women on the whole reacted more strongly than men. An exception can be found among the partners, where the widowers manifest virtually the same level of difficulties as widows. This accounts for the interaction effect between kinship and sex. The scores of the mothers, in particular, surpass those of all other groups. They are still very attached to their lost child, manifesting a strong yearning, and difficulty to concentrate on the demands of daily life. At the other extreme we find the men loosing a parent to be the least affected group.

At fourteen months after the loss, the differences between the kinship groups in difficulty with detachment is still very clear. The differences between the modes of death are, however, no longer significant. The interaction between kinship and sex is more marked at fourteen months than four months after the loss. In every kinship group, women show more difficulties with detachment than men, except in the partner group: at fourteen months the widows show considerably less problems than widowers, dropping to the level of sisters and daughters. Like at four months, age of respondent as a covariate contributed significantly, but explained only a modest proportion of the variance on the LDS.

At both points in time, the relationship to the deceased (the combination of kinship and sex) plays an important role: it explains 20.4% of the variance at four months and 24.2% at fourteen months after the loss, clearly overshadowing the role of mode of death in difficulty with detachment.

---

4   Age, in this and the following analysis, was entered *after the* main effects, since it is closely related to kinship group: e.g. the parent-group as a natural group is of an older age than the group children of the deceased. Entering the covariates after the main effects takes this difference into account.

Table 5.3

Analysis of covariance on difficulty with detachment (LDS) at 4 and 14 months after the loss, with mode of death, kinship and sex independent, and age of the respondent as a covariate

	Variable	Variance explained	Signific.
Detachment at 4 months	Mode of death	6.7%	p=.000
	Kinship	15.4%	p=.000
	Sex	2.6%	p=.001
Kinship x	Sex	2.4%	p=.014
Mode of death x Kinship x	Sex	3.2%	p=.027
Covariate:	Age of respondent	2.6%	p=.001
Total variance explained (incl. interactions):		38.1%	
Detachment at 14 months	Mode of death	0.3%	N.S.
	Kinship	16.1%	p=.000
	Sex	2.3%	p=.003
Kinship x	Sex	5.8%	p=.000
Covariate:	Age of respondent	2.3%	p=.003
Total variance explained (incl. interactions):		35.7%	

Following the norms given by Van der Wal (1988), we can also take a closer look at the subsample that shows a relatively large difficulty with detachment. In Fig. 5.4, the percentage that shows moderate to severe difficulties with missing the deceased (LDS score > 8) is presented for each combination of kinship and mode of death.

At four months after the loss, the majority of the widowed and parents belongs to this group. The overall level of emotional and cognitive attachment is highest among bereaved from a traffic-fatality. The most affected subgroups are people who lost a spouse or child in a traffic accident: 78%, respectively 93% of those groups still evidence moderate to severe difficulties four months after the loss.

Ten months later the situation has changed considerably. The overall percentage showing strong attachment to the deceased drops from 48.7% to 32.0%. The percentage is, however, still over 50% among parents and more than 30% among the widowed. Compared to the rest of the sample, there is a remarkable drop in the percentage having troubles among the parents and spouses in the traffic-fatality group. The percentages for these kinships are now virtually the same in all modes of death. It is also noteworthy that the percentage having difficulties among the parents bereaved after suicide hardly decreases, and even increases among parents in the long-term illness group, where the fathers generally manifest an increase (+1.8) in reactions. One of them explicitly stated that he ran out of energy: *'My work is very demanding. We* [he and his wife] *have gone through a lot these last months. I have postponed my grief, but now my reserves are running out..'*. In general, there was the impression that many of the fathers had tried to support their wives emotionally and practically during the first months after the loss, and that the onset of their problems was somewhat delayed. Among siblings and children, more problems with detachment were evidenced by the ones who frequently had contact with the deceased.

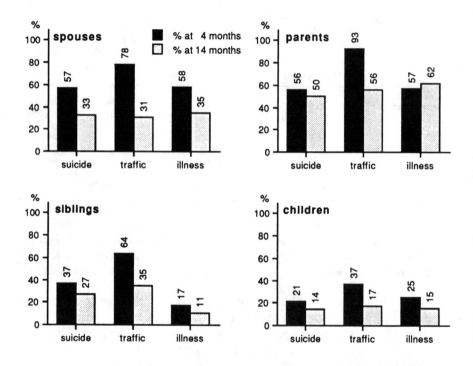

Fig. 5.4   *Respondents experiencing moderate to severe difficulty with detachment per kinship group (percentages)*

Looking at the decrease in reactions between the situation at the two points in time, it appears that there is a general decline in all relationship groups[5]. The mean drops

---

5   The term relationship-group will be used to designate the combinations of kinship to the deceased and sex (with the categories widowers, widows, fathers, mothers, brothers, sisters, sons and daughters).

from 8.9 to 6.7 (t=8.64, df=270, p=.000). In some groups the difference in reactions is more marked, however, than in others.

In order to get a better view on the changes in reactions between the two interviews, the model of Uniken Venema - van Uden (1990) (described in the beginning of this chapter) was applied to assign every respondent to one of five dynamic classes: unchanged no or little difficulty (class 1), significantly less difficulty (class 2), unchanged moderate difficulty (class 3), significant increased difficulty (class 4), and unchanged severe difficulty with detachment (class 5) .

Table 5.4 lists the composition of each of these classes by relationship to the deceased and mode of death. Looking first of all at the total percentages for each class, it appears that 41% of the sample shows a significant decrease in reactions between the two interviews. On the other hand, 10% deteriorate significantly. The rest of the sample (49%) is to be found in the unchanged classes, where 20% show virtually no problems at either point in time, leaving 19% with unchanged some or moderate problems, and 10% with continued severe problems with detachment.

As can be seen, members of each relationship group and mode of death are spread over all the dynamic classes. Exceptions are class 1, in which are no sons of the deceased, and class 5 of unchanged no difficulty, where no mothers are found.

About one-third of the widowers shows unchanged moderate difficulty with detachment from their wife. Among the widows, the majority (52%) is found to improve significantly. Forty-five percent of the fathers show improvement, but there are also 24% who manifests more severe grief reactions. Forty-nine percent of the mothers evidence unchanged severe difficulty, or significant deterioration at fourteen months. The major part of the brothers has either no problems at both interviews (32%) or has improved significantly at fourteen months (50%). Significant improvement is shown by the mode of the sisters (44%), brothers (50%) and daughters (37%).

Inspecting the distribution of the different modes of death over the dynamic classes, there appears not to be much difference, except for the much larger proportion of bereaved from a traffic-fatality evidencing significant improvement.

In order to discover which effects were significant in distinguishing deterioration, unchanged functioning and improvement, the classes 1, 3, and 5 which manifest no significant change, were put together and compared with the classes which showed significant deterioration (class 4) or significant improvement (class 2). The resulting variable was examined in a log-linear analysis together with mode of death, kinship group and sex.

Table 5.4

Composition of the five dynamic classes on difficulty with detachment (LDS) by relationship and mode of death[6]

Class:	1 Unchanged no/little difficulty	2 Significant improvement	3 Unchanged some/moder. difficulty	4 Significant deterioration	5 Unchanged much difficulty
By relationship					
Widowers	3 (12%)	7 (28%)	8 (32%)	1 (4%)	6 (24%)
Widows	4 (12%)	17 (52%)	9 (27%)	1 (3%)	2 (6%)
Fathers	3 (10%)	13 (45%)	5 (17%)	7 (24%)	1 (3%)
Mothers	0 (0%)	12 (32%)	7 (19%)	5 (14%)	13 (35%)
Brothers	12 (32%)	19 (50%)	3 (8%)	3 (8%)	1 (3%)
Sisters	8 (22%)	16 (44%)	6 (17%)	3 (8%)	3 (8%)
Sons	15 (47%)	11 (34%)	3 (9%)	3 (9%)	0 (0%)
Daughters	10 (24%)	15 (37%)	11 (27%)	4 (10%)	1 (2%)
By mode of death					
Suicide	18 (23%)	27 (35%)	18 (23%)	8 (10%)	7 (9%)
Traffic-fatal.	12 (14%)	49 (56%)	10 (12%)	8 (9%)	8 (9%)
Illness	25 (24%)	34 (32%)	24 (23%)	11 (10%)	12 (11%)
Total per class	**55 (20%)**	**110 (41%)**	**52 (19%)**	**27 (10%)**	**27 (10%)**

The results show a best-fitting simple model with a main effect for mode of death, and a main effect for kinship. The likelihood ratio chi-square of this model is 35.18 (df= 36, p=.507), indicating no significant difference between the expected cell frequencies (on the basis of the model) and the observed cell frequencies. A larger proportion of the bereaved after a traffic-fatality manifest a significant decrease in grief symptoms compared to the other modes of death. The main effect of kinship group on change is especially reflected in the high percentage of parents deteriorating between the two interviews (see also Table 5.4).

---

[6] The percentages listed are row percentages.

We can also graphically represent the combination of scores and dynamic class. In Fig. 5.5, the diagonal lines represent a Cohen's d value of -0.5 and +0.5. Translated into scores on the LDS, they correspond to a raw difference score between the two measurements of -2.8 and +2.8 respectively. The group centroids for the relationship groups and the modes of death are plotted. They are formed by the mean score of each group on each measurement[7].

Every relationship group on the whole shows a decrease in reactions, although in some groups this is very small, particularly among the mothers (mean d = -.22). Interestingly, the widows manifest the largest significant (mean) drop in reactions (mean d = -.80), while their male counterparts as a group evidence unchanged moderate difficulty.

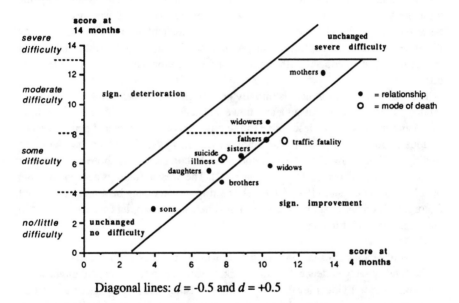

Diagonal lines: d = -.5 and d = +0.5

Fig. 5.5 *Visual representation of the dynamic classes for changes in difficulty with detachment between four and fourteen months after the loss, with the group-centroids for the relationship groups and the modes of death*

The drop in reactions among the bereaved after a traffic-fatality is clearly reflected in the plot: their mean on the LDS drops 3.7 points in comparison with 1.5 points

---

7   These points have to be considered in a descriptive sense, since no correction has been made for the unequal distribution of the kinship groups over the modes of death.

among the bereaved from suicide and 1.4 points among the bereaved from a long-term illness.

Conclusion

As could be expected, difficulty with detachment appears to be very common among bereaved family members in the early period after the loss.

The widowed and partners evidence the severest problems with detachment, the siblings less, and the children of the deceased least of all. The bereaved parents continue to have great difficulties with detachment. They seem to be unable to 'let go' of their child. The fact that there is hardly any change in this situation between the two interviews underlines the problematic situation of this group. This result is in line with the findings of other studies (see Section 3.3.5). The position of siblings between widowed and children concerning their difficulty with detachment, may illustrate the wrongful neglect of this group in empirical research. Siblings who had frequently been in contact with the deceased seem especially prone to have more difficulties.

Difficulty with detachment is initially greater among the bereaved after a traffic-fatality. This difference disappears, however, at fourteen months. This finding is surprising in view of the descriptive (non-comparative) literature and commonsense notions about sudden losses. The findings are, however, in accordance with the findings of Farberow et al. (1987), and seem to come close to those of Barrett & Scott (1987) in this respect (see Section 3.3.2). The present findings also corroborate the observation of Ball (1977-1978), suggesting that age may be a more important factor than mode of death with regard to the intensity of the grief reaction, at least in the longer term after the loss.

In terms of change for the better or for the worse, it is clearly the bereaved after a traffic-fatality who evidence the most marked decrease in reactions, although, when we look at the individual level, there is still a considerable percentage of this group deteriorating significantly (14%) or showing moderate difficulty with little or no change (20%).

5.1.4   Impact of the loss-event

The reactions to a loss can also be examined in terms of post-traumatic stress. The death of a family member may imply a shock, and lead to a Post Traumatic Stress Disorder (APA, 1987) in the bereaved.

The Impact of Event Scale

Post-traumatic stress was measured with our own translation of the Impact of Event Scale (Horowitz et al.,1980; Van der Wal, Cleiren et al., 1988).

The Impact of Event Scale (IES) consists of two subscales. The first assesses the degree to which the bereaved shows intrusive thoughts, troubled dreams and strong pangs or waves of emotions about the event (IES-Intrusions). The other subscale measures evasive thoughts and behavior with regard to the event, such as denial of the consequences and meaning of the event, blunted sensation, and behavioral inhibition (IES-Avoidance). The items are comments with regard to the life event. The respondent was asked to indicate how frequently those comments were true over the past seven days, including the day of the interview. Scoring categories were: 'not at all', 'rarely', 'sometimes' and 'often'. As in the original scale, the item-categories were scored respectively 0, 1, 3, and 5[8]. During the trial of our instrument, it became clear that the phrasing in the past tense gave rise to time compression: respondents tended to apply their answer to a period of time longer than one week. In order to avoid this, the scale was reformulated in the present tense. This elicited the desired effect[9].

For the *Intrusions* subscale, the item-total correlations ranged from .45 to .64 at the first interview, and from .45 to .70 at the second. Cronbach's coefficient α was .79 respectively .84, and $R_{T1.T2}$ was .67. Typical items for the Intrusions subscale, having the highest item-total correlation were:

'Pictures about it keep popping into my mind.' (T1: r=.64, T2: r=.68)
'I have waves of strong feelings about it.'   (T1: r=.60, T2: r=.70)
'Any reminder brings back feelings about it.'   (T1: r=.56, T2: r=.64)

For the *Avoidance* subscale, the item-total correlations ranged from .38 to .64, at the first interview, and from .27 to .55 at the second. Cronbach's α was .73 respectively .74. $R_{T1.T2}$ was .57. The three items with the highest item-total correlation were:

'I try not to think about it'   (T1: r=.52, T2: r=.55)
'I try not to talk about it'   (T1: r=.46, T2: r=.50)
'I try to remove it from my memory'   (T1: r=.48, T2: r=.53)

---

[8] The unequal spacing between the categories was considered to better reflect the distance between the contents of the categories and elicited a better interpretable factor structure (N.Wilner, personal communication).

[9] The complete scale is described in Van der Wal, Cleiren, Han & Diekstra, 1987.

As in the original scale-evaluation (Horowitz et al., 1979), the two subscales were significantly correlated at both interviews (r=.43 respectively r=.52, Horowitz 1979: .42). This implies that they share 16% of the variance. This can be considered a low enough percentage to treat them as conceptually different dimensions.

The psychometric evaluation of both scales indicates that the scale-score gives a good indication of the concepts involved.

Results: Intrusions

Intrusive thoughts were common among the bereaved. The mean score of our sample on the Intrusions subscale was 16.9 (s.d.=8.2) at the first interview and 14.2 (s.d.=8.8) at the second.

Typical intrusive thoughts and images consisted of confrontations with the absence of the deceased and were often experienced as painful. A widow, whose husband had always been slightly disabled and had to walk with a stick, suffered frequently from auditory delusions: *'He used to go out for a little walk through the village at four o'clock and was usually back by five o'clock, before diner. Now, around that hour, I often think I hear his characteristic walk and tapping of his stick at the front door.'*

Table 5.5

Analysis of variance on intrusive thoughts (IES-I) at 4 and 14 months with mode of death, kinship and sex as independent variables

	Variable	Variance explained	Signific.
IES-I scores at 4 months	Mode of death	1.5%	N.S.
	Kinship	11.4%	p=.000
	Sex	5.8%	p=.001
Kinship x Sex		2.8%	p=.012
Total variance explained (incl. interactions):		27.4%	
IES-I scores at 14 months	Mode of death	0.4%	N.S.
	Kinship	15.2%	p=.000
	Sex	4.4%	p=.000
Total variance explained (incl. interactions):		26.5%	

Differences between groups in the intensity of intrusions were assessed with an analysis of variance with mode of death, kinship and sex as independent variables (see Table 5.5), showing main effects for kinship and sex on both interviews. Age of the respondent, when introduced as a covariate, did not contribute significantly at either interview.

At four months, the analysis of variance shows that kinship and sex account for a considerable part of the variance. Parents are the ones who suffer most from intrusive thoughts, followed by spouses, siblings and children. Women generally score higher, except among the spouses, where widowers have virtually the same mean intrusion score. This accounts for the interaction-effect kinship x sex at four months.

Sisters and daughters experience about the same level of intrusions as the widows. The modes of death do not differ significantly on this variable. The pattern resembles the results found for the LDS. This is not surprising, since both scales correlate respectively .68 and .70 on each measurement. The scores on the IES-I appear to be independent of the age of the respondent.

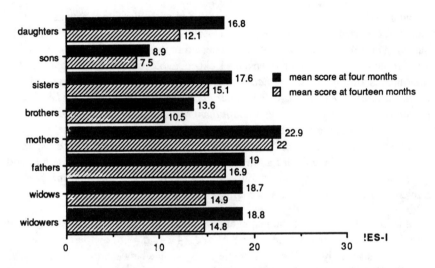

Fig. 5.6 *Intrusive thoughts about the loss for each relationship group four and fourteen months after the loss* [10]

Looking at the differences between the groups at fourteen months, we see that the interaction between sex and kinship has disappeared, although the pattern of mean scores still shows relatively high scores for the widowers.

Comparing the scores of the sample at both interviews, it appears the mean score of the sample has dropped from 16.9 to 14.2 (t=6.2, df=277, p=.000). Although significant, the absolute drop is not very large (see also Fig. 5.6). Since no norm

---

[10] Since no norm scores were available for this version of the IES, the dynamic class model will not be employed here.

scores were available for the subscales of the IES, the model of dynamic classes could not be employed here. The differences between groups in the amount of change were assessed in an analysis of covariance with Intrusions at fourteen months as a dependent variable and Intrusions at four months as a covariate.

There appeared to be no significant difference between the modes of death in the amount of change, but a significant difference between the relationship groups (F=2.9, df=7, p=.007). Mothers and fathers, in particular, manifest a relatively smaller decrease in intrusions than the other relationship groups.

Results: Avoidance

Avoidance of thoughts and behavior that reminded of the deceased, such as intrusive thoughts, occurred frequently. They were closely, and sometimes explicitly, related to the avoidance of the painful emotions connected to the loss. A mother, who lost her 19 year old daughter after a burdensome sickbed, avoided going out shopping in the first months after the loss: *'She had beautiful long blonde hair. Every time I go into town, I see lots of young girls with her hair and of her age. Every time my heart skips a beat 'Is it her..?' I get very angry about them being alive while L. is dead... it is so unfair..'.* The example also shows that intrusions and avoidance are closely related, and one may follow as a reaction to the other. Avoidance may also be experienced as a derealization, and persist for a long time after the loss. A widow, whose husband committed suicide, acknowledged fourteen months after the death: *'I am still pushing it away, one day I will have to wake up.'.*

Avoidance is a common phenomenon at both points in time. The mean score of the sample at four months is 16.8 (s.d.=8.6) and 14.2 (s.d.=8.8) at fourteen months. This implies a highly significant decrease in avoidance between the two interviews (t=6.42, df=278, p=.000). The decrease occurs in all groups: there are no significant differences in the amount of change between the modes of death or between the relationship groups.

In Table 5.6 the results of an analysis of variance on Avoidance are listed. All between-group differences on the IES-Avoidance scale are less marked than those on Intrusions. At four months, mode of death, kinship and sex each have small but significant effects. Of the modes of death, bereaved after a traffic-fatality score highest (m=12.1), followed by bereaved from suicide (m=10.9) and a long-term disease (m=8.9). Sisters of persons who died in a traffic-fatality are the highest scoring subgroup (m=18.4, s.d.=9.7), followed by widows bereaved from the same mode of death (m=18.1, s.d.=10.4). No interactions were found, and age of the bereaved had no significant contribution.

Table 5.6

Analysis of variance on Avoidance (IES-A) at 4 and 14 months with mode of death, kinship and sex independent

	Variable	Variance explained	Signific.
IES-A scores at 4 months	Mode of death	2.8%	p=.009
	Kinship	3.4%	p=.010
	Sex	3.4%	p=.001
Total variance explained (incl. interactions):		16.8%	
IES-A scores at 14 months	Mode of death	0.9%	N.S.
	Kinship	4.7%	p=.004
	Sex	2.9%	p=.004
Total variance explained (incl. interactions):		13.5%	

Fig. 5.7 lists the mean scores for the relationship groups on Avoidance. Closer examination of the sisters subsample (scoring high both on Intrusions and Avoidance) reveals that they often shared the same household as the deceased, and many of them had had an intense contact with their deceased brother or sister, although the

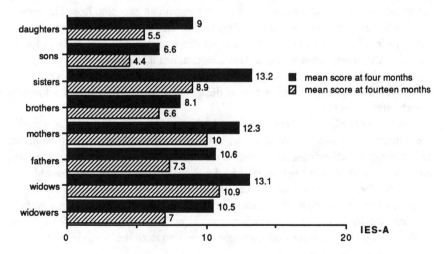

Fig. 5.7 *Avoidance (IES-A) in each relationship group at four and fourteen months after the loss*

frequency of the contact had generally not been very high. More often than any other relationship group (including the mothers), they saw their deceased sibling as being dependent on them, and being dominant in the relationship.

As for the Intrusions scale of the IES, an analysis of covariance was conducted on the Avoidance score at fourteen months with the score at four months as a covariate. This was done to assess possible differences in change between the relationship groups or the modes of death. No significant differences were found: the decrease in avoidance appeared to be about the same for the different subsamples.

Next to the thoughts and behaviors assessed by the Avoidance subscale, other evasive behaviors were also reported. In some cases, bereaved did not want to meet friends of the deceased, fearing the pain that this would bring about. Others moved, or changed the interior of their home. One widow could not bear to listen to the radio, fearing to hear the favorite music of her husband. These findings seem to distinguish the character of avoidance from that of intrusions: avoidance is more clearly a coping strategy, and may be employed voluntarily, in contrast to intrusions which are, by definition, involuntary.

Conclusion

The Impact of Event Scale is designed to measure the impact of traumatic events. Conceptually, one might expect to find higher levels of post-traumatic stress among bereaved after an unexpected loss in comparison with an expected loss. The present data, however, show another picture. Bereaved of all modes of death show virtually the same level of intrusions: the impact of the shock seems to be equally large for the bereaved after a long-term illness and the unnatural death causes.

   Although the avoidance component of the stress response, initially, is significantly higher for the bereaved from unnatural death, this difference disappears fourteen months after the loss.

   The steep drop in the scores may be an indication that avoidance acts as a coping mechanism to cushion the initial blow, in order to allow the bereaved to continue functioning, and allowing a more gradual processing of the loss on the cognitive and emotional levels. Rather than denial, avoidance may thus serve as an adjustable and necessary filter to process the massive change brought about by the loss. The results indicate that natural and, to some extent, expected loss must not be underestimated in its traumatic impact. Although not a general effect, in a number of cases a strong tendency to avoid thoughts and situations associated with the death leads to social withdrawal and isolation.

The kinship groups differ considerably in the amount of intrusions, with parents and spouses showing the highest levels. The differences in avoidance are smaller. Women show a somewhat more intense stress response than men. The sisters of the deceased show a relatively very high level of intrusive thoughts, which is of the same magnitude as in the widows. It seems the sisters quite often had a relationship in which they felt close to the deceased, while they also more than any other relationship group reported that the deceased had been dominant and dependent in the relation. It appears that the sisters tended to feel responsible for deceased, and have trouble breaking away from this attitude.

Comparing the results with studies among patient groups who sought help after a loss reveals, not surprisingly, that the level of traumatic stress reactions in our sample is generally somewhat lower: Brom & Kleber (1985) found a mean of 26.2 on Intrusions and 20.8 on Avoidance. Zilberg, Weiss & Horowitz (1982) found a score of 21.2 on Intrusions, and 20.6 on Avoidance. The fact that the present study uses a community sample rather than a patient sample may account, to a large extent, for this difference. The perspective is clearer when we compare their results with the spouses and partners in our sample who applied for psychiatric and psychological care after the loss. This subsample (n=20), at four months after the loss, had a mean score of 20.1 on the Intrusions scale, and 15.3 on the Avoidance scale. The values on the Intrusions scale for this group are higher, and closer to those in the aforementioned studies. It must be noted that the diminished time-compression (by our translation of the IES in the present tense) may have contributed to a relatively lower score in comparison with the use of the original scale.

5.2   Functioning in terms of health

In this section, the measures of general psychological and physical health will be discussed. These measures do not directly refer to the loss: they are not grief-specific scales. This enables a comparison with populations other than the bereaved.

5.2.1   Depression

An important indicator of psychological well-being is the extent to which the bereaved is depressed. Depressed mood is regarded as one of the most common phenomena after loss, with sadness, tearfulness, problems with sleeping and listlessness as the easiest observed components. However, depression, in contrast to depressed mood, consists of more elements. Full blown depression, among other things, comprises a specific (negative and selective) perception of the environment, negative beliefs about oneself and one's own abilities to cope with life, and pessimism with regard to the future. Suicidal ideation is common among the severely depressed. Depression is furthermore related to degraded physical condition and immunologic change, which make the depressed person more vulnerable to illness (Laudenschlager, 1988).

Beck Depression Inventory

The level of depressive symptoms was measured with the 13-item version of the Beck Depression Inventory (Beck & Beck, 1972; Bouman et al., 1985). The scale contains items dealing with negative mood and views of oneself, others, and the future. Each item consists of four statements which are ordinally scored from 0=no indication of depression to 3=strong indication of depression. The respondent is requested to choose the statement which applied most to his or her condition during the last week, including the day of the interview. The higher the score, the stronger the depressive symptom is present in the subject.

The scale appeared to be highly reliable at both interviews, eliciting Cronbach's alphas of respectively .87 and .88 (see also Appendix 1). The correlation between the scores at the successive interviews was .72. The psychometric evaluation indicates that the scale is highly suitable as a measure for depressive symptoms. The items with the highest item-total correlations are:

BDI 11	Work retardation	(T1: r=.69, T2: r=.70)
BDI 4	Dissatisfaction	(T1: r=.63, T2: r=.64)
BDI 2	Pessimism	(T1: r=.59, T2: r=.62)
BDI 12	Fatigueability	(T1: r=.57, T2: r=.60)
BDI 1	Sadness	(T1: r=.54, T2: r=.57)

The highest correlating items are connected to mood and general functioning, rather than to more stable constructs about one's person, such as feelings of guilt, and a distorted self-image. Van Egmond (1988) found the latter constructs to be particularly associated with suicidal ideation among a sample of depressed women (n=123).

Results

The mean level of depressive symptoms was relatively low on both interviews: 4.0 (s.d.=3.7) at the first, and 3.4 (s.d.=3.6) at the second interview. There are, however, considerable differences between the subsamples.

Analysis of variance with mode of death, kinship and sex independent (see Table 5.7) showed, at four months, a significant difference between the different modes of death.

Table 5.7

Analysis of variance on the BDI at 4 and 14 months with mode of death, kinship and sex independent

	Variable	Variance explained	Signific.
BDI scores at 4 months	Mode of death	1.9%	p=.032
	Kinship	7.8%	p=.000
	Sex	4.7%	p=.000
Kinship x	Sex	2.3%	p=.039
Total variance explained (incl. interactions):		22.3%	
BDI scores at 14 months	Mode of death	0.7%	N.S.
	Kinship	12.1%	p=.000
	Sex	2.6%	p=.004
Total variance explained (incl. interactions):		20.3%	

On the whole, the bereaved in the traffic-fatality group showed the highest level of depressive symptoms (m=5.1), followed by bereaved from suicide (m=4.0) and bereaved from a long-term illness (m=3.3). More important variables differentiating on depressive symptoms are, however, kinship and sex: together they account for 14.8% of the variance in depressive symptoms. Mothers are the most affected group, with a score of 7.6 evidencing a mean level of 'moderate depression', according to the norms of Beck and Beck (1972). The mothers of children who committed suicide or died in a traffic accident are the most depressed (respectively m=8.2 and m=9.2). Age of the deceased and the bereaved, entered as a covariate in analysis of covariance, did not reach significance.

Ten months later, there no longer appears to be a main-effect of mode of death on depressive symptoms (see Table 5.7). The parents still evidence the highest depression scores (m=6.0), followed by widowed (m=3.8), siblings (m=2.4) and children (m=1.8). As at four months, inserting age of the respondent as a covariate does not change the results.

Another way of looking at the results is to apply the norms of Beck & Beck (1972). The scores were categorized as follows: 0-4 not or hardly depressed, 5-7 mildly depressed, 8-15 moderately depressed, and 16-39 severely depressed. In Fig. 5.8, the level of depression is shown in percentages and absolute figures.

In the sample as a whole, 17% appears to be moderately to severely depressed at four months. This decreases to 13% at fourteen months. It is important, however, to consider the kinship-groups in this respect: 22% of the widowed and 29% of the parents are moderately to severely depressed at four months, while among siblings and children this percentage is much lower: 13% and 8% respectively.

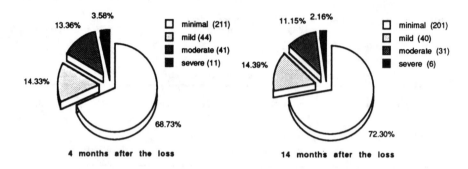

Fig. 5.8 *Sample divided up according to the level of depressive symptoms*

Among the widowed, the percentage evidencing moderate to severe depression is 22% at four months, and 15% at fourteen months. It is the bereaved in the suicide subsample who show the largest proportion with moderate to severe depression (see Fig. 5.9). The difference with the other modes of death is, however, greater at four months than at fourteen months. The rise in the number of depressed among widowed after a long-term illness (from 7% to 14%) is also noteworthy.

The parent subsample shows the highest proportion depressed at both interviews, and even a slight increase: 29% at T1 and 30% at T2. Again, the increase in depressive symptoms is most marked among the bereaved after a long-term illness.

Among siblings and children of the deceased, the proportion of depressed is much lower than in the aforementioned groups. At four months, 13% of the siblings are depressed, decreasing to 7% at fourteen months.

For the children, these percentages are 8% and 4% respectively. In both groups, the percentage at four months is highest for the siblings and children bereaved after a traffic accident. At thirteen months this difference has disappeared.

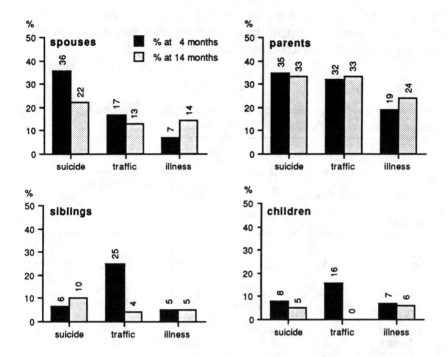

Fig. 5.9 *Respondents evidencing moderate to severe depression at four and fourteen months after bereavement (percentages)*

As was done for the difficulty with detachment, a closer examination was performed on the changes between the two points in time with the model of Uniken Venema - van Uden (1990). Every respondent was assigned to one of five dynamic classes: unchanged not depressed (class 1), significant improvement (class 2), unchanged moderately/mildly depressed (class 3), significant deterioration (class 4) or unchanged severe depression.

Table 5.8 lists the composition of each of those classes by relationship to the deceased and mode of death. Looking at the percentages for each class, it appears that the majority (60%) of the sample is to be found in the 'unchanged not depressed' class 1.

Virtually all the men who lost a parent can be found in this class, in contrast to only 28% of the mothers. A significant improvement is found among about one-third of the widowers and the sisters of the deceased. Unchanged mild or moderate depression is evidenced by 12% of the sample. One-fourth of the mothers, and 27% of the widowers are in this class. Furthermore, 8% of the bereaved show a significant increase in depressive reactions between the two interviews. A relatively large number of parents are found in this deteriorating class. Only 1% of the entire sample (three parents) show unchanged severe depression.

Table 5.8

Composition of the five dynamic classes on depressive symptoms (BDI-13) by relationship and mode of death[11]

Class:	1 Unchanged no depression	2 Significant improvement	3 Unchanged light/moder. depression	4 Significant deterioration	5 Unchanged severe depression
By relationship					
Widowers	10 (39%)	8 (31%)	7 (27%)	1 (4%)	0 (0%)
Widows	22 (63%)	5 (14%)	6 (17%)	2 (6%)	0 (0%)
Fathers	18 (62%)	3 (10%)	1 (3%)	6 (21%)	1 (3%)
Mothers	10 (28%)	9 (25%)	9 (25%)	6 (17%)	2 (6%)
Brothers	30 (77%)	4 (10%)	2 (5%)	3 (8%)	0 (0%)
Sisters	19 (51%)	12 (32%)	5 (14%)	1 (3%)	0 (0%)
Sons	31 (94%)	1 (3%)	1 (3%)	0 (0%)	0 (0%)
Daughters	26 (62%)	9 (21%)	3 (7%)	4 (10%)	0 (0%)
By mode of death					
Suicide	51 (66%)	11 (14%)	7 (9%)	7 (9%)	1 (1%)
Traffic-fatal.	44 (50%)	23 (26%)	15 (17%)	4 (5%)	2 (2%)
Illness	71 (63%)	17 (15%)	12 (11%)	12 (11%)	0 (0%)
Total per class	**166 (60%)**	**51 (18%)**	**34 (12%)**	**23 (8%)**	**3 (1%)**

Looking at the visual representation of the dynamic classes with plotted group-centroids for each relationship group (see Fig. 5.10), the only marginal change in depressive symptoms between four and fourteen months after the loss becomes clear.

---

[11] The percentages listed are row percentages.

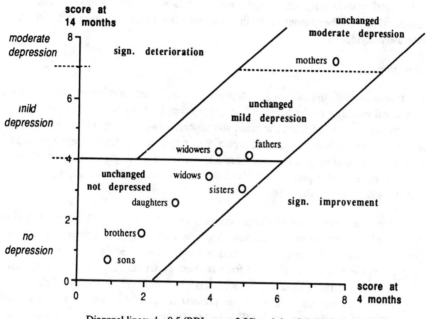

Diagonal lines: *d* = 0.5 (BDI-score -2.35) and *d* = -0.5 (BDI-score +2.35)

Fig. 5.10 *Visual representation of the dynamic classes for change in depression between four and fourteen months, with the group-centroids for each relationship group*

The diagonal lines represent a change of -2.35 points or 2.35 points on the BDI-13 scale (*d* = 0.5 and *d* = -0.5), while the horizontal lines indicate the norm scores for depression. All the centroids are in the unchanged no-depression, or light/moderate depression areas. The centroids for all modes of death (not plotted here) also fall into the 'unchanged no depression' class 1.

In order to find systematic differences between groups in the direction of change, log-linear analysis was performed to find a parsimonious description of the data. In order to assess change only, and not the absolute level of depressive symptoms, the dynamic classes 1, 3 and 5 (indicating stability) were taken together. A series of models was hierarchically tested, including this recoded dynamic class variable with changing combinations of mode of death, kinship group and sex. This resulted in a simplest acceptably fitting model (likelihood ratio chi-square=32.3, df=28, p=.26) with an interaction of kinship and sex (=relationship) with dynamic class, and a main effect of mode of death on dynamic class: a larger proportion of the bereaved after a traffic-fatality show a significant decrease in depressive symptoms at 14 months when compared to the other modes of death, while the illness-bereaved more often show an increase in symptoms.

Conclusion

The results indicate that, although a depressed mood is common in our sample, only a very small minority of the bereaved becomes severely depressed upon bereavement. This can be concluded from the scale sumscores, as well as from the pattern of the scores on the individual items. Complaints center more often on emotional and physical exhaustion, than on aspects known to be strongly related to clinical depression. A similar pattern has also been found in other studies among bereaved (e.g. Breckenridge et al., 1986).

The mean scores for men and women are very close to the mean BDI-score found in the normal (non-bereaved) population. When we look at specific kinship groups, we get a somewhat different picture: Kerkhof (1985) measured depressive symptoms among suicide attempters referred for treatment to an academic hospital (n=100). Their scores, on the BDI-21, indicated moderate depression among 20% of the attempters. Among the parents in the present sample, this percentage is higher fourteen months after the loss (24%). In the higher regions there is, however, an important difference: Kerkhof found severe depression among 24% of his sample, whereas, among the parents in our study, this is only 6%. The percentages for all the other kinship groups in our sample is even lower. This forms an indication that the incidence of severe depression is relatively rare, but that parents, especially mothers, run a relatively higher risk of developing depression.

Although there is a small initial difference in depressive symptoms between the modes of death, this difference does not persist at fourteen months.

One reason for concern is the relative lack of change or even, in some cases, the increase in the level of depressive symptoms among more than half of the mothers and in one-third of the fathers and widowers. Projected into the future, it seems that depressive symptoms in these groups are less likely than the direct loss-reactions to wear off. Mothers must clearly be seen as a high-risk group for developing moderate to severe depression.

The results for the subsample of widowed can be compared with other studies in which the BDI was employed. Farberow, Gallagher, Gilewski & Thompson (1987) found, among their sample widowed from suicide and natural death causes, a percentage of 16% that were moderately to severely depressed. Although this percentage is somewhat lower than in our sample, this may be caused by the fact that their study was conducted two months after the loss. Since in several studies, and also in our sample, there is a decrease of depressive symptoms over time, the difference may be due to this time effect. Stroebe, Stroebe & Domittner (cf. Stroebe 1987) found, in their sample, 14% of the widowed to be moderately to severely depressed four to six months after the loss, a percentage substantially lower than the one found in the present study. A possible reason may be the relatively lower response percentages of the aforementioned studies; which may result in a different composition of the samples in terms of mental health.

5.2.2   Suicidal ideation

As noted before, thoughts about not wanting to live anymore, or having phantasies about ending one's life, may occur after the loss, and are considered to be common in severe depression. It is also known that the suicide rate is higher among bereaved than non-bereaved (see Section 3.3).

KONSUI scale

Thoughts about committing suicide were measured with a changed version of the KONSUI scale (Kerkhof, 1985). The scale consisted of 11 questions assessing the presence of specific suicidal thoughts, all methods of committing suicide. The scoring categories were: 0: 'never', 1: 'once', 2: 'more than once'. The respondent was asked to answer the questions for the time period after the loss at the first interview, and for the time between the two interviews during the second interview.

One item (thinking about burning oneself), was eliminated from the scale since it had zero variance. The resulting 10 item scale had a reliability of .69 at the first interview, and .68 at the second.

Suicidal thoughts were relatively rare in our sample. The mean for the scale was .26 (s.d.=1.2) at four months, and .27 (s.d.=1.2) at fourteen months. The items with the highest item-total correlations were:

'I have thought of taking poison'   (T1: r= .66, T2: r=.68)
'I have thought of wounding myself' (T1: r= .61, T2: r=.71)

The psychometric evaluation indicates that this scale appears suitable as a measure for suicidal ideation.

Apart from the assessment of suicidal thoughts, the respondents were also asked if they had actually performed one or more of the acts described in the scale. Since the presence of actual suicidal actions was very low, construction of a suicidal action scale was not feasible.

Results

Suicidal ideation was not exceptionally high in the sample: at both interviews 9% of
the sample had at least once thought about ending their lives. Many stated, however,
that it had only crossed their mind, usually in the first days after the loss which they
often described as a period of disorientation and despair. They often added that they
would never 'do such a thing'.

Analysis of variance indicated no systematic differences between the modes of death,
kinship groups, or the sexes. Neither did age of the respondent, age of the deceased
and educational level covary significantly.

At fourteen months, the bereaved were asked if they had ever, since the loss, wished
their life was over, or had thoughts about 'not caring if they did not wake up again in
the morning'. Thus, the accent was on a general feeling of being tired of life, rather
than on concrete thoughts about methods of committing suicide. 33% of the parents,
35% of the spouses, 22% of the siblings and 11% of the children had had this kind of
thoughts at least once in the year after the loss. There is a systematic difference
between the modes of death in this respect (Chi-square 16.6, df=6, p=.011): spouses
and parents more often have this type of thoughts.

Looking more closely at the case histories of the bereaved who evidence relatively
strong suicidal ideation, it appears that in some cases these bereaved had already been
depressed and suicidal before the loss. One spouse had met his wife in a psychiatrical
hospital where they were both under treatment. When she committed suicide, it was a
kind of relief for him, and he also felt a certain admiration that she had had the
courage to act. He wanted to give his life yet another chance but: *'If my life goes on
the way it is now, I will make an end of myself in two years' time'*.
   In some cases, other (multiple) problems seemed to play a more prominent role in
the state of the respondents, such as divorce, multiple losses, or drug dependence.

Among the bereaved after a traffic-fatality, fantasies of suicide were often related to
the way the other person had died. One man, whose sister was run over by a car, had
strong thoughts that her car, which he had inherited, was intended to kill him. A
young woman who lost her brother: *'I often think about taking the same route as she
did, and that it doesn't matter to me at all if they run me over'*.
   One mother, who lost her 22 year old son in a car accident, had thought a lot about
different methods of committing suicide. *'I think about it a lot, but I would never dare
to do it. I would leave other people in such great pain. They need me.'*

On the other hand, however, there were also five respondents who attempted suicide during the period of the study. Four of them were bereaved from suicide, two after a long-term illness. We shall examine these in some more detail.

In four cases, these attempts seemed to be related to previous problems rather than to the loss. One daughter whose mother died after a long-term disease, wounded herself and took an overdose of medicine. She was involved in a tiresome divorce procedure, and the loss of her mother (72) did not pose any problem to her. A man whose girlfriend had committed suicide had also taken an overdose of medicine. He had already been psychiatrically treated before the loss for severe depression. A woman, whose husband killed himself, took too much pills. After a separation from her husband for one year, they had tried to live together again. This failed after four weeks, upon which he took his life.

There were three respondents who attempted suicide *without* an apparent previous history of severe problems. One man tried to shoot himself, but could not bring himself to pulling the trigger. His wife had died after falling from the balcony of their apartment. He was suspected of murder, and although, finally, the conclusion of the police was suicide, he was pursued by feelings of guilt, and withdrew from social contacts. Another respondent was a mother whose son died of AIDS. She had started suffering severe psychological problems upon the onset of the disease. After the loss, she tried to take an overdose of medicine, but was stopped by her husband.

Conclusion

Although a vague desire about 'wanting to put an end to it all' occurred fairly frequently among the bereaved, explicit suicidal thoughts were rare. Six of the bereaved attempted suicide, but only two of these attempts seemed to bear a relationship to the loss event. Four of the bereaved after suicide attempted suicide themselves. For two of them, their own psychiatric history appears to play a major role in this. Two of the bereaved after an illness also attempted suicide. Thus, the danger of suicide among the bereaved may be considered as small but real, and perhaps somewhat higher for those who are themselves bereaved after suicide. The numbers are too small, however, to draw conclusions and to make reliable comparisons with epidemiological studies in this area.

Having responsibility for others, such as for one's partner and especially one's children, appears to act as an important buffer between suicidal ideation and the suicide act, and is often described as such by the bereaved themselves. On the other hand, most of the suicide attempters did not feel they had someone they had to care for, and generally lived alone.

The finding in epidemiological studies that the suicide risk is greater shortly after the loss may be reflected in the increased suicidal ideation reported in our sample. Also the finding of Bunch et al. (1972) that previous psychiatric breakdown was more frequently found among bereaved who committed suicide than in those who did not, is corroborated by the present findings.

5.2.3   Feeling in control

The feeling that one is in control of one's life, and will be able to cope with the demands of the future has been described as a central theme in the adaptation to a loss (Hansson and Remondet, 1988; Van der Wal, 1988). Also, in an attribution-theoretical sense, this aspect is considered important (cf. Stroebe & Stroebe, 1987). The measure in our study is somewhat different in nature. It means to assess the expectancy of maintaining or regaining control over one's situation, rather than the attribution of control.

Sense of Control Scale

The scale consisted of the unweighted sumscore of five items, assessing the thoughts of the subjects about their own situation. The respondents were asked to what extent a series of statements applied to them. The alternatives ranged from 0: 'does not apply to me' to 2: 'applies largely or fully to me'. In a principal components analysis, the scale appeared to be uni-dimensional. The reliability was .59 at the first interview and .62 at the second. The items correlating highest with the scale's sumscore were:

'I think in the end I will get over this blow.'   (T1: r=.36, T2: r=.42)
'I feel that, compared to
   others in the same situation, I'm not doing so badly.' (T1: r=.41, T2: r=.51)

From the above evaluation, it can be concluded that the scale forms an acceptable measure of estimated control. Van der Wal (1988) applied the following norms to the scale, which will also be applied here: 0-5: low control, 6-7: moderate control, 8-10: high control.

Results

In general, the bereaved felt moderately in control of their situation. There was no significant difference between the mean scores at each interview (m=7.7, s.d.=2.2 at T1, m=7.8, s.d.=2.2 at T2).

Four months after the loss, analysis of variance shows no significant difference between the modes of death, kinship groups or the sexes. At fourteen months, there is a small but significant difference between the kinship groups. The amount of variance explained by kinship is 7.1%. There is also an interaction-effect of kinship and sex: although in most of the kinship groups the men feel slightly more in control than the women, among the spouses this is the other way around. Widowers feel less in control of their situation.

As before, the bereaved were assigned to one of five dynamic classes on the basis of their level of experienced control at both interviews (see Table 5.9).

Most of the respondents show an unchanged high level of control at both interviews. It is remarkable that many of the widows (69%) show an unchanged positive view of the future and of their ability to cope. Looking at mode of death, the major part of the bereaved after a long-term illness also show unchanged high control.

Only 34% of the sample show a significant change in score between the two interviews. Twenty-one percent show increased control at the second interview. Many traffic-fatality bereaved can be found in this group.

In comparison with the other relationship groups, a relatively large part of the mothers (25%), daughters (20%) and widowers (19%) has a decreased feeling of control at fourteen months. In the unchanged low control group, also, a relatively larger part of the widowers and mothers can be found.

In Fig. 5.11, a graphical presentation is given of the dynamic classes on sense of control. In order to assess systematic differences in the direction of change, the dynamic classes which indicate stability of the situation (classes 1, 3 and 5) were taken together and compared to the significantly deteriorating (class 4), and the significantly improving (class 2) groups.

In a log-linear analysis, a series of models was tested, including this recoded dynamic class variable, with changing combinations of mode of death, kinship group and sex. An acceptably fitting and simple model (Likelihood ratio chi-square=49.5, df=42, p=.20) contained only a strong main effect of mode of death on change in control: a larger proportion of the bereaved after a traffic-fatality show a significant increase in feeling in control, in contrast with the other modes of death.

Many of the bereaved who evidenced a low sense of control felt they had lost grip on their lifes. Sometimes this was associated with helplessness, and neglect for themselves and their homes. A mother who lost her son after suicide: *They are all*

Table 5.9

*Composition of the five dynamic classes on sense of control (Sense of Control Scale)
by relationship and mode of death[12]*

Class:	1 Unchanged high control	2 Significant increase	3 Unchanged moderate control	4 Significant decrease	5 Unchanged low control
By relationship					
Widowers	8 (31%)	5 (19%)	3 (12%)	5 (19%)	5 (19%)
Widows	22 (69%)	6 (19%)	2 (6%)	2 (6%)	0 (0%)
Fathers	15 (52%)	6 (21%)	4 (14%)	2 (7%)	2 (7%)
Mothers	11 (31%)	7 (19%)	3 (8%)	9 (25%)	6 (17%)
Brothers	18 (49%)	11 (30%)	5 (14%)	2 (5%)	1 (3%)
Sisters	13 (36%)	7 (44%)	5 (14%)	7 (20%)	4 (11%)
Sons	21 (68%)	5 (16%)	1 (3%)	3 (10%)	1 (3%)
Daughters	22 (56%)	10 (26%)	1 (3%)	4 (10%)	2 (5%)
By mode of death					
Suicide	34 (47%)	14 (19%)	9 (12%)	12 (16%)	4 (6%)
Traffic-fatal.	35 (41%)	31 (36%)	6 (7%)	8 (9%)	6 (7%)
Illness	61 (57%)	12 (11%)	9 (8%)	14 (13%)	11 (10%)
Total per class	**130 (49%)**	**57 (21%)**	**24 (9%)**	**34 (13%)**	**21 (8%)**

*very nice to me. I can talk about it whenever I want, but I don't think I can ever get
over this.'* She still experiences strong and quickly alternating emotions. The suicide
has also brought her in conflict with her religious beliefs.

In the case of some respondents, the loss of control was also apparent in their
behavior during the course of the interview, reflected in the tendency to relate, in a
chaotic manner, what had happened to them. Some showed the tendency to jump
back and forth in time in their description of the events, and had difficulty with
following the (chronological) order of the interview.

---

[12]   The percentages listed are row percentages.

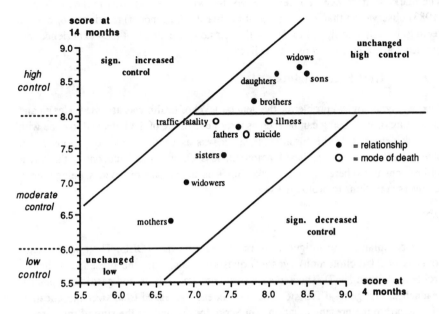

Diagonal lines: *d* = -0.5 (Sense of Contr. Scale -1.1) and *d* = +0.5 (Sense of Contr. Scale +1.1)

Fig. 5.11 *Visual representation of the dynamic classes for sense of control (Sense of Control Scale) between four and fourteen months, with group-centroids plotted for each relationship group and mode of death.*

Conclusion

The bereaved evidence a generally optimistic belief in their ability to cope with the loss in the long run. The most marked sex-differences are found among the widowed and the parents. Widowers feel less in control, and deteriorate more often than widows in this respect. The widows, on the contrary, evidence the highest level of control of the situation, compared to the other relationship groups. The mothers evidence the lowest level of control. In comparison with the other modes of death, a larger part of the bereaved after a traffic-fatality experience significantly increased control.

The data seem partly consistent with the literature. They corroborate the findings on massive feeling of loss of control for mothers, but not for fathers (cf. Osterweis et al., 1984).

The marked difference between widows and widowers confirms Parkes & Weiss' (1983) observation that, coming out of the marital (dependent) relationship, women seem to be better equipped to deal with their new role, and that they experience less problems in taking control over their lives.

5.2.4   Health complaints

Next to psychological problems, the general level of health was assessed. Health and the feeling of well-being can be seen as a resource of the of the bereaved to cope with the task-demands of the loss. This aspect was assessed by two questions about physical and psychological health before the loss. On the other hand, and in the way it will be considered here, it can be looked upon as an outcome of the loss, being related to adverse reactions to prolonged stress.

VOEG

Health complaints and fatigue were measured with the VOEG. The questionnaire consists of 21 dichotomous (yes/no) questions, assessing the presence of health problems (Dirken 1967). The items are mainly related to heart and gastric complaints, headaches, and general fatigue. The respondent was asked to answer the question with regard to the present situation. The score for the scale is the sum of the number of 'yes' responses. According to Gazendam & Van Egmond (1987), who studied the conceptual validity of the VOEG, the scale measures a general feeling of well-being.

Principal components analysis on the first measurement resulted in 4 factors with eigenvalue larger than 1, but according to the 'elbow-criterion' only one major factor fitted the data. The four factor solution coincided with the four principal areas of functioning assessed by the VOEG listed above. Since the 1-factor solution also was satisfactory, while also better reflecting the 'general' health situation, it was decided to use the sumscore of the 21 items. The reliability of the VOEG was satisfactory: .74 at T1 and .88 at T2. The items with the highest item-total correlations were:

'Do you fairly often have a feeling of pain in the region of heart
  or chest?'   (T1: r=.55, T2: r=.57)
'Do you often have a feeling of fatigue?'   (T1: r=.60, T2: r=.57)
'Do you find yourself tiring earlier than you
  consider normal?   (T1: r=.57, T2: r=.59)
'Do you fairly often feel listless?   (T1: r=.55, T2: r=.58)

The psychometric evaluation shows that the scale can be considered as a good measure of experienced health and can be used in further analysis.

Results

The mean score of the sample was 5.4 (s.d.=4.9) at four months, and 4.5 (s.d.=4.4) fourteen months after the loss. This decrease was significant (t=3.02, df=276, p=.003). On both interviews, there are no differences in general health between the modes of death (see Table 5.10).

Table 5.10
Analysis of covariance on general health (VOEG) at 4 and 14 months with mode of death, kinship and sex as independent variables and age of the respondent as a covariate

	Variable	Variance explained	Signific.
Health scores at 4 months	Mode of death	0.7%	N.S.
	Kinship	2.6%	p=.034
	Sex	6.9%	p=.000
Covariate:	Age of respondent	0.3%	N.S.
Total variance explained	*(incl. interactions):*	15.7%	
Health scores at 14 months	Mode of death	0.5%	N.S.
	Kinship	4.3%	p=.004
	Sex	6.5%	p=.000
Covariate:	Age of respondent	1.5%	p=.033
Total variance explained	*(incl. interactions):*	17.5%	

Kinship only contributes marginally in the analysis of variance, with parents in particular evidencing more problems than the other groups, and children having the least problems in this area. The most significant difference is found between the sexes: women, in both interviews, score more than 2 points higher than men (m=6.6 respectively 4.0 at four months and m=3.3 respectively 5.5 at fourteen months). Age of the bereaved (introduced as a covariate after the main effects) is not significantly related to general health four months after the loss.

Among the parents, there was even a moderate negative relationship between age and health complaints at four months: the younger parents evidenced relatively more health problems (r=-.25). At fourteen months there is a slight contribution of age of the respondent (var. expl.= 1.5%, p=.033). Examining the role of age of the deceased in the same way reveals a somewhat larger, though still marginal association with health complaints (var. expl.= 2.8%, p=.000). Older age of the deceased is related to more health problems in the bereaved.

At both four and fourteen months, mothers of the deceased in particular report more problems than the other kinship groups (see Fig. 5.12), while the scores of adult children figure at the level of the general population mean. The mothers clearly evidence most health problems, while the sisters tend to score in the same range as the widows in this respect. As can also be seen in the figure, health complaints tend to diminish over time. With the mothers, however, the decrease is only minimal.

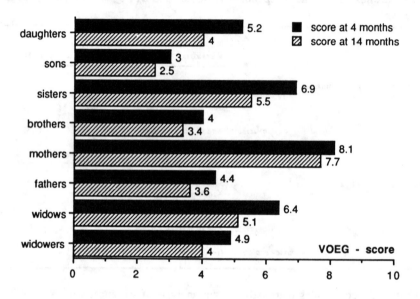

Fig. 5.12 *Mean score on the VOEG health problems scale for each relationship group, four and fourteen months after the loss*

Conclusion

The level of health complaints in the sample was higher than was found in a representative sample of the Dutch population (M=3.3, cf. CBS, 1984). The tendency for the women to evidence a higher level of health complaints (m=3.8 against men m=2.9) is also comparable to population differences. It is thus unlikely that there is a differential effect of bereavement on health complaints of men and women. The differences between the kinship groups are marginal, although the difference increased at fourteen months after the loss. Systematic differences between the modes of death are absent.

Compared to certain other, clinical samples, the score is relatively low. Kerkhof (1985) found a mean score of 9.1 (s.d.=5.3) on the VOEG among suicide attempters, four weeks after their dismissal from the hospital., and Visser (1983), in a sample of chronically ill and physically handicapped, found a mean score of 9.9 (s.d.=4.6). None of our subsamples evidences scores in this range, although the mean score for the mothers of 8.1 (s.d.= 6.2) is not very much lower. Interestingly, the mean score of the fathers is much lower. Age seems not to be strongly related to the level of health problems.

The physical well-being of the children seems only to be slightly affected by the loss. The differences between the relationship groups tend to increase in the interval between the two interviews. It is possible that the differential effects of the loss for the different kinship groups may become more clearly visible in the long-term.

5.2.5   Use of intoxicating substances

The consumption of and/or addiction to psychotropic substances can be considered to be riskful behavior that may have short and longer-term health consequences for the bereaved.

Measures of use of intoxicating substances

The consumption of alcohol, tobacco, drugs, and medicine since the moment of death were measured with single questions. For each substance, the frequency and quantity of consumption at the present time were measured.

The consumption of alcohol was measured with two questions: one assessing the frequency of the consumption of alcoholic drinks, and a second asking the number of drinks at each occasion. The two questions were combined and recoded in 10 categories, ranging from 1: 'never' to 10: 'every day consumption / more than five consumptions'.

Medicine intake was measured by asking the frequency of medicine intake for each medicine he or she used (with a maximum of five) at the time of the interview. The categories for each medicine ranged from 1:'less than once a week' to 5:'more than once a day'. The score on medicine intake was formed by adding the scores on the five questions. If a respondent used no medicine, he obtained a score of zero on the scale. In a principal components analysis, the scale appeared to be uni-dimensional. The reliability was .72 at T1 and .80 at T2, and the correlation between the two measurements was .69 (see also Appendix 1 and 2).

Tobacco consumption was measured with a single item, asking for the total number of pipes, cigarets or cigars (each counting for one unit) smoked per day. The answer categories ranged from: 1: 'less than one a day' to 5: 'more than 25 a day'.

The use of narcotics was originally measured in the same way as medicine intake. Since the incidence of drug consumption was very low, construction of a scale was impossible, thus a more impressionistic view will be given here.

The respondents were asked, for each substance, if there had been an increase or decrease in consumption since the time before the loss.

Results

Medicinal consumption

More than one-third (34%) of the bereaved used medicine at least once a week. There was no significant difference between the mean medicine consumption at four months and fourteen months.

The consumption of medicine was clearly highest among parents and spouses of the deceased. Analysis of covariance was performed to test for differences between groups. This confirmed the significant difference between the kinship groups, with kinship accounting for 9.1% of the variance (F=10.9, df =3, p=.000). There was a significant correlation between age of the respondent and the consumption of medicine at both measurements: older age was accompanied by increased medical consumption (r=.35 respectively .40). Also when entered in the analysis of covariance as concommittant variable -after the main effects for mode of death, kinship and sex-, age yielded a (somewhat weaker) relationship (F=20.0, df =1, p=.000; variance explained=5.6%)

Medicinal consumption was highest among the mothers, who at four months had a mean score of 4.7 (s.d.=5.6), the equivalent of about one medicine used several times a day. They are followed at some distance by the widows (m=3.8, s.d.=5.5). Of the men it is the widowers who have the highest medicinal intake (m=3.7, s.d.=5.2). No systematic difference in change was found between the modes of death or the sexes at both interviews.

On the whole, the sample reported an increase in the use of medicine at four months after the loss as compared with the time before the loss (see Table 5.11). It must be noted, however, that the major part (about 85%) of the bereaved did not report a significant change at all at either interview. An analysis of covariance resulted in systematic differences between groups (age of the bereaved was introduced as a covariate). After the loss, in general, an increase in medicine consumption was more often reported by the bereaved of the unnatural modes of death (F=3.99, df=6, p=.02). The increase in medicine consumption among parents turned out to be higher than for the other kinship groups (F=3.16, df=3, p=.025). There was no systematic difference between the sexes, nor any interaction effects. The age of the respondent was not related to change in intake at four months.

Table 5.11

Reported changes in medicinal consumption in comparison with the time before the loss (row percentages)

Kinship:		Decrease	Same level	Increase
		Change in medicinal consumption		
Spouses	4 months:	10%	78%	12%
	14 months:	9%	82%	9%
Parents	4 months:	3%	70%	27%
	14 months:	14%	72%	14%
Siblings	4 months:	2%	86%	12%
	14 months:	5%	90%	5%
Children	4 months:	0%	95%	5%
	14 months:	3%	92%	5%
Total:	4 months:	13%	77%	10%
	14 months:	14%	75%	11%

At the second interview, ten months later, in many cases the consumption had decreased to the pre-bereavement level according to the bereaved. However, in the sample as a whole, there was no decrease in the absolute level of medicine intake between the two interviews. The difference between the modes of death was still significant (F=3.73, df=6, p=.025), but now the order was reversed: at fourteen months more bereaved after a long-term illness reported an increase, while a decrease was relatively more frequent among the bereaved of suicide and traffic-fatalities. The older, more often than the younger bereaved, tended to stay at an elevated level of medicinal intake (F=9.95, df=1, p=.002).

Tobacco consumption

Forty-three percent of the respondents smoked at least one cigaret (or equivalent) a day. The mean number of cigarettes, pipes or cigars in the smokers' group lay between 15 and 25 at the first interview. Fourteen months after the loss, there was a decrease: the mean was, then, between 5 and 15 tobacco consumptions a day. Since the standard deviation is quite high however, this is only a trend (t=2.11, df=269, p=.04). The number of non-smokers also increased from 57% to 61%. Many of the respondents indicated that there had been an increase in comparison with the time before the loss, but they tried to bring it down again. The bereaved after suicide smoked significantly more than those in the other groups at both interviews. Men smoked more than women at four months, but they fell back to the same level as women at fourteen months. There was no systematic difference between the kinship groups.

In comparison with the time before the loss, there is more often an increase in smoking four months after bereavement (in 14%) rather than a decrease (in 3%). The increase is most marked among the bereaved after a traffic-fatality: 18% reported an increase in comparison with the time before the loss, and none of them a decrease. A decrease is more often reported by the bereaved from long-term illness (in 6%). There are no significant differences between the kinship groups or the sexes, nor is there a relationship with age in this respect.

Fourteen months after the loss, increased and decreased smoking are reported equally often: in 9% of the sample. No significant differences between groups are found.

Alcohol consumption

At four months, the consumption of alcohol was much higher among men (m=4.6, the equivalent of more than two consumptions a day) than among women (m=2.5, the equivalent of about two consumptions, almost 6 days per week), sex accounting for 14.5% of the variance on this variable. At fourteen months, the mean for the men is 4.6, and 2.9 for the women, sex explaining 12.6% of the variance.

At four months, alcohol consumption was, relatively speaking, highest among children of the deceased. The effect of kinship accounted, however, for only a small percentage of the variance (3.2%). At fourteen months, it appears there was a decrease among the children, while the parents, spouses and siblings stayed at the same level. The differences between the kinship groups have thus disappeared. There is no significant difference in alcohol consumption between four months and fourteen months.

In comparison with the time before the loss, the bereaved hardly report any increase in alcohol consumption (see also Table 5.12). At four months, a decrease in consumption is more often reported by bereaved after long-term illness (Chi-square=13.4, df=4, p=.001). At fourteen months after the loss, 75% state that their alcohol consumption is on the pre-bereavement level, 11% state it has increased, and

14% report a decrease. As at four months, at fourteen months bereaved after long-term illness more often report a decrease in alcohol consumption in comparison with the time before the loss, whereas an increase is more often found among the bereaved after a traffic-fatality.

Table 5.12

Reported changes in alcohol consumption in comparison with the time before the loss (row percentages)

		Change in alcohol consumption		
Mode of death:		Decrease	Same level	Increase
Suicide	4 months:	4%	88%	8%
	14 months:	7%	87%	7%
Traffic	4 months:	14%	72%	14%
	14 months:	15%	70%	16%
Illness	4 months:	19%	73%	8%
	14 months:	18%	71%	11%
Total:	4 months:	13%	77%	10%
	14 months:	14%	75%	11%

Drug use

It appeared that the respondents who took psychotropic drugs were already using them before the loss. Eight of the respondents use soft drugs (hash and marihuana) and three both soft and hard drugs (cocaine, heroine). In some cases, there had been an increase in drug consumption after the loss, but also decreases had occurred. A man who lost his brother: *To enjoy a joint you have to be in a good mood. In this situation, I only feel more down when I smoke.* There was no systematic rise or fall in the consumption of drugs in comparison with the time before the loss, or between the two interviews.

Conclusion

Like Valanis et al. (1987), in a sample of bereaved spouses, we found no systematic increase or decrease in alcohol consumption among the bereaved in comparison with the time before the loss. Between the two interviews, the level of alcohol intake also, apparently stays virtually the same. An initial higher level of intake among adult children at four months has disappears at fourteen months.

A possible problem in interpreting the results is the knowledge that the self-reported level of alcohol and other drug consumption is often unreliable, generally because of the negative image this conveys, and may therefore lead to an underestimation of the real consumption. It is difficult to say to what extent this is true of the present study.

The level of medicine intake is, in general, fairly high in the sample. An increase in medicinal consumption is less often reported by the long-term illness group, but the absolute post-bereavement level of consumption is virtually equal for each mode of death. This indicates that a higher level or increase in consumption among the illness-bereaved may have occurred during the illness period. The increase in the consumption of medicines with age seems to parallel the findings for the population at large. Since women in representative population samples generally seem to have a higher medical consumption, the fact that there is no difference in the use of medication in our sample may indicate a more substantial increase in medicine intake for men compared to women.

The consumption of narcotics is relatively rare, or rarely admitted. There is no apparent change in intake after the loss, nor between the interviews.

In general, there appears to be a somewhat higher substance use in the early months after the loss which, subsequently, diminishes. Higher consumption appeared to serve as a way to control nervousness and discomfort. Many of the bereaved stated that they had consciously brought down, or tried to bring down their medicine intake or smoking after the first months since they felt it was no good. Excessive smoking was more often considered to be a problem by the bereaved themselves, than a high level of medicine intake or drinking.

5.3   Social functioning

The quality of social functioning was measured with the Need for Emotional Support Scale, the Social Integration Scale, the Social Activity Scale and the Negative Reactions Scale. Each of these scales assesses social functioning from the viewpoint of the bereaved. This means that the scales concentrate on the bereaved's needs and feelings about the social situation rather than the situation itself.

5.3.1 Need for emotional support

Need for Emotional Support Scale

The need for emotional support was measured with scales of our own design. The Need for Emotional Support Scale (NESS) is a scale consisting of four items designed to measure the need for emotional support from the environment. The respondent was asked to express his or her present need for different types of emotional support. The answer categories were 0: 'no need', 1: 'some need', 2: 'great need'. The normscores for the scale as proposed by Van der Wal (1988) are 0-2: '(virtually) no need' 3-5: 'moderate need' and 6-8: 'great need'.

Inspecting the correlation matrix of the four items, we found that they correlated between .08 an .44, with a mean inter-item correlation of .30 at four months, and .28 at fourteen months. Cronbach's coefficient α was .64 at four months and .62 at fourteen months. The item-total correlations ranged between .32 and .53. The two items correlating highest with the scale were:

'Do you have the need to be able to express freely
your feelings and thoughts to others?'   (T1: r=.53, T2: r=.48)
'Do you have the need to talk about the memories
you have of ...[name of the deceased].?'   (T1: r=.46, T2: r=.49)

Considering the above psychometric evaluation, it can be stated that the scale is an acceptable measure of the need for emotional support.

Results

The mean score for the total sample is 4.3 (s.d.=2.1) at four months, and 3.8 (s.d.=2.0) at fourteen months. This decrease in the need for emotional support is significant (t=4.5, df=266, p=.000) but not very substantial. On the whole there is a moderate need for support.

Looking at the analysis of covariance for this variable (Table 5.13), with mode of death, kinship and sex as independent variables, and age of the respondent as a covariate, it appears that the percentage of variance explained by relationship to the deceased (the combination of kinship and sex) is again relatively large (variance expl.= 11.8%). The role of mode of death, although significant, is relatively small.

At four months, the mothers and the daughters of the deceased, in particular, express a relatively strong need for emotional support in comparison with the other groups. The women in general score higher on the NESS, except for the spouses group, where the widowers score higher. This also causes the significant interaction effect in the analysis of covariance (see Table 5.13). The greatest need for support is expressed by the mothers whose children committed suicide (m=6.3, s.d.=2.6). Least affected are the sons of deceased irrespective of the cause of death (m=2.8, s.d=1.6). Four months after the loss, the need for emotional support is somewhat lesser among bereaved after a long-term illness than among the unnatural death groups. This difference, however, is only significant on the 5% level.

Table 5.13

Analysis of covariance on need for emotional support (NESS) at 4 and 14 months after the loss, with mode of death, kinship and sex independent, and age of the respondent as a covariate

	Variable	Variance explained	Signific.
Need for emotional support at 4 months	Mode of death	1.7%	p=.049
	Kinship	1.7%	N.S.
	Sex	2.6%	p=.001
Kinship x	Sex	7.5%	p=.000
Covariate:	Age of respondent	1.8%	p=.001
Total variance explained	*(incl. interactions):*	21.1%	
Need for emotional supp. at 14 months	Mode of death	2.0%	p=.043
	Kinship	3.5%	p=.012
	Sex	6.2%	p=.000
Kinship x	Sex	5.2%	p=.001
Covariate:	Age of respondent	2.8%	p=.003
Total variance explained	*(incl. interactions):*	23.6%	

Ten months later, the bereaved after a traffic-fatality are the ones who are most in need of emotional support (m=4.2), followed by the bereaved from suicide (m=3.9) and the bereaved after a long-term illness (m=3.4). Now the differences between the relationship groups are even stronger, accounting for 14.9% of the variance. Parents show the highest scores, followed at some distance by siblings, children, and the spouses, who score relatively low in comparison with their scores on the other outcome measures.

The change in the need for emotional support was examined with the model of change and norm scores. Every respondent was assigned to one of five dynamic classes: unchanged little or no need for emotional support (class 1), a significant decrease (class 2), unchanged moderate need (class 3), a significant increase (class 4) or unchanged great need for emotional support (class 5).

Table 5.14 lists the composition of each of these classes by relationship to the deceased and mode of death.

Many of the sons of the deceased show unchanged little need for emotional support (class 1), while the proportions for the other relationship groups are markedly lower. There are many more men in this class (74%) than women. Decreased need for support (class 2) is evidenced by almost one-third of the widows, widowers and fathers. Unchanged moderate need (class 3) is experienced by 23% of the bereaved, with large proportions of the widows, brothers and sisters belonging to this class. An increased need for emotional support (class 4) is felt by one-fourth of the mothers, who make up the largest proportion of this class. The majority of the mothers falls into the 'unchanged great need' category (class 5). A large proportion of the daughters can also be found here (44%), and more than one-third of the fathers (39%).

As previously, a log-linear analysis was performed to assess differences in the direction of change by recoding the classes into three categories: deterioration, stability and improvement. Analysis of a series of models containing the different combinations of mode of death, kinship and sex showed a best-fitting model including a main effect for mode of death and an interaction effect of kinship and sex (or a main effect for relationship to the deceased). The likelihood ratio chi-square of this model is 26.9 (df= 38, p=.526). The bereaved after a traffic-fatality show a significant decrease in need for support less often than the bereaved in the other groups.

From the visual representation in Fig. 5.13 of the classes on the need for emotional support, it is clear that, with the notable exception of the widows, the women manifest a stronger need for support than the men. There seems to be little systematic difference in change for any of the relationship groups. A decrease in need for support is found more often among men than among women. The centroids for the modes of death (not plotted here) lie all close to each other in class 3 (unchanged moderate need).

The principal source of emotional support to the bereaved often are the next of kin. Since with the death of a family member *all* family members suffer a loss, this support system is under pressure after bereavement. Signs of this were found in different groups. Parents losing a child often reported the asynchronicity of their needs, finding it difficult to be of any any help to the other. Sometimes there were tensions between widow(er)s and the family in law. On the other hand there was also the impression that the bond between bereaved family members grew stronger. Like a

Table 5.14

Composition of the five dynamic classes of need for emotional support (NESS) by relationship and mode of death[13]

Class: By relationship	1 *Unchanged no/little need*	2 *Significantly decreased need*	3 *Unchanged moderate need*	4 *Significantly increased need*	5 *Unchanged much need*
Widowers	3 (12%)	7 (28%)	6 (24%)	3 (12%)	6 (24%)
Widows	3 (9%)	10 (31%)	11 (34%)	6 (19%)	2 (6%)
Fathers	6 (21%)	8 (29%)	2 (7%)	1 (4%)	11 (39%)
Mothers	3 (8%)	2 (5%)	4 (11%)	9 (24%)	19 (51%)
Brothers	6 (16%)	10 (26%)	13 (34%)	3 (8%)	6 (16%)
Sisters	3 (9%)	6 (17%)	12 (34%)	3 (9%)	11 (31%)
Sons	13 (42%)	5 (16%)	4 (13%)	6 (20%)	3 (10%)
Daughters	1 (2%)	10 (24%)	8 (20%)	4 (10%)	18 (44%)
By mode of death					
Suicide	12 (16%)	21 (29%)	9 (12%)	9 (12%)	22 (30%)
Traffic-fatal.	7 (8%)	12 (14%)	25 (29%)	12 (14%)	31 (36%)
Illness	19 (18%)	25 (23%)	26 (24%)	14 (13%)	23 (21%)
Total per class	**38 (14%)**	**58 (22%)**	**60 (23%)**	**35 (13%)**	**76 (29%)**

55 year old woman who lost her oldest brother told: '*His death has made us* [the other brothers and sisters] *realize how important we are to one another. Now we regularly go out together for a weekend to walk, talk and laugh a lot.*'.

Conclusion

The bereaved in general evidence a moderate need for social support, which is stronger at four months than at fourteen months. Daughters and mothers of the deceased express a relatively stronger need for emotional support in comparison with the other groups. The bereaved after a traffic-fatality also experience a relatively stronger need for support, and they show a much smaller decrease in need over time than bereaved from the other modes of death. The need for support is relatively small

---

13 The percentages listed are row percentages.

among widows: at both interviews they evidence less need than sisters and daughters of the deceased, who after the mothers are the most affected relationship group in this respect.

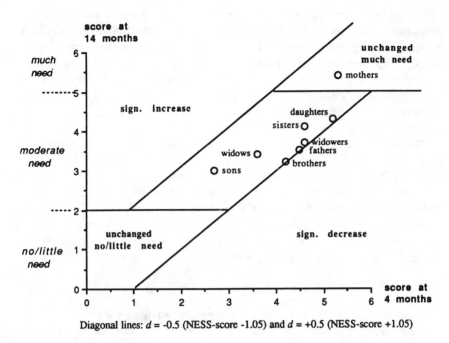

Diagonal lines: $d = -0.5$ (NESS-score -1.05) and $d = +0.5$ (NESS-score $+1.05$)

Fig. 5.13 *Visual representation of the dynamic classes for the change in need for emotional support between four and fourteen months, with the group-centroids for each relationship group*

Stroebe & Stroebe (1987) found that men were less motivated than women to use social support in coping with traumatic life events. In the present study, this observation is confirmed in the parent, sibling and child groups. Among the spouses, however, it appears that it are especially the widowers who show a relatively strong need for emotional support. This finding can probably be explained by the fact that, in our society, the wife is often the principal provider of emotional support for the man, while the woman often relies on other sources. Loss of one's wife may thus constitute a major loss of emotional support, which is far more important than in other relationships.

5.3.2   Social integration

Social Integration Scale

A general feeling of security, being part of a group, and being involved in intimate relationships was measured with the Social Integration Scale (SIS) of our own design (Cleiren, Van der Wal & Diekstra, 1988). This scale consists of three items: the first assessing the feeling of being loved by someone, the second the feeling of being valued by others, and the third the feeling of being part of intimate social relationships. The respondent was asked to answer the questions with regard to the present situation. The answer categories ranged from 0: 'not at all' to 4: 'very strongly'. The scale scores ranged from 0 to 12.

The correlations between the items of the Social Integration Scale ranged from .41 to .52 at four months, and from .40 to .54 at fourteen months. On the basis of these relatively high correlations, it was decided to form a scale from the unweighted sumscore of the items. The reliability of the Social Integration Scale was satisfactory at both measurements with Cronbach's α .71 at four months and .72 at fourteen months, and with the item-total correlations at both interviews ranging from .49 to .59. From the above evaluation, it was concluded that the SIS is a satisfactory instrument for measuring social integration.

Results

The social integration of the bereaved can generally be termed good: the mean score was 9.7 (s.d.=2.3) at four months and 9.9 (s.d.=2.2) at fourteen months. There was no significant change in social integration (t=-.62, df=264, p=.54) between the two points in time.

Analysis of variance reveals minor systematic differences between the groups at four months (see Table 5.15). The total amount of variance explained is not significant however. The bereaved from suicide generally feel somewhat less integrated than those in the long-term illness group and the bereaved after a traffic-fatality. The absolute level of integration is, however, high for all three modes of death. As could be expected, the spouses feel less socially integrated in comparison with the other kinship groups.

Fourteen months after the loss, the difference between the modes of death has disappeared. Looking at the mean scores, it appears that the level of integration has somewhat improved among the bereaved in the suicide group (m=9.2 respectively 10.0), whilst the other modes of death show virtually the same level of integration at both times of interview. At fourteen months, the children appear significantly more integrated than the other groups. The spouses remain the relatively least integrated group. All effects are small, although the difference between the kinship groups is somewhat more pronounced.

Table 5.15

Analysis of variance on social integration (SIS) at 4 and 14 months after the loss, with mode of death, kinship and sex independent

	Variable	Variance explained	Signific.
Social integration at 4 months	Mode of death	2.9%	.011
	Kinship	2.9%	.027
	Sex	0.0%	N.S.
Total variance explained (incl. interactions):		11.1%	N.S.
Social integration at 14 months	Mode of death	0.4%	N.S.
	Kinship	4.2%	p=.008
	Sex	0.0%	N.S.
Total variance explained (incl. interactions):		16.1%	p=.007

For the widowed, the feeling of being socially isolated is often related to specific events and situations, such as having to go to a birthday gathering alone, or coming home and finding no one there. A widow (45) had lost her husband after an illness and wanted very much to be with other people but: *'Going there while before you have always gone there together, it makes me feel superfluous. They put up with me, but do not really need me.'*. The older widowed several times mentioned the weather or season as having an influence on their possibilities of entering in contact with people. An older man: *'I am really waiting for the summer so I can go out walking again and have a chat here and there.'*.

The widowers evidence the lowest level of social integration at both interviews: m=8.5 (s.d.= 3.2) and 8.4 (s.d.= 2.9) respectively. We also looked at the difference in change in social integration between the two interviews by conducting an analysis of covariance with the Social Integration score at fourteen months as a dependent variable, and the score at four months as a covariate (relationship and mode of death independent). There was a significant difference between the relationship groups in the amelioration of integration. From a multiple classification analysis, the widowers appeared to contrast markedly with the other relationship groups. Given their low initial score, they did worse than expected at the second interview. The children seem to make an improvement in social integration fourteen months after the death, while the other groups show somewhat increased isolation (see Fig. 5.14).

It appears that the bereaved who feel isolated often withdraw from social intercourse, sometimes as a result of negative experiences with other people close to them. They often are more depressed, and find themselves incapable of enjoying the contact with others. A man whose wife (48) died after an illness: *'I had a dinner with other members of the family, but I did not feel related at all to those people. They were there just laughing and enjoying themselves. I felt as if I was sitting on an island, not at all a part.'*. Quite frequently, however, after the loss there was an improvement in integration, due to different causes. One of these causes seems to be the change of role within the family. The oldest daughter (34) of a women who died after a traffic accident said: *'Because of her death, it is now me who is the center of the family. My relationship with the others has improved a lot.'*. For others, the reason for the improved integration lay more in their own, changed perspective on the priorities in life. A daughter who lost her mother after an illness: *'After this you see the triviality of so many things. It makes you enjoy each other much more.'*.

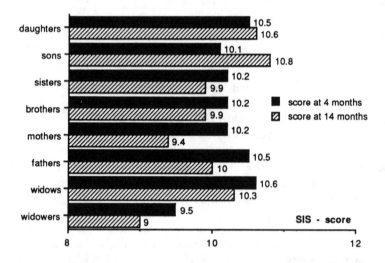

Fig. 5.14 *Mean scores on the Social Integration Scale at four months and fourteen months by relationship to the deceased*

Extremely low social integration (SIS-score < 3) was only found in three cases. A lack of social integration was not always experienced as a problem by the bereaved. Some bereaved had clearly been very much on their own before the loss, like one older mother (83) who, having lost her son to cancer, said at the first interview: *'We lived in the same house but were entirely independent of each other. I didn't know anything about his life, actually. I do everything on my own, but I like it that way.'*.

Ten months later, she was living in a home for the aged, but chose to leave, because she was not independent enough.

Conclusion

Social integration is generally satisfactory in the sample, both at four and at fourteen months after the loss. There is, however, a decrease in the integration among the spouses and the parents. This may be due to a somewhat decreasing attention paid to the bereaved by the environment as time passes. Often the feeling of 'emptiness' became more marked when life followed its daily course.

The finding that the widows feel not less integrated than the other kinship groups is somewhat surprising in view of earlier findings. A massive loss of a sense of security, to which this group might be prone according to some researchers (comp. Lopata ,1973b, 1979), does not seem to occur in our sample. This difference may be due to socio-cultural differences. Widowers feel less integrated than widows, and are the least integrated group in the sample. This may reflect the important (culturally defined) role of their wife as their main provider for emotional security.

5.3.3 Social activity

The extent to which one engages in (diverting) social contacts was measured with the Social Activity Scale (SAS).

Social Activity Scale

The Social Activity Scale (Van der Wal, Cleiren et al., 1988) consists of 6 items, checking engagement in specific social activities with others inside and outside the home. The respondent was asked to answer the questions with regard to the past week, including the day of the interview itself. The answer categories ranged from 0: 'does not apply to me' to 2: 'applies largely or fully to me'.

Inspection of the correlation matrix revealed that inter-item correlations ranged between .06 and .50, with a mean inter-item correlation of .26 at four months, and .24 at fourteen months. Cronbach's α was considered sufficiently large (.67 at four months and .65 at fourteen months) to construct a uni-dimensional Social Activity Scale. The item-total correlations ranged from .28 to .51. On this basis, it was decided to use the unweighted sumscore of the scale, resulting in a scale range of 0 to 12. Typical items, correlating high with the scale's sumscore were:

'Spend time with friends or acquaintances' (T1: r=.46, T2: r=.51)
'Invite people to my home'. (T1: r=.48, T2: r=.45)

Reviewing the psychometric evaluation of the scale it was concluded that the SAS is an acceptable scale to measure social activity, and that it can be used in further analysis.

Results

The level of social activity in the sample is moderate, although the bereaved appear to differ considerably in their level of activities. The mean score for the scale was 7.4 (s.d.=8.4) four months after the loss and 7.7 (s.d.= 7.7) at fourteen months. This small increase, which is significant at p=.05, indicates that the bereaved in general progressively (re-)engage in social contacts.

Analysis of variance (see Table 5.16) revealed no systematic differences between groups at four months. At fourteen months, the kinship groups show different levels of engagement in social activities. Among the kinship groups, it is above all the parents who have a lower level of social activity (m=6.9, s.d.=2.8), followed by the spouses. Widows tend to engage much more frequently in social activities (m=8.3, s.d.=2.7) than their male counterparts (m=6.2, s.d.=3.2). Most socially withdrawn are the spouses in the suicide group (m=5.4, s.d.=2.9). Together with the relatively low level of social activity among the siblings in the long-term illness group, this accounts for the significant interaction effect between mode of death and kinship.

Table 5.16

Analysis of variance on social activities (SAS) at 4 and 14 months after the loss, with mode of death, kinship and sex as independent variables

	Variable	Variance explained	Signific.
Social activities at 4 months	Mode of death	0.8%	N.S.
	Kinship	0.1%	N.S.
	Sex	4.1%	N.S.
Total variance explained	*(incl. interactions):*	9.2%	N.S.
Social activities at 14 months	Mode of death	0.1%	N.S.
	Kinship	4.1%	p=.009
	Sex	1.3%	N.S.
Mode of death x	Kinship	5.6%	p=.018
Total variance explained	*(incl. interactions):*	14.3%	p=.025

The accent of social activities among the bereaved initially seems to be more on receiving people at home than on going out. The initiative in the early time after the loss generally comes more from the environment than from the bereaved themselves.

Some of the respondents reported that they had actively retreated from former activities. A man whose wife died after an illness: ' *It wouldn't work out if I went out, I wouldn't say anything anyway'*. Some found that after the loss, their position in social life had changed. A woman bereaved after suicide: *'It's just a fact that the more activities you undertake, the more you get beaten.'*. However, this is not always the case. A lot of bereaved did not lead a very busy social life, regardless of the loss, and felt no urge to engage in friendships and social exchange.

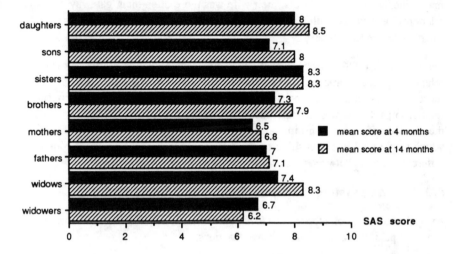

Fig. 5.15 *Mean scores on the Social Activity Scale at four months and fourteen months by relationship to the deceased*

In all relationship groups there is an increase in social activity, except among the widowers, who show a decrease in social involvement in comparison with the situation at four months after the loss (see Fig 5.15). Differences in change between the relationship groups and the modes of death were assessed by ANCOVA on the SAS at fourteen months with the score at four months as a covariate. From this, a significant interaction between mode of death and relationship appeared (F=2.1, df=14, p=.015). Inspection of a multiple classification analysis showed that improvement in social integration occurred considerably faster among the widowers bereaved after an illness, than among widowers in the unnatural death groups. One explanation might be that these widowers often already had to get by socially without their wives before the loss, and thus had had more time to acquire the social skills and contacts than the widowers in the other groups.

Conclusion

The absolute level of social activity in the sample is high, although it is clear that this aspect is initially less in the foreground in the period immediately after the loss. Initially, there is little difference between the kinship groups. As time passes, however, some signs of differential (re)engagement in social contacts occurs. While the bereaved in general show increased social activity, the widowers show a decrease. Their female counterparts, on the contrary, seem to do very well in this respect. This may indicate that for widowers, their wife was more often their 'gateway' to social relationships, and that with the decreasing attention from the environment, they are to a certain degree left helpless.

Sarason et al. (1987) observed that support measures may be biased towards the relationships that women tend to find supportive and that, while men possibly value more contacts which take their minds off troubles, women seek more confiding relationships. In the present scale this aspect was explicitly avoided by leaving open the character of the relationship. Indeed, in contrast to the need for emotional support, which might tend to be sensitive to sex differences in needs, no overall consistent difference appears between men and women here.

5.3.4   Aggravating reactions of the environment

As well as a source of support, the social environment may also be experienced as a source of painful avoiding, and negative reactions.

Aggravating Reactions Scale

Negative and painful reactions were measured with the Aggravating Reactions Scale of our own design. The scale consisted of 5 items questioning the frequency of different negative reactions from the people around them. The answer categories were: 0: 'never'; 1: 'rarely'; 2: 'sometimes'; 3: 'often'. The scale appeared internally consistent, with item-total correlations ranging from .23 to .54 at T1 (Cronbach's α=.65) and .21 to .52 at T2 (Cronbach's α=.64). The items which had the highest correlations with the scale were:

'How often do you encounter reactions of incomprehension?'

(r=.54 respectively .49)

'How often did people, in their contact with you, avoid talking about ..[name].. or about the death of ..[name].. '   (r=.49 respectively .48)

'Does it happen that people with whom you had contact before now avoid contact?'

(r=.39 respectively .52)

Along with this, the respondents were asked to indicate to what extent they were disturbed by these reactions. The answer categories went from 0: 'not at all' to 3: 'severely'.

Results

In general, the number of aggravating reactions is not very high. The mean score for the Aggravating Reactions Scale was 3.9 (s.d.=3.3) at the first interview, and 3.5 (s.d.=3.3) at the second. This decrease is not significant (t=1.11, df=259, p=.27). The reaction most frequently encountered among the bereaved (among 49% at four months) was that people suddenly cut off their conversations when the bereaved approached them.

The degree to which negative reactions distressed the bereaved was .65 (s.d.=.9) four months after the loss and .64 (s.d.=.9) at fourteen months, which is quite low.

The content of the reactions can roughly be grouped in two classes, which are often related.

One class of reactions comprises insensitivity to the needs and problems of the bereaved. A man whose son died in a car-crash said: *'Sometimes people at my work say "It will wear off", more to get rid of the subject than because they are really concerned'* . A daughter whose father committed suicide felt abandoned by her environment. *'I was always open to every one else's problems. Now something has happened to me and no one shows up.'*. On the other hand a 'businesslike' way of acting is often felt as tactless. Often, it seemed the bereaved felt more hurt by people staying away or reacting insensitively than by those who did not know what to do, but at least tried.

Another class of reactions seems to originate from embarrassment and not knowing what to do. This is also often seen as the reason for people 'not showing up', and is felt by many bereaved. The bereaved often feel they have to make the first step to reestablish the contact. A widow: *'They just count you out. On a social evening of the musical society of which we both were members, I came in and the room fell silent. Everyone looked away and no one greeted me. I became so angry that I yelled: " It may well be that you find this difficult, but that is no reason to avoid me like the plague!" After that I had less problems..'*. A widower, coming back to the office for the first time after the loss, had a similar experience of his colleagues negating him. *'After that I went to every single one of them to tell them I was back. As long as it was me who started the conversation, it went all right.'*.

The new marital status of young widows sometimes led to being regarded as 'available' to other former friends. A woman who lost her man, with whom she had led a very active social life: *'Old [male] friends of my husband pass by much more often now to "comfort" me. Recently one said he loved me, and made a pass at me.*

That is the last thing I want at the moment.'. On the other hand, the widowed sometimes felt they were regarded as a 'threat' by the person of the same sex when they visited befriended couples.

Aggravating reactions seemed to be experienced throughout our sample. Differences between the groups were again assessed with analysis of covariance at 4 and 14 months after the loss (see Table 5.17). At four months there are no significant differences between the modes of death, the kinship groups or the sexes. There are, however, differences between younger and older respondents: the younger report significantly more aggravating reactions (expl.. var. 9.2%, F=28.7, p=.000).

Ten months later, the role of age is again highly significant (10.6% var. expl., F=34.7, p=.000). At the second interview, there is, furthermore, a clear difference between kinship groups: partners and parents report relatively more reactions than siblings and children of the deceased. Examination of the mean scores shows that, in the last two groups, there is virtually no drop in the reactions experienced by the spouses, while the other groups show a (small) decrease.

Table 5.17

Analysis of covariance on aggravating reactions reactions at 4 and 14 months after the loss, with mode of death, kinship and sex independent

	Variable	Variance explained	Signific.
Aggravating reactions at 4 months	Mode of death	0.2%	N.S.
	Kinship	1.6%	N.S.
	Sex	0.1%	N.S.
Covariate:	Age of respondent	9.2%	p=.000
Total variance explained	*(incl. interactions):*	14.5%	p=.008
Aggravating reactions at 14 months	Mode of death	0.5%	N.S.
	Kinship	8.5%	p=.000
	Sex	0.3%	N.S.
Covariate:	Age of respondent	10.6%	p=.000
Total variance explained	*(incl. interactions):*	25.3%	p=.000

Looking at the degree to which the respondents are perturbed by these reactions, a slightly different picture emerges. Most of the respondents seem not to be very much disturbed by negative reactions (T1: m=.65, s.d.=.9, T2: m=.64, s.d.=.9). There is a significant, but rather small difference between the modes of death (expl. var. 2.9%,

F=4.6, p=.011), with the bereaved from suicide having the most trouble with negative reactions, followed by bereaved from a traffic-fatality and those after a long-term illness.

At fourteen months, the difficulty experienced with negative reactions seems to run parallel to the amount of reactions, and follows the same pattern: no differences between the modes of death are found (in contrast to the situation at four months), and parents and spouses have more difficulties with these reactions than the other bereaved.

Although the mean score of the bereaved in the traffic-fatality group is at the same level as in the others, the number of people having severe problems with these reactions is significantly smaller than for the other modes of death: while 14% of the suicide-bereaved and 12% of the bereaved after a long-term illness report severe perturbation by negative reactions at at least one of the interviews, this figure is only 3% in the traffic-fatality group.

The negative reactions more often came from people outside the circle of family and close friends. In many cases, it was people at work, acquaintances, and sometimes institutions which reacted negatively to the bereaved. Sometimes they also came, however, from people who were closer to them. The bereaved often re-evaluated their relationship with friends on the criterion of the possibility to talk with them about the loss. A woman who lost her son by suicide: *'My friends have left me. On New Years Eve, a few months after he died, they all wished me a happy New Year, but no one would talk about the grief'*. This example also illustrates that *not* reacting to the loss was often seen as a denial of the importance of the death to the bereaved, and felt as an aggravating reaction.

In many cases, it appears that the loss lead the bereaved to discover who were their real friends and who were not. Quite often, there were painful surprises with people whom one trusted to be available for support while, on the other hand, new 'real' friendships came out and deeper relationships were established.

Conclusion

Negative and frustrating reactions from the environment are often experienced by the bereaved, but they are rarely severely perturbed by those reactions. In contrast to what is often assumed, it seems that bereaved from suicide do not have to cope with more negative reactions in comparison with the other modes of death. There is a slight indication that at four months they may be more sensitive than the other groups to the adverse reactions. This difference disappears, however, at fourteen months. Younger bereaved experience more frustrating reactions and feel more affected by them. The latter are sometimes related to negative reactions, or lack of understanding on behalf of their parents.

In comparison with the findings in other studies, less stigmatization is found in the present sample. Lindemann & Greer (cited in Osterweis et al., 1984) state that in suicide bereavement there is a stronger tendency to look for a scapegoat within the family, and a search to blame someone for not recognizing the impending suicide, or not paying enough attention to the needs of the deceased. The present results give no indication that any systematical differences of this is kind exist here. Barrett & Scott (1987) found more feelings of shame, stigmatization and rejection, among suicide-bereaved as compared to other causes.

The reason for the marked differences with the cited studies may lie in the better representativity of the present sample, but it may also be caused by a real difference. Attitude of the environment, and thus also aggravating reactions, may be narrowly related to sociocultural norms. The difference with our study may be due to differences between the United States and the Netherlands in the acceptation of suicide.

5.4   Age of deceased and functioning

In the discussion of the outcome variables, age of the respondents was added to the analysis as a covariate. Age of the deceased could not be introduced at the same time, since there was a high degree of co-linearity between these variables, resulting in uninterpretable results.

To check for the role of age of the deceased, each analysis of covariance was also conducted with this variable as a covariate. It appeared that in many cases, age of the deceased explained a larger part of the variance than age of the respondent. Since the correlation between age of the deceased and age of the bereaved is high, the effects are hard to separate and a source of the age effect is hard to determine statistically. Perhaps some of the equivocal results in studies regarding the role of age arise from this compound of age with the situation.

The finding that age of the deceased is generally more strongly related to adaptation may indicate, however, that the impact of a loss may be more dependent on the age of the deceased (and thus be an effect of untimeliness of the death) rather than the age of the bereaved. For example: when a widow is bereaved at a young age, her husband was most probably young as well. In comparison with an older widow, there may be important differences in the context as well as in the life phase. The young widow may face a long period of child-rearing as a single parent, and experience concurrent financial and social stresses. In the case of an older widow, the children may have households of their own, and she may be more 'cared for' than her younger counterpart.

Combining statistical and conceptual data in this way, we may argue that the origin of the age-effect in bereavement has to be ascribed to the deceased dying at a younger or older age, rather than to the age of the bereaved.

5.5   Attitude to the task-demands of bereavement

In order to assess the attitude of the bereaved to the loss, we measured three types of feelings with regard to the loss: anger, guilt and relief.

5.5.1   Anger

Feelings of anger are often regarded as a protest against the loss. It has been found that it may be directed towards different persons, objects or circumstances which may be held responsible for the death. Anger may also be experienced as a more general feeling, without a concrete aim or switching from one object to another.

Anger Scale

Feelings of anger during the week preceding the interview were measured with the Anger Scale. This scale is a selection of the 'state' version of the Z.A.V., a questionnaire for self-analysis (Van der Ploeg, Defares & Spielberger; 1982), this being a translation of Spielberger's State Trait Anxiety Scale. Respondents were asked to what degree a series of statements applied to them over the last seven days, including the day of the interview. Answer categories ranged from 0: 'not at all' to 3: 'very much'. On the first interview, Cronbach's α was .83, on the second measurement .75. $R_{T1.T2}$ was .35.

The items with the highest inter-item correlations were:

'I am furious'	(T1: r=.70, T2: r=.56)
'I would like to yell at someone'	(T1: r=.70, T2: r=.67)

The above psychometric evaluation indicates that the scale is highly suitable as a measure for anger.

Results

The major part of the sample does not experience strong feelings of anger, neither at four months, nor at fourteen months after the loss. The scale mean of the sample at four months is 1.4 (s.d.= 2.4), and at fourteen months 1.0 (s.d.=1.8).

Analysis of variance revealed no significant differences between the modes of death or the kinship groups. There is a slight difference between the means of the long-term illness and the unnatural death groups, but this does not reach significance. At four months, women show slightly more anger (F=6.47, df=1, p=.011) than men. Age of the respondent did not significantly covary with the scores on the Anger Scale at either interview. One subgroup with exceptionally high scores are the daughters whose father or mother committed suicide. This group had a mean score of 3.7 (s.d.=4.9) at T1, but this fell back to 1.0 (s.d.=1.1) at T2. Inspection of this group does not show a common ground or object of their anger.

Also, at fourteen months, the analysis of variance shows no systematic differences between the independent variables, although a trend for women to be slightly more angry than men persists (respectively m=1.13 and m=.76). The mean of the sample as a whole drops significantly between the two interviews (t=2.72, df=274, p=.007).

Van der Wal (1988) calibrated the scale, with a score of 0 taken as 'not angry', 1 through 3 as somewhat angry, 4 through 12 as 'angry', and 13 through 20 as 'very angry'. The percentages of our sample falling into each of these categories is shown in Fig. 5.16. At fourteen months, none of the respondents falls in the category 'very angry'. The percentage experiencing anger among the long-term illness-bereaved is lower (although not reaching significance) especially in the 'somewhat angry' category.

From the explanations of the respondents about the subject of their anger, it appeared that, as expected, the anger was directed towards a variety of subjects. These subjects corresponded partially with the mode of death.

   The bereaved from suicide, not unexceptionally, were angry at the deceased for doing this to them. A man whose brother had shot himself in the head at home was angry about the way he had committed suicide. The room in which his brother had shot himself was full of blood, and even parts of his brother's brain were splattered around. He was very angry with the police as well, who had left him to clean up the room in the state they had found it.

   A women who had lost her mother after suicide was very angry with her. As she kept watch over the body, she did not want to look at her mother's face: *'I could feel her jeering at me: "I succeeded, after all.".'* . Since, in many cases, the deceased had been under psychiatric treatment before death, some had also feelings of resentment towards those who had taken care of him or her.

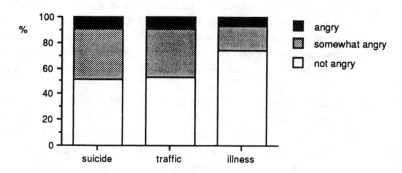

Fig. 5.16 *Feelings of anger for each mode of death fourteen months after the loss (percentages)*

Among bereaved from traffic-fatalities where another (guilty) party was involved, anger was often directed towards this person. In several cases, it was not the responsibility for the accident itself which made them angry, but the conduct afterwards. A man, whose sister had been killed crossing a road on her bicycle, was filled with rage towards the woman who had run her over: *'She did not ever let us know she was sorry for what had happened. One month later, her lawyer came to us with a demand to pay for the damage to her car'*. Sometimes, bereaved were angry with the people from the ambulance company, or the hospital for not arriving in time.

Bereaved after a long-term illness were sometimes angry with the hospital staff, or the doctor or specialist who had treated the deceased during his or her illness. Sometimes the reasons for these feelings lay in the lack of attention for the patient. More often, respondents complained about lack of information from the family doctor or surgeon about diagnosis and progress, and a lack of being involved in decisions about treatments and risks of certain treatments of the disease. In most cases, however, this did not lead to strong feelings of anger.

Conclusion

Feelings of anger are present across the whole sample, with no systematic differences between kinships or modes of death, although those in the unnatural death groups seem somewhat more angry shortly after the loss. The objects of anger are diverse, but tend to be somewhat similar for each mode of death. The anger is rarely directed towards the deceased, but rather, the circumstances surrounding the loss. None of the respondents evidences excessive feelings of anger.

Although anger is generally regarded as a normal component of the grief response, strong anger does not appear here as such. This finding is interesting, since it corroborates the position of anger in our model as reflecting the attitude to the loss. Rather than covarying with the formal aspects of the task-demand of the loss (mode of death and kinship), it appears here to be a personal way of coping with the situation.

In some respects, the results differ from the findings of other research: Sanders (1983) found more anger among bereaved from sudden deaths. In other studies, differences were found between kinship groups: Fish (1986, in Sanders 1988) found greater anger among mothers. Miles & Demi (1984) and Osterweis et al. (1984) found more anger in parents than among spouses. A possible reason for this may be that, in the Anger Scale, we chose not to explicitly point to the loss and its circumstances as a source or reason for the anger. In this way, our scale also measures anger when attributed by the bereaved to other causes.

5.5.2   Guilt feelings

Blaming oneself for the death of the other person is an attitude with different aspects. First of all, there may be a component of factual or juridicial guilt, e.g being the driver that caused the accident in which a copassenger died. Guilt can also be psychologically defined. The bereaved may reproach themselves with things done or neglected that might have prevented the death. This type of guilt was operationalized in the study.

Guilt Scale

Feelings of guilt with regard to the (circumstances of) death were measured with the Guilt Scale of our own design (Van der Wal, Cleiren et al. 1988). This scale consisted of two items, with which the respondent was asked to agree or disagree:

'I wonder what I have done wrong.'   (m=.53, s.d.=1.2)
'I feel guilty about the death.'   (m=.32, s.d.= .9)

The five answering alternatives ranged from 0: I totally disagree to 4: I totally agree. The intercorrelation of the items was .60. The above evaluation indicates that the two-item scale is acceptable as a measure of specific (death-related) guilt feelings. The unweighted sumscore of the items was used in further analysis, with a range of 0 through 8.

Results

In general, strong feelings of guilt were rare. Guilt feelings, not surprisingly, are much more prominent among bereaved from suicide (see also Fig. 5.17). As can be seen in Table 5.18, there was a highly significant difference between the modes of death: bereaved from suicide felt more guilty (m=2.0, s.d.=2.3) than those bereaved after a traffic-fatality (m=.4, s.d.=1.3) and after a long-term disease (m=.4, s.d.=1.1). The kinship groups also differed significantly from each other. Guilt feelings were relatively strongest among parents, followed by widowed, siblings and children. There were no interaction effects.

Table 5.18

Analysis of covariance on guilt feelings at four months with mode of death, kinship and sex as independent variables, and age of the deceased as a covariate

	Variable	Variance explained	Signific.
Guilt scores at 4 months	Mode of death	18.0%	p=.000
	Kinship	5.8%	p=.000
	Sex	0.3%	N.S.
Covariate:	Age of deceased	1.9%	p=.006
Total variance explained (incl. interactions):		29.9%	

There was no systematic difference between men and women in the level of guilt feelings. Analysis of covariance revealed a small but significant contribution of age of the deceased: younger age of the deceased is related to stronger feelings of guilt (r=-22, p=.000).

Figure 5.17 shows the scores of the kinship groups and modes of death on the guilt scale. The mean scores of the bereaved from suicide are markedly higher. All the means for the bereaved from other modes of death fall into the category '(virtually) no guilt feelings'. Applying the norms given by Van der Wal (1988) to these data, we find that the parents of children who committed suicide experience moderate feelings of guilt.

As with anger, the reasons for feeling guilty differed with the modes of death. Among the bereaved from suicide, feelings of guilt were principally related to two different aspects: the process which led to the suicide and the suicide event itself. Some bereaved who had lived together with the deceased accentuated situational factors. One brother said: *'If I had come home a bit earlier it wouldn't have happened'*, and a widow: *'I just could not be there all the time to watch over him. I sometimes had to go out shopping.'*

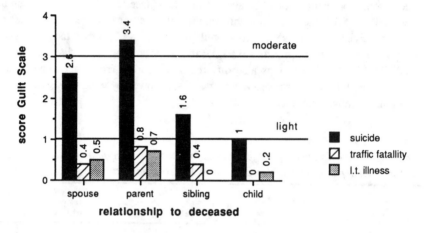

Fig. 5.17 *Feelings of guilt by kinship group and mode of death (mean scores)*

Other bereaved after suicide reproached themselves with not having seen the signs: *'He had always said that one day when he found the courage, he would kill himself. I never believed that he meant it...'.*

Bereaved from the other modes of death generally experienced little feeling of guilt. Among bereaved from traffic victims, it is more often situational factors they feel guilty about. A woman who lost her husband in a car accident: *'We had had a fight just before he left, he was very angry when he stepped into his car. The moment I heard he had died I thought: It is my fault, he was thinking about me.'.* The father of a little boy who died in the street in front of his home reproached himself for not having forbidden his son to play there.

Among the bereaved after a long-term disease, only 13.9% experienced mild to moderate feelings of guilt. Guilt, when present, was often expressed by the fact that people asked themselves whether they had done something wrong when taking care of the patient, or felt that it would have been better to live in a healthier environment. Other doubts were more related to aspects in the relationship. A son: *'I should have seen more of her during her illness.'*

In many instances, people used rationalizing strategies to reduce feelings of guilt. In several cases, the bereaved from suicide regarded the death as the direct consequence of psychiatrical illness. A man whose sister committed suicide: *'You have to think there was nothing you could do, that she was mentally ill, otherwise you become crazy yourself.'* Another brother reacted to the guilt items with: *'I didn't understand her at all, her way of thinking, how she acted. In the past I had tried to help her, but it was no use. There was just nothing I could do.'.* In many instances, the bereaved after a long-term disease reacted with a firm 'no' to the guilt questions, illustrating this with remarks such as: *'I did everything that was in my power to do. I gave him/her the best possible care during the illness'.* Often, they added that it was beyond their power to control death.

Conclusion

The results corroborate the finding in other studies that guilt plays a more important role in bereavement after suicide than after other modes of death. The reasons for feeling guilty differ considerably with the bereaved, but are mostly related to regrets about specific things they had done or omitted to do.

Our findings also confirm the observations in other studies, that parents evidence relatively more guilt (see Section 3.3.5). The coping strategy of 'rationalizing' to fend off guilt, as mentioned by Miles and Demi (1984) appeared to be used by many of the bereaved. The most common type of guilt was, as in their study, the feeling of being (partly) responsible for the death of their child. When the deceased died at a younger age, the bereaved tended to feel more responsible for the death.

5.5.3   Relief

The attitude to the loss is also reflected in the degree of relief the bereaved experiences after the loss.

Relief Scale

With the Relief Scale of our own design (cf. Van der Wal, Cleiren et al.; 1988), the degree of relief over the death of the deceased was measured during the first interview. The scale consisted of three statements, with which the respondent was asked to agree or disagree. The alternatives ranged from 0: I totally disagree to 4: I totally agree. The items, all correlating above .80 with the sumscore, were:

'With the death of ..., a weight has fallen off my mind.'
'The death of ... gives me, in spite of everything, a certain feeling of relief.'
'With the death of ... a burden has fallen from me.'

The scale proved to be highly reliable and uni-dimensional (α = .92). This indicates that the scale is highly suitable as a measure of relief.

Results

The mean score on relief for the whole sample was 4.2 (s.d.= 4.8), indicating that feelings of relief were quite common among the bereaved. Analyzing the differences between the groups with an analysis of covariance, it appeared there were significant differences between the modes of death in the amount of relief the death had brought about (see Table 5.19). The kinship groups and the sexes did not differ systematically in relief. Older age of the respondent was somewhat, but not strongly, related to greater relief.

Van der Wal (1988) calibrated the scale as follows: 0: 'no relief at all', 1- 5: 'some relief', 6-9: 'moderate relief', and 10-12 'great relief'. A mean score indicating 'moderate relief' is found among the bereaved after a long-term illness, and among spouses and children of those who committed suicide. The parents and siblings in this group show somewhat (but not significantly) less feelings of relief. These scores stand in a marked contrast to the bereaved after a traffic accident, who virtually never evidence strong feelings of relief (see also Fig. 5.18).

Table 5.19

Analysis of covariance on feelings of relief, four months after the loss, with mode of death, kinship and sex independent, and age of the bereaved as a covariate

	Variable	Variance explained	Signific.
Relief at 4 months	Mode of death	19.4%	p=.000
	Kinship	0.7%	N.S.
	Sex	0.2%	N.S.
Covariate:	Age of respondent	1.1%	p=.036
Total variance explained (incl. interactions):		26.9%	

As was found for feelings of anger and guilt, the subject of feelings of relief differed according to the mode of death.

Among the bereaved from suicide, the reasons for relief lay mostly in the end of a prolonged period of trouble, stress and worry. Often, there had been multiple suicide attempts or threats. A daughter who lost her mother to suicide: *'During the final years I felt powerless to do anything. She was so depressed. Every time I heard the telephone ring my heart pounded. I was very restless....Now it is so much easier.'.*

In another case, the deceased had always leaned heavily upon her daughter. *'She was so demanding! If it had lasted much longer, it would have driven me mad..'*.

Feelings of relief were the rule rather than the exception in the long-term illness group. For many respondents, the long-term tensions and uncertainties about the illness weighed heavily. Some of them, especially those who took care of the patient themselves, said that, in the end, they even wished for the patient to die. Often with the remark: *'You couldn't call it living anymore '*. When asked about it, they often said they had been on the verge of a breakdown themselves. The general impression is that the longer the patient had been ill, the more relieved the bereaved were at the time of the interview (r=.30, p<.001).

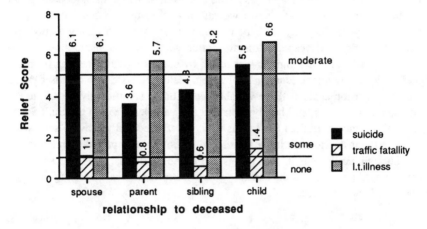

Fig. 5.18 *Feelings of relief by mode of death and kinship to the deceased, four months after the loss (mean scores)*

Closer examination of the rare cases where relatively strong feelings of relief were present in the traffic-fatality group reveals that they are generally connected to prior worries or problems in the relationship. The parents of a 29 yr. old son who died in a motorcycle accident felt, next to deep grief, relief also. His father: *'He had given us much worry in the past. He was active in the squatters' movement, and was addicted to heroin. He was always very reckless on the road, and I often feared he might have an accident. He was always so restless, and rarely seemed to be happy.'* . A 19 year old daughter, whose father was run over by a car, also had feelings of relief: *'I miss him of course, but he always controlled me in everything. He was a real household tyrant. It is a relief not only to me but also for the others* [sister and mother]*.'* .

In one case, the deceased had been very ill for a long time and his wife (69) had always taken care of him. Their relationship had been loving, but comradely, more than anything else. With his knowledge, she had resumed contact with a lover from her youth, a long time before the accident. After his death, she had the feeling she could start a new life.

It has been assumed that feelings of relief after a loss may lead to a sense of guilt in the bereaved. In some psychoanalytic views, it is presumed that relief represents the bereaved's wish for the death of the deceased. Since this is an intolerable desire the bereaved would, as a consequence, feel guilty about this (unconscious) death wish, and/or attribute the death to his or her wish. Contrary to this, it seems, relief and guilt were not directly related in any way in our sample. The correlations were virtually zero. This was true for the sample as a whole, as well as within each mode of death and kinship group. However, since we saw here that the reasons for relief are diverse, it may be that only the type of relief associated with highly ambivalent feelings towards the deceased or dissatisfaction with the relationship gives rise to feelings of guilt. This assumption was tested by predicting guilt feelings from the Relief Scale score *and* the score on Ambivalent feelings towards the deceased[14] in a multiple regression analysis. Both variables contributed significantly (p<.05) to the prediction, but together, still hardly explained any variance (5%) on the Guilt Scale. With ambivalence partialled out in this way, relief appeared to have a somewhat stronger relationship to guilt in the opposite direction (with a partial correlation of -.13), although hardly salient. This means that to the extent that there was an effect, more guilt was predicted for the bereaved who felt strong ambivalent feelings towards the deceased and *little* relief.

Conclusion

Relief is a very common feeling both among suicide and long-term illness bereaved. The reasons given for relief among the suicide-bereaved resemble strongly those among the long-term illness bereaved: in both groups the death means an end to the worrying and fear of what is going to happen. Another similarity is the relief occasioned by the knowledge that the deceased is at last free of his or her suffering: free, in the case of a long-term illness, from physical pain, and in suicide from psychic pain. Also, in the case of suicide, the bereaved were often caught up in a situation of burdensome (emotional) care.

Among the bereaved after a traffic accident, relief, if present, is less likely to be related to the factors surrounding the event of the loss, but rather seem to be related to a burdensome preceding situation.

Thus, the reasons for relief are generally connected to the end of an unbearable or hopeless situation, rather than relief over the death in itself. In some cases, relief is

---

[14]   See Section 7.1.1 for a description of this scale.

found in being free of a dominating parent or spouse, as was observed by Parkes & Weiss (1983). In many cases, however, the reasons for relief are found in situational, rather than relational aspects. No relationship could be found between relief and guilt feelings.

5.6   Summary

At the end of this long analysis, we will now summarize our main findings. In this chapter, a systematic comparison was made between the three modes of death, between the different kinship groups and between the sexes in functioning after bereavement. We will look at the overall systematic differences. First, we shall focus on the sample as a whole, and then discuss the role of kinship and mode of death in functioning after bereavement. In the last subsection, we will describe the findings in terms of the contribution of our main independent variables ordered by dimension of functioning.

5.6.1   Functioning after bereavement: the general picture

Four months after the loss, the general impression of the sample is one of intensive involvement and preoccupation with thoughts about the loss.

Most of the bereaved, by four months after the death, seem to have developed a fairly good picture of what has happened to them. A substantial minority, however, is still frequently wondering what has happened and continues to be uncertain about circumstances and cause of death. The bereaved are often preoccupied with the question of the meaning of the loss, and more generally, the meaning of their very existence. Rather than finding an answer to these questions, it appears that acceptance of the impossibility of this, sometimes accompanied by a different view of life, leads to a diminishing preoccupation at fourteen months after the loss.

Difficulty with detachment is very common in the early period after the loss. At fourteen months, 20% of the sample still has either great difficulty with detachment, or deteriorates significantly in this respect. Closely reflecting this situation is the level of shock reactions. A substantial part of the sample can, on the basis of their scores on the IES, probably be diagnosed as suffering a post-traumatic stress syndrome.

Only a minority of the bereaved experience extreme psychological and physical health problems, although health too is clearly affected by the loss. At four months, in particular, it is clear that many are going through a difficult time. Physical health seems somewhat lower than in the Dutch population. The most characteristic complaints seem to reflect the physical effects of prolonged stress. The overall level of health complaints diminishes somewhat between four and fourteen months. In many cases, there is evidence that the bereaved's health was already affected during the time before the loss. Medicine and substance-use seem to increase shortly after the loss and to gradually increase to pre-loss levels. Medicine consumption is strongly related to age of the bereaved.

In terms of psychological health, it seems that a depressed mood, accompanied by emotional and physical exhaustion, prevails in our sample. Only a few bereaved, however, become severely depressed upon bereavement. Suicidal ideation in terms of concrete plans or methods is rare. If present, the onset of suicidal thoughts usually started before the loss, and was often unrelated to it. The desire that 'it would be all over with', or sometimes wishing one were dead, were frequently reported in the first days after the loss, but had subsided for most of the bereaved at the time of the interview.

Serious problems in social functioning are not common. Although, in general, there is a strong need for emotional support, most of the bereaved, even those who lose a spouse, feel relatively well socially integrated and develop a moderate level of social activity. However, the overall level of social functioning seems to *decrease* somewhat, in contrast to the other dimensions of functioning.

5.6.2   Kinship and adaptation

The reactions that pertain directly to the loss are the ones that covary most strongly with kinship (see also Table 5.20). We see the parents and spouses, in general, systematically evidencing more intense reactions than siblings and children of the deceased. Here, we will describe our main conclusions for each kinship group, giving a short recapitulation of the condition for each.

Spouses

Not surprisingly, the widowed reacted strongly to the loss of their spouse. Both widows and widowers frequently ruminate about the circumstances, cause and meaning of the loss in the early months, while this decreases for most of them over the year. They have great difficulty turning their thoughts away from the deceased. At fourteen months, one third still has moderate to severe problems with detachment. They frequently suffer from intrusive thoughts about the loss and, to a lesser extent, avoid confrontations with it. In contrast to the other bereaved family members, at four months the men and women do not much differ in the level of loss-reactions. Widows, however, at fourteen months, show remarkably decreased difficulty with detachment in comparison to the widowers.

Health among the widowed seems somewhat deteriorated, but not very strongly, in general. Here, a number of differences between men and women appear. Interestingly, the differences are in the opposite direction for physical health on the one hand, where the widows seem more affected, and psychological health on the other hand, where widowers show more complaints.

In terms of depression, the widowers seem to do somewhat worse than the widows, although for both, severe depression is rare. Suicidal ideation is frequently present shortly after the loss, but is not specific, and seems to have virtually disappeared at four months. The expectancy for doing well in the future differs considerably between widows and widowers. The vast majority of the widows have good hopes for the future and gain confidence with time. The majority of the widowers, however, evidence only moderate, low, and often decreasing control at both interviews.

Although the relationship with the spouse before death was not always optimal, it is clear that most of the widowed had lost their most important confidant and friend. Here again, it is clear that the loss of a spouse seems, socially, to have more severe implications for men in comparison to women. This is illustrated by the relatively higher need for support among widowers, especially shortly after the loss. Also, in terms of social activities, there is a difference: here it is the degree of reintegration that differs between the sexes. While the widows (like all other groups) have become more socially active at fourteen months after the loss, the widowers more often tend to withdraw. The same is found for social integration. Widowers tend to feel much more isolated, and many of them show no improvement between four and fourteen months after the loss. The widows feel more integrated and recover more quickly.

Parents

Parents who lose their child, by virtually all standards of functioning, are clearly the most affected group of all: 93% of the parents who lose a child after a traffic accident still have moderate to severe difficulties with detachment from their child after four months.

More than a year after the loss, half of the parents are still often or continually occupied with the meaning of the loss, with most reporting that the death of their child makes no sense to them at all. A majority still have moderate to severe difficulty with detachment from their child, and more than one third have severe difficulty both at four and fourteen months, or experiences increasing difficulty. Intrusive thoughts are stronger among them than among the widowed at both interviews, and they show little decrease in intrusions over time. Avoidance of thoughts about the loss does occur frequently, but is not very different from the level in other groups. Guilt feelings, especially in the case of suicide, are more frequently found among parents than in the other relationships.

Depression is invariantly high among the parents at both interviews. About one third is moderately to severely depressed at both points in time. Recovery over time seems only limited. Social activity is relatively low and hardly increases over the first fourteen months.

The situation of the mothers, in particular, can be qualified as worrisome. This is perhaps best illustrated by quoting some of the data reported in the preceding sections: 35% of the mothers show no signs of a decreasing attachment to their child, while the group as a whole is characterized by a moderate (unchanged) depression at four and fourteen months. They often tend to have little or no hope for recovery in the future. Mothers also have the highest level of physical health complaints, with a mean score approaching that of suicide attempters and chronically ill, while the level of medicinal consumption was high. More than half of the mothers at both interviews reports being in great need of emotional support.

The picture of the parents is one of despair, and they often encounter great problems, or even inability to redirect their lives. The possibility of growth resulting from the loss -sometimes mentioned in the literature- is virtually absent in this group. As one father who had lost his 2-year old son due to a severe brain dysfunction, put it, fourteen months after the loss: *'It does not make you stronger. You get tougher, and weaker'*.

Siblings

Less affected than the parents and spouses are the siblings of the deceased. Extreme problems are less likely to occur in this group. There is, however, a strong contrast between the men and the women.

The brothers in general do not suffer major problems on any of the measures of functioning. They show only a little loss-reactions at four months after the loss, and also a significant decrease in reactions over time. Their health and social functioning seem unaffected on the whole.

However, the sisters generally have more problems, and appear to be even slightly more affected than the widows in most of the aspects of functioning. Many of them show a high level of intrusive thoughts, and difficulties with detachment of the same magnitude as the widows. The sister group at four months shows the highest level of avoidance of all.

Health, also, seems quite often strongly affected: the sisters express less confidence in the future, are initially more depressed, and have more health complaints than the widows. On a social level, like the other groups, most of them seem not to have many problems. However, many sisters feel a considerable need for emotional support which shows little change over time. On the other hand, they often already show a high level of social activity at four months, and a reasonable level of social integration.

It appears that the sisters often felt close to their deceased brother or sister, although as a rule the frequency of contact was not high. They often tended to see the deceased as dominant, but also as dependent on them. The picture is one of close emotional, rather than practical, involvement with the deceased.

Women in particular thus seem prone to have difficulties after the loss of a brother or sister. The high level of problems in this group is alarming, and certainly unexpected in view of the scarce attention that has been given to bereaved siblings in the literature. The position of siblings between widowed and children concerning their loss-reactions and health illustrates the wrongful neglecting of this group in empirical research.

Children

The least affected, considered as a group, are the adult children of the deceased. Four months after the loss, the major part is not very occupied with questions about the loss, and does not show a high level of difficulties with detachment and shock, although the daughters are more affected than the sons.

Both physical and psychological health can be termed good for most of those who lost a parent. The daughters show a relatively high need for emotional support, especially four months after the loss, but both social integration and social activities seem hardly affected. The findings for the children are in line with findings of other studies.

5.6.3   Mode of death and adaptation

The mode of death often appears to have more influence on the themes of the bereavement process than on its intensity. As we saw before, the differences between the modes of death are mostly minimal. For that reason, in this section, we will only highlight those aspects which seem to differ and are more or less characteristic for the specific modes of death.

Suicide

The bereaved after suicide are often searching to make out what has happened, and especially in what state of mind the deceased was at the time of the suicide. The quest for the motivation of the suicide and underlying reasons is combined with a broader search for the meaning, and often with their role in it. Feelings of guilt are, not surprisingly, most prominent in this group. Most of the parents of children who committed suicide appear to be increasingly preoccupied with the question of why this had to happen, and usually find no answer. In the other kinship groups, the search for meaning is quite intense in the early time after the loss, but extreme preoccupation occurred markedly less frequently after fourteen months.

Both the level of difficulty with detachment and the level of shock reactions do not seem to reflect an atypical bereavement process among the suicide-bereaved. The magnitude of their problems most resembles those of the bereaved after long-term illness. This is also true for the amount of relief they feel after the death. Most of the suicide-bereaved had gone through a very burdensome time before the loss. Many had worried a lot about the deceased, had been fearful of suicide, and had often gone through intensely stressful episodes with the deceased. A qualitative difference with the situation of the long-term illness bereaved is that the problems were mostly found in the affective and relational area, while, in the long-term illness group, problems concentrated more on physical and psychological exhaustion. There is a sense of relief, as well as the consolation that the deceased is finally free of his or her psychic suffering.

Although severe health problems and depression were not more frequent among the suicide-bereaved, there is some indication of a higher suicide risk in this group. Four suicide-bereaved (as opposed to only one non-suicide-bereaved) had attempted suicide themselves after the loss. In two cases, their own psychiatric history appeared to play a major role, but in the other two cases this was not clear. Although in general there does not seem to be an excess of psychological problems among the suicide-bereaved in terms of depression, we may suspect a relatively higher suicide (attempt) risk. A possible explanation for this is that in the case of suicide bereavement, the bereaved are also presented with a specific way of coping with problems: by stepping out of life. This may function as a model for solving their own (grief) problems.

In terms of social functioning, it seems there is no massive social 'stigmatization' of the suicide-bereaved. Social activity is no lesser than in the other modes of death. The social integration seems not to be markedly different either, although at four months after the suicide, the mean is somewhat lower than in the other groups. Although the absolute level of aggravating reactions is not different among the suicide-bereaved in comparison to both other groups (a finding which is quite astonishing in view of the literature on suicide bereavement), the suicide-bereaved in general feel somewhat more affected by it. This may indicate that suicide-bereaved are generally not treated much differently from other bereaved, but are more vulnerable to the negative reactions of the environment.

Guilt feelings, not surprisingly, play a far more important role in bereavement after suicide than after other modes of death. Severe feelings of guilt are, however, relatively rare. They are often related to the question concerning what they could have done to prevent the deceased from taking this step. On the other hand, many of the suicide survivors, after some time, conclude there was finally nothing they could have done to prevent it. The results corroborate the finding in other studies, that guilt plays a more important role in bereavement after suicide than after other modes of death.

Traffic-fatality

As with the suicide-bereaved, preoccupation with the search for what has happened occurs frequently in the traffic-fatality group, although slightly less often then with the suicide-bereaved. The bereaved after a traffic-fatality too are unable to find meaning in the loss, and when they stop ruminating over it, it is more often because they have given up than because they have found a explanation or reason.

The reactions of bereaved after a traffic-fatality are also characterized by more difficulties with detachment than in the other groups at four months. They evidence, however, a more marked decrease in reactions than the other groups, which means that they do not significantly differ from the two other modes of death at fourteen months. When we look at the individual level at fourteen months, there is still, however, about one-third of this group that evidences moderate or increasing problems with detachment. There are also somewhat higher initial reactions of avoidance than in the other groups, while intrusive thoughts about the death occur, in general, as frequently as in the bereaved after other modes of death.

Both at four and at fourteen months after the loss, the psychological and physical health of bereaved in this group does not differ systematically from the other modes of death. Depression among siblings and children is, initially, somewhat higher than in the other modes of death, but at fourteen months, this decreases to a comparable level.

Relief after the loss is rare in the bereaved after a traffic-fatality. When present, it is virtually always related to a burdensome preceding situation, although not related to the loss itself as in the other two modes of death. Sometimes relief is felt about the consolation that, given the accident and the injuries, the deceased did not have to go on living severely handicapped.

Guilt is not often felt by the bereaved after a traffic-fatality, although somewhat more strongly than in the illness group. The parents, especially when their child was young, sometimes reproached themselves with not paying attention at the moment it happened or not warning their child enough about the dangers of the traffic.

Long-term illness

Although the cause and circumstances of death may seem clear in the case of death after an illness, preoccupation with the search for a picture of what has happened, is only somewhat less important in this group than among the bereaved after an unnatural death. The subject of rumination, here, has more often to do with the cause of the illness rather than the cause of death itself. This seems to concur with a search for the meaning of the death, which is virtually as strong as among the bereaved in the unnatural death groups. The bereaved have difficulties finding any meaning in the loss, particularly when the deceased was fairly young. Dying from an illness at a young age can in fact also be considered as unnatural.

The long-term illness-bereaved in general do not to a great extent differ from the unnatural modes of death in the intensity of their reactions to the loss. The illness-bereaved appear to have as much trouble with detachment from the deceased as the suicide-bereaved. Although slightly less avoidance is evidenced by the illness-bereaved at four months, the post traumatic stress reactions at fourteen months are at the same level as those in the other groups. At both points in time after the loss, the post traumatic stress response seems to occur as frequently as in the unnatural modes of death. This finding is interesting, since it implies that the consequences of an expected, natural death may be as traumatic as those of an unexpected and/or violent mode of death. Maybe the intense contact that often developed during the illness makes the contrast with the subsequent absence of the deceased even sharper, thus constituting a relatively great shock.

Psychological and physical health is, generally, not systematically different from that connected with the other modes of death. Initially, depression is somewhat lower among the illness-bereaved, but at fourteen months there appears to be an increase in the proportion of depressed spouses and parents, in contrast to the other modes of death. This corresponds with the findings of Lundin (1984b) that there are no long-term differences in health between bereaved after expected and unexpected deaths (see Section 3.3.7).

In terms of social functioning the illness-bereaved do not form a special group either. The mean level of need for emotional support is moderate, and slightly lower than with the unnatural modes of death. Social integration and social activities are at roughly the same level, however.

Many of the long-term illness bereaved feel very relieved after the loss. The reasons for relief seem unambiguous in this group: the death means an end to the worrying and fear of what is going to happen. The deceased is seen as finally freed from his or her suffering. Relief was also felt from the burdensome care, which had occupied 24 hours a day for some bereaved.

5.6.4 Systematic differences between groups on the dimensions

In the preceding sections, we presented some characteristic findings for each of the kinship groups and each mode of death. In this section we will look at this from a more comparative point of view. Table 5.20 lists the main results of the analyses of variance that were performed in the preceding sections.

Table 5.20

Overview of the significant differences between the groups on the dependent variables (only main effects are listed)

	Kinship		Sex		Mode of death	
	4 Months	14 Months	4 Months	14 Months	4 Months	14 Months
Loss related variables:						
Occupation circumst. of death	*	***	*	*	***	--
Search for meaning	***	***	--	**	*	--
Detachment from deceased	***	***	***	**	***	--
Intrusive thoughts	***	***	***	***	--	--
Avoidance	**	**	***	**	**	--
Health measures:						
Depressive symptoms	***	***	***	**	*	--
Suicidal Ideation	--	--	--	--	--	--
Sense of control	--	***	--	--	--	--
Medicine use	***	***	--	--	--	--
Alcohol use	**	--	***	***	--	--
Tobacco use	--	--	*	--	*	*
Somatic complaints	*	**	***	***	--	--
Social functioning:						
Need for emotional support	--	*	***	***	--	*
Social integration	--	*	--	--	--	--
Social activity	*	**	--	--	--	--
Negative reactions	--	***	--	--	--	--
Perturbation by reactions	--	***	--	--	*	--
Attribution of loss:						
Anger	--	--	*	--	--	--
Guilt feelings	***		--		***	
Relief	--		--		***	

Note: -- = not significant, * = trend (p<.05), ** = p<.01, *** = p<.001

Since the data were not analyzed in a multivariate way, and as we are making multiple comparisons here, it is preferable to employ the somewhat sharper ($p<.01$) criterion for significance. Significance at the 5% level will be considered, here, as only a trend.

Looking at the general image for the loss-related variables, there appear to be fairly large differences between the kinship groups and between the sexes on most of them. Exceptions are feelings of anger and relief, which seem to be more equally spread out over the sample. Roughly speaking, the image which appears on most loss-related variables is one with parents being the most affected group, followed by spouses, siblings and children. With regard to the role of mode of death, it appears that the traffic-fatality bereaved initially react more vehemently than both other groups, with the suicide-bereaved evidencing about the same level of reactions as illness-bereaved. The avoidance component of the stress response is at first significantly higher for the bereaved from unnatural death. It must also be noted that the magnitude of the differences between the modes of death at four months is not very large in comparison with the role of kinship and sex of the bereaved.

The results indicate that a natural, and to some extent expected, loss such as death after a long-term illness must not be underestimated in its traumatic impact. An important finding for all loss-related variables is that, although there are sometimes significant differences between the modes of death four months after the loss, these seem to have disappeared ten months later.

On the measures of general health, a comparable image appears. Here too, the differences are most marked between the sexes and between the kinship groups, while interactions between the latter are common as well. In general, there is the impression that women show more health deterioration than men, except for the widowed, where the widowers seem more affected than their female counterparts. Interestingly, and somewhat in contrast with the findings on the loss-related variables, there is no highly significant difference between the modes of death on any of the health measures, either at four months or at fourteen months.

The measures of social functioning show a somewhat different picture. In general, at four months, the differences between groups are small or absent with a notable exception for the women evidencing a markedly stronger need for emotional support than the bereaved men. On all measures of social functioning, the widowers take a special position: they usually evidence the least favorable scores of all relationship groups, in contrast with their female counterparts, who seem to cope without major impairment of social functioning. At fourteen months, there appears to be a stronger differentiation between the relationship groups on all social functioning variables, while the order of ranking parallels the one on the loss-related and health variables. Again, the differences between the modes of death on the aspects of social functioning are minimal.

Finally, looking at the variables addressing the attitudes to the loss, we see (with the exception of the significantly higher guilt among spouses and parents) little differences between kinship groups and sexes, but some significant differences between the modes of death. The contrasts here can be ascribed to the higher level of feelings of guilt among the suicide-bereaved, and a lower level of relief among the bereaved after a traffic-fatality.

In the next chapter, we will look at the relationships between the three dimensions of functioning, which we discussed in this chapter in terms of their different aspects.

Chapter 6

The Structure of Functioning

In this chapter we will be discussing the relationships between the aspects of functioning, which were presented in a univariate way in the preceding chapter. Here we will attempt to answer the second question of our study:

> *How do the different aspects of functioning after bereavement relate to each other?*

We will translate the aspects of the three dimensions of functioning (which were formulated in Chapter 2, and discussed in detail in the preceding chapter) into three corresponding scales, which can be examined in a multivariate manner.

After discussing the construction of these scales, functioning of the bereaved on each dimension will be examined in relation to the other dimensions, and we will again compare the positions of the kinship groups and the modes of death, thus examining the findings of the preceding chapter in a multivariate perspective.

6.1   Construction of the three dimensions of adaptation

In Section 2.9 we defined three dimensions of functioning that together form the picture of adaptation after the loss: a loss reactions dimension, a health dimension and a social functioning dimension. As we stated there, these dimensions are not independent of each other[1]. Since, however, there is a conceptual difference between them, and we are interested in how they relate to each other, we decided to construct a uni-dimensional measure for each dimension separately, after which the relationships between the dimensions could be examined more in detail. In order to be able to conceptually construct similar scales for each measurement, only variables measured at both interviews were entered for analysis.

The Reactions dimension

The variables dealing with reactions directly pertaining to the loss-event are the Leiden Detachment Scale, the IES-Intrusions Scale, the IES-Avoidance Scale, occupation

---

[1]   The exact relationships between the measures of functioning can be found in the correlation matrix (Appendix 1).

with questions about the cause of death, and occupation with the search for meaning of the loss.

The sumscores of the scales were entered as variables in a principal components analysis (PCA). The results of analysis of these 5 variables showed a one factor solution explaining 50% of the variance at four months and 56% at fourteen months. With reliability analysis, the scale was refined in order to obtain optimal variance and Crohnbach's α. The sumscores of the scales involved were translated to z-scores in order to assign equal weight to each of the scales in the resulting sumscore. This was done for each measurement independently[2].

The resulting scale, evidencing optimal reliability at both four and fourteen months, consisted of four variables: difficulty with detachment (LDS), intrusive thoughts (IES-I), avoidance (IES-A) and occupation with the meaning of the loss. Preoccupation with the cause of death was excluded, since it did not contribute sufficiently to the scale. An individual's score on the Reactions dimension was formed by the unweighted sumscore of the (standardized) scores on these four variables. The scale proved reliable with a Crohnbach's α of .74 at four months and .81 at fourteen months.

The resulting scale was checked for possible multi dimensionality by entering the 23 individual items in a principal components analysis instead of the sumscores for the scales. This showed no anomalies on either measurement. Due to the standardization, the mean of the scale was .00. The standard deviation was 3.0. A low score on the Reactions dimension indicates little psychological reaction to the loss, whereas a high score indicates considerable reactions and preoccupation.

The Health dimension

Another adaptational dimension we defined in Section 2.9 concerns the maintaining or (re)building of a satisfactory level of psychological and physical health. This health dimension of functioning was operationalized in the measures of depressive symptoms (BDI), suicidal ideation (KONSUI), the sense of being in control (Sense of Control Scale), somatic complaints (VOEG), use of intoxicating substances[3] (alcohol, tobacco and medicine use) and the change in use of these substances.

As was done for the Reactions Dimension, all measures were entered in a principal components analysis. This resulted in one medium-sized factor, explaining 25% of the variance at both measurements. A somewhat smaller second factor appeared

---

2   In this procedure, information on the absolute difference in score between both measurements is lost. Since we will only be working with the dimensions in a correlational sense, this is considered of minor importance. One disadvantage of calibrating the scales on the first measurement to maintain this information is that, the proportional weight of the scales within each dimension becomes unequal for each measurement, leaving us with conceptually different, and therefore incomparable measures for each interview.

3   In abbreviated form this will be referred to as 'substance-use'.

which explained about 15% of the variance. After Varimax rotation of the two-factor solution it appeared that the second factor was virtually only defined by the measures of use of intoxicating substances, except for medicine use, which loaded higher on the first factor. Since inspection of the correlation matrix (see Appendix 2) revealed only very low correlations between the substance-use measures and the other functioning variables, it was decided to drop the second factor from further analysis.

Consequently, the remaining five scales for depressive symptoms (BDI), somatic complaints (VOEG), suicidal ideation (KONSUI), Sense of Control and Medicine Use were entered in a reliability analysis. No further variables were eliminated from the scale, which elicited a Crohnbach's α of .66 at four months, and .68 at fourteen months.

Entering the 54 individual items of the resulting scale in a principal components analysis, to check for possible multiple factors showed no anomalies. An individual's score on the health dimension was formed by the unweighted sumscore of the five (standardized) constituting scales. The mean score on this dimension was 0.0. The standard deviation was 3.2 at four months and 3.3 at fourteen months. A low score on the Health dimension means there are little or no physical and psychological health problems. A high score indicates severe health problems in these areas.

The Social Functioning dimension

The third adaptational goal mentioned in Section 2.9 is maintaining or rebuilding meaningful and supportive relationships with others. The aspects of social functioning which were assessed are the need for emotional support (NESS), social integration (SIS), social activity (SAS), and the presence and evaluation of negative reactions from the environment. Inspection of the correlation matrix, as well as principal components analysis showed no clear factorial structure at either point in time. However, the Social Integration Scale and the Social Activity Scale came out as independent factors at both four months and fourteen months. Their correlation on both measurements was considered sufficiently high (.27 respectively .38) to combine them into a single scale representing Social functioning.

Principal components analysis of the resulting scale on item level (9 items) showed only one major principal component. As with both other dimensions, the score on the Social functioning dimension was computed by adding the standardized sumscore of the two measures involved. However, in order to bring the direction of the scale in line with the Health and Reactions dimensions, the scale was reversed. Thus, a low score on the Social Functioning dimension indicates little problems in social contacts and integration, whereas a high score indicates loneliness and social isolation. At both interviews, the mean score of the scale was 0.0, with a standard deviation of 1.6.

6.2   Interrelatedness of the dimensions of adaptation

In this section we will look in more detail at the relationship between the different dimensions of functioning, using the measures constructed in the last section.

As could be expected, the three dimensions of functioning are interrelated. The reactions to the loss are more closely related to the level of psychological and physical health than to social functioning (see Table 6.1). The correlations at four months were bivariately tested[4] against those at fourteen months to determine whether they differed significantly between the two measurements. It appeared that the bivariate

Table 6.1
Correlations between the dimensions of functioning at four months and fourteen months after the loss

At 4 months:	Health	Social func.	At 14 months:	Health	Social func.
Reactions	.49 (p=.000)	.07 (p=.124)	Reactions	.53 (p=.000)	.15 (p=.008)
Health		.27 (p=.000)	Health		.41 (p=.000)

relationships between loss reactions, health, and social functioning do not significantly differ between the two measurements[5]. At fourteen months, the correlation between social functioning and health, in particular, seems to have become stronger. The difference did not, however, reach significance, although there was a trend (z=-1.81, p=.035) for the correlation between social functioning and health to increase. On the whole, the correlations between the measures are somewhat higher at fourteen months in comparison to four months after the loss.

The auto-correlation between the scores on loss reactions at four months and at fourteen months is high (r= .74). For the health dimension, this correlation is even higher (r=.80). The relationship between social functioning at both interviews is somewhat lower (r=.50).

---

4   cf. Hays, 1980, p. 467.
5   A sharper significance criterion of p<.01 was employed for the three combinations because of the use of multiple univariate tests.

It would be interesting to consider the level of functioning in these three areas with regard to the differences between the modes of death and the relationships to the deceased. A technique particularly suited to make this visible is PRINCALS.

The PRINCALS technique

PRINCALS stands for 'principal components analysis by means of alternating least squares'. As with normal principal components analysis, it is designed to adequately represent the relationships between variables in a smaller number of components or dimensions[6]. With the PRINCALS method, one can analyze data with mixed measurement levels at the same time. Numerical data (e.g. length), ordinal data (such as scales with answering categories never/sometimes/often/always) and nominal data (such as kinship to the deceased) can be entered in the analysis. With this aim in view, the categories of the variables are quantified in an iterative process, which searches to find a least-squares solution by alternately optimizing in an across-variables manner and an across-subject manner. In this way, persons (objects) who resemble each other in terms of similar scoring patterns acquire similar quantifications, whereas persons with different patterns obtain different quantifications. In cases where a solution with more than one dimension is chosen for a PRINCALS, with mixed variables, the solution is not nested, as in principal components analysis. The scores on a specific dimension will then vary according to the number of dimensions chosen[7]. When a variable is entered as a single ordinal in the analysis, PRINCALS will look for an optimal solution, with the restriction that for each dimension the order of the quantified variables has to be the same as for the original ones, and that the quantifications for the variable are identical for each dimension. This implies that the distances between the categories may differ, but will always be on one line. When a variable is entered as 'multiple nominal' in the analysis, PRINCALS will compute different quantifications for each dimension, and the order of the observed categories will not be respected.

An interesting aspect of PRINCALS is that a mean quantification for each dimension can be computed not only for each person (the object score, equivalent of a factor score) but also for the categories (the category quantifications) of each variable. The values of these quantifications can be plotted, and examined in a visual way, which is especially informative in case of a two dimensional solution. The plot thus allows us to examine the relationships between nominal, ordinal and numeric variables at the same time.

---

6   Note that the term "dimension" here is used in another sense than in Chapter 3 and the previous sections. The dimensions of functioning may be represented in a smaller number of (data analytical) dimensions.
7   For a more elaborate explanation of the technique, see Gifi, 1985.

A PRINCALS analysis was performed, entering mode of death, and relationship to the deceased as active, nominal variables. The number of days between loss and interview[8] and the three dimensions of functioning, both at four months and at fourteen months were also entered. This was done in order to account for possible changes in the correlations between these dimensions.

Before entering the dimensions of adaptation in the analysis, each variable was recoded into five equally filled classes, thus forming ordinally arranged groups. In each of the recoded variables, category 5 consists of the worst functioning 20% in our sample, whereas in category 1 we find the 20% that function best.

As a rule of thumb for the number of dimensions to be taken in PRINCALS, Gifi (1985) suggests retaining the dimensions for which the eigenvalue is larger than $1/m$, where m is the number of variables entered for analysis. In the present analysis, the eigenvalue thus had to be larger than 0.1. By this rule, and in terms of interpretability, a two-dimensional solution appeared suitable for presenting the data. In Table 6.2, the measurement level and component loadings of the variables in the PRINCALS analysis are listed. The first dimension is clearly dominated by adaptation in terms of health and loss reactions. These appear to be closely interrelated. The second dimension is dominated by social functioning.

Interpretation of the PRINCALS category quantifications plot

A better view of the solution can be obtained by looking at the plot of the PRINCALS category quantifications for this solution (see Figure 6.1). In this way, the dimensions of functioning can be visually examined in relationship to both mode of death and relationship to the deceased.

In general, the closer two categories or variables lie together in the plot, the stronger they are related to each other. When we choose a two dimensional PRINCALS solution, it is possible to plot the category quantifications in a picture. In cases where a variable is entered at a single ordinal level, a straight line can be drawn though the quantifications of the of a variable. The length of this line indicates the importance of the variable in the interpretation of the dimension(s): the longer the line, the more important the variable's weight in the solution. When a variable is entered as multiple nominal, in a two dimensional solution the categories can be plotted as points in the chart. Also, for multiple nominal variables, we can state that (globally) the more the category quantifications differ from zero, the more important the role of the variable in the solution.

---

8   Since there was some between-subjects variation in time between the loss and the interview, the role of this variation may give an indication for the direction of change at each measurement.

Table 6.2

Measurement level and component loadings of the variables in the PRINCALS analysis

Variable	Measurement level	Dim. 1	Dim. 2
Mode of death	Multiple nominal	–	–
Relationship to deceased	Multiple nominal	–	–
Loss reactions T1	Single ordinal	.77	-.35
Loss reactions T2	Single ordinal	.79	-.26
Health T1	Single ordinal	.80	.05
Health T2	Single ordinal	.80	.15
Social functioning T1	Single ordinal	.34	.63
Social functioning T2	Single ordinal	.40	.66
Number of days since loss T1	Single ordinal	-.32	.24
Number of days since loss T2	Single ordinal	-.12	.27

Eigenvalues: .34 and .17   (total fit = .50, total loss = 1.50)

At the origin (0,0) of the plot, we find what could be termed the 'mean situation' of the sample in terms of the variables entered in the analysis. The further a category quantification lies from the origin (0,0) of the plot, the more this category differs from the overall situation of the sample. For the interpretation of this distance, we have to look at its position in relation to the two axes and to the other variables in the plot.

The relationship of a specific category with regard to one of the dimensions of functioning (the lines drawn in the plot) and the dimensions of the solution is given by the perpendicular projection of the category on the line in question. In this way we see, for instance, that the bereaved after a long-term illness at fourteen months have a 'mean position' around the seventh and eighth decile (around category 4) on problems in social functioning, whereas when projected on the Health dimension at fourteen months, they fall around the fifth and sixth decile (category 3).

Although the component loadings of the number of days between loss and interview are too low to be of importance to the solution, it is interesting to see that the variation in time between loss and interview (the dashed line marked 'time T1' in the plot) is initially related to differences in loss reactions: the shorter the time after the loss, the stronger the loss reactions. At the second interview, the variation in time since the loss (the dashed line marked 'time T2' in the plot) is more indicative for differences in social (re)integration: follow-up interviews that were conducted a longer time after the loss tended to show a somewhat better level of social functioning among the bereaved.

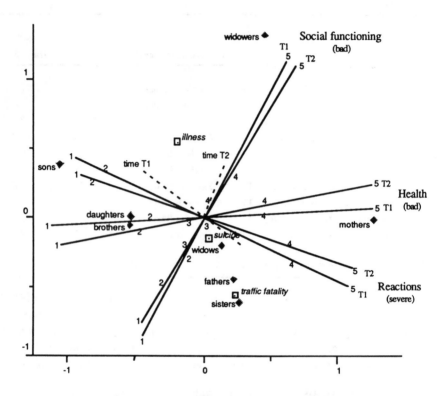

Fig. 6.1   *Plot of the two-dimensional PRINCALS solution (category quantifications of the three dimensions of functioning, mode of death, and relationship to the deceased)*

The results of the PRINCALS solution closely reflect those of the ANOVA analyses in the preceding chapter. Comparing the roles of mode of death and relationship to the deceased in the plot, it becomes clear once again that relationship to the deceased, in general, plays a more important role than mode of death in functioning after bereavement. This is reflected in the relatively large values of the category quantifications of the relationship categories[9].

---

9   See for instance the positions of the sons and the widowers in Fig. 6.1.

Relationship to the deceased and overall adaptation

It appears that the relationship groups generally spread along both axes of the plot. On the horizontal axis, which reflects functioning in terms of both loss-reactions and health, we find a clearly different ranking of the relationships from that of the vertical axis, which is primarily defined by social functioning. Looking at the perpendicular projections of the modes of death on the dimensions of functioning, we see that they tend to differ somewhat in the severeness of loss reactions and in social functioning. In terms of health there is, however, no systematic difference.

Now, we will look somewhat closer at the positions of the individual relationship groups. To explore the contrasts between the modes of death, oneway analyses of variance for each dimension were conducted with Scheffé's test, to discover where the highest significant contrasts between the modes of death could be found. A significance level of $p < .01$ was chosen for Scheffé's test for contrasts, since multiple independent comparisons were being made.

At the low end of the Reactions and the Health dimension, we find the sons of the deceased, evidencing relatively little or no loss reactions or health problems. At four months, their reactions contrast strongly with those of parents, spouses, and sisters of the deceased. They also evidence a moderately favorable level of social functioning.

Generally somewhat more affected in health and reactions than the sons are brothers and daughters of the deceased. They score somewhat better, however, in terms of social functioning.

Among widowers, there is a clear differentiation between their functioning in terms of loss reactions, health and social functioning: whereas, like the widows, they evidence relatively moderate direct reactions to the loss, they are among the most affected in terms of health, and clearly do worst in terms of social functioning (see the perpendicular projections on the corresponding vectors).

The widows, fathers and sisters of the bereaved occupy virtually the same, moderately affected, position in terms of loss reactions and health. Sisters show relatively strong reactions, and deteriorated health, falling in the same range as the widows and fathers, but as a group are among the socially best integrated.

By far the most affected group, both in terms of health and loss reactions are, as we saw before, the mothers. In terms of social functioning they are also among the most affected, at some distance from the widowers. The Scheffé tests showed that they contrasted highly significantly with most other groups in health and loss reactions at both interviews.

Mode of death and overall adaptation

Looking at the positions of the category quantifications for the modes of death, some interesting differences appear. In this case also, we explored the contrasts with a Scheffé test.

Bereaved from a traffic-fatality show, relatively, the most severe loss reactions and contrast significantly with the illness-bereaved at four months ($F=9.17$, $p=.000$), but no systematic difference can be found at fourteen months ($F=2.09$, n.s.). In terms of social adaptation there is a trend ($F=3.12$, $p=.046$) towards better functioning of the bereaved after a traffic-fatality in comparison to the other modes of death, although no specific contrast reaches significance. The reverse seems true for the bereaved after a long term illness: they evidence the least severe loss reactions, but show more social dysfunction in comparison with the other modes of death. Suicide occupies an intermediate position. There appears to be no significant differentiation between the modes of death in terms of health at either point in time. This is also confirmed by analysis of variance.

At fourteen months after the loss, none of the differences in functioning between the modes of death reaches significance any longer in the oneway- analyses of variance, and Scheffe's test does not reveal any significant contrasts between them. This can also be seen in Fig. 6.1, where the perpendicular projections on the dimensions of adaptation at fourteen months lie closer together than at four months. Comparing in this way the vectors for the dimensions of functioning at four months with those at fourteen months, it appears that there is a decrease in the differences between the modes of death on all three dimensions of functioning. This is in line with the general univariate findings in Chapter 5 (see Section 5.6).

6.3   Conclusion

The first conclusion that can be drawn from the analyses in this chapter is that, to a certain extent, the dimensions of functioning are independent of each other. Although loss-reactions and health are interrelated, social functioning seems to be more or less independent, especially from loss reactions. The fact that the rank order of the relationship-groups is often different for each dimension, underlines the idea that a conceptual differentiation is meaningful.

Looking at the dimensions of adaptation after bereavement, it appears that the loss reactions are closely related to health. The quality of social functioning is more or less independent from loss reactions, but somewhat related to health. From the correlation between the scores at four months and those at fourteen months we can state that the health of the bereaved shortly after bereavement is a very strong predictor for long term health, with a proportion of shared variance of $(.804)^2 = 65\%$. In terms of loss reactions, long-term functioning can also be predicted quite accurately from the early situation, with a shared variance of $(.740)^2 = 55\%$. Social functioning at fourteen months is less predictable from the situation at four months, explaining only 25% of the variance. The finding that the three dimensions of adaptation are interrelated, but still show a considerable amount of non-shared variance, calls attention to the fact that adaptation may vary along different lines. The difference in rank order of the modes of death on the different dimensions accentuates this relative independence (see also Section 6.2).

As in Chapter 5, we see confirmed here that many of the differences in functioning can be attributed to kinship, sex, and, to a much smaller degree, to mode of death. The different position of the male and female members of each kinship group is also noteworthy. The pattern of functioning differs widely between the sexes, especially between widows and widowers, mothers and fathers, and brothers and sisters.

It appears that men do better in all kinship groups, except for the spouses group, where widowers evidence somewhat more health problems and considerably greater difficulties in terms of social functioning than their female counterparts. In terms of social functioning, it furthermore appears that in every kinship group, except in that of parents, women are *better* off than the men.

In the PRINCALS analysis there is, again, a clear indication that mothers and widowers are the relationship groups most at risk for developing problems in adaptation. Mothers seem to be most at risk for severe loss reactions and health problems. Their problems in social functioning appear to be somewhat lesser however. Widowers evidence most problems in the area of social functioning, and show (in some lesser degree than mothers) health problems. In contrast, they show much fewer loss reactions: on this dimension they are among the lower-scoring part of the sample. The present multivariate picture also shows, in concordance with the findings in Chapter 5, that sisters evidence a far higher level of loss reactions and health problems than the brothers of the deceased, and turn out to be a relatively high risk group.

Comparison with other studies

The finding in literature that parents are the most affected kinship group has to be nuanced on the basis of the present data. The mothers are by far the most affected group in terms of loss reactions and health. There is, however, a marked difference between them and their husbands. The level of adaptation among the fathers is comparable to widows and sisters of the deceased, while the widowers, in terms of health and social functioning, seem more strongly affected than the fathers.

The difference between fathers and mothers is in line with the observations of Fish (1986, in Sanders 1988) that mothers are more strongly affected than fathers and suffer from greater social isolation.

Our findings with regard to the role of kinship in general seem to corroborate the results reported in the study of Zisook & Lyons (1988). Their (somewhat ambiguously defined, one-item) criterion for unresolved grief is probably best reflected in our Reactions dimension. Their study resulted in the conclusion that there were no differences between kinship groups in terms of health and psychosocial functioning[10], but that the occurrence of 'unresolved grief' was most frequent among parents losing a child, followed by spouses, then siblings and, least problematic in this respect, children of the deceased. Although their conclusion is analogous to the present findings, they unfortunately did not take into consideration or mention differences between men and women within each kinship group, which appears to constitute a major difference with our study.

A remarkable new finding here is the frequent occurrence of problems among sisters of the bereaved. This (sibling) group, which has hitherto hardly been studied, seems to run a high risk of suffering health problems after the loss, and an even higher risk than fathers and widows of evidencing strong loss reactions. It is possible that this may at least partially corresponds with Zisook & Lyons' (1988) findings. They found that, when only the most recent death was considered, the incidence of 'unresolved grief' was almost identical for siblings and spouses who applied for psychiatric care. However, since, as mentioned above, in their article they made no distinction between brothers and sisters of the deceased, more precise comparison is not possible.

The findings concerning adult children of the deceased are largely consistent with what has been found in other empirical studies. They parallel those of Sanders (1979-1980) and Owen et al. (1982-1983), who found adult children to be the least affected group in comparison with other family survivors.

The absence of clear differences in health between the different modes of death, especially fourteen months after the loss, is consistent with the findings of other studies (Barrett and Scott, 1987; Shepard & Baraclough, 1974; McNiel et al., 1988; Demi, 1984; Trolley, 1986; Pennebaker and O'Heeron, 1984; Farberow et al.,1987). Van der Wal (1988), analyzing a set of variables somewhat different from those of the present sample, also found that there was little difference between suicide and traffic-fatality bereaved on a series of outcome measures. He also found bereaved from suicide to be somewhat, but not much, less socially integrated.

---

[10] For a comment on another possible interpretation, see Section 3.2.

Chapter 7

A Prospective Study on Functioning

In this chapter we will try to discover predictors which, in an early period after the loss, form an indication for the quality of middle and longer-term functioning among the bereaved. This pertains to the third question we formulated:

> *In what way is functioning after bereavement related to the characteristics of the loss, the situation in which it occurred, and the resources available to the bereaved?*

Apart from the scientific or heuristic value, early recognition of risk indicators may serve a practical goal. If we can localize in an early phase of bereavement the pre-bereavement characteristics and factors which are indicative of longer-term adaptation, it may enable caregivers to be alert to specific persons at risk for developing problems in functioning. It may also enable specific preventive action with risk groups.

An attempt will be made to prospectively estimate adaptation after bereavement in terms of loss-reactions, health and social functioning from a combination of the task-demands of bereavement, social support, material resources, and aspects of the attitude towards the loss. Multiple linear regression analysis will be used. In the next section, the potential predictor variables are presented. A number of variables will be described in some more detail since they were not evaluated in the preceding chapters. In Section 7.3, the multiple linear regression technique will be described, and the steps and procedure that was followed. In the final sections, predictions will be made for each criterion of functioning independently.

7.1   Potential indicators of adaptation

In this section, we will present the variables that will be taken into account in the regression equations as predictors[1] for loss-reactions, health and social functioning. The predictor variables are operationalizations of most of the task-demands and

---

[1]   The term 'predictor' will be used here in the technical sense in the context of the regression technique.

resources that were presented in Chapter 2. They are considered to be potential indicators of adaptation, and will be treated here as independent variables.

The characteristics of the task-demands, especially the quality and characteristics of the relationship as well as stress before the loss, are likely to differ according to the kinship groups and the modes of death. In order to check this, an analysis of variance was performed for each of these variables with mode of death, kinship and sex as independent variables, which will be listed after each description. In Section 7.2 we will summarize these findings.

7.1.1   Task-demands

As we saw in Chapter 2, the task-demands bereavement imposes on the bereaved may differ in type, number and pattern. Mode of death and kinship to the deceased have already been discussed as important aspects of the type of task-demand. The pattern and type of task-demands is also determined by sociodemographic characteristics and quality of the relationship with the deceased. Concurrent demands, which may not be related to the loss itself, must also be taken into account: other problems and impaired health before the loss may contribute to subsequent dysfunction.

In the Leiden Bereavement Study the following characteristics of the task-demands were operationalized:

Sociodemographic variables

- *Gender* of the deceased and the respondent[2]
- *Same sex* a constructed variable which indicates if the deceased and respondent were of the opposite sex (value 1) or of the same sex (value 2)
- *Age* of the deceased and the respondent

All sociodemographic variables were measured with single items. The characteristics of the sample with regard to sex and age of bereaved and deceased have already been described in some detail in Chapter 5.

Quality of the relationship

The quality and characteristics of the relationship between bereaved and deceased were assessed with a number of scales which will be described here. Differences between the modes of death and the kinship groups were assessed for every variable

---

2   In the analysis for the spouses, only gender of the respondent was entered.

by means of individual ANOVA's. Significant differences will be mentioned, and are listed in Table 7.2.

Frequency of contact

The frequency of contact (including writing and phoning) between the bereaved and the deceased during the last half-year before the loss was measured with a single question. The answering categories ranged from 1: 'a few times a year or less' to 6: 'daily'. As could be expected, there was a highly significant difference between the kinship groups (see Table 7.2). Spouses and parents had had the most frequent contact with the deceased, while children and siblings had a less frequent contact. The bereaved after suicide reported somewhat less contact with the deceased during the last half-year before the loss in comparison with the other modes of death. The illness-bereaved usually had a more frequent contact, often related to an intensified care for the dying relative.

Relationship satisfaction

The extent to which the bereaved were satisfied in the relationship with the deceased was measured by use of four statements with which the respondent was asked to agree or disagree on a five-point scale ranging from 0: 'disagree completely' to 4: 'agree completely'. The items were: 'Our relationship was close', 'We formed a real team', 'We had a good relationship' and 'Our relationship made me happy'.

The scale proved to be very reliable. The mean inter-item correlation was .64, and Cronbach's α .87. The statement with the highest item-total correlation (.73) was 'We had a good relationship'. The scale ranged from 0 (a very bad relationship) to 16 (a very good relationship). The mean score of the sample was 12.4 (S.d.= 4.5).

Satisfaction with the relationship was highest among spouses and parents. The bereaved after suicide in general were markedly less satisfied with the relationship than the other two groups. Many of them reported frequent quarrels and tensions over an extended period of time. Sometimes they even said they had no relationship at all, or had been suffering from it.

Intimacy

The intimacy of the relationship with the deceased person during his or her life was measured with a four-item scale. The respondent was asked to describe the deceased in terms of four dichotomies, each describing a certain aspect of the relationship. The dichotomies were: being open versus being closed, giving him/herself in the relationship versus avoiding deeper contact, being distant versus confidential, and cold versus compassionate. The respondent was asked to point out the position of the deceased on a five-point scale for each dichotomy.

The scale proved to be reliable with a mean inter-item correlation of .48 and Cronbach's α of .79. The item with the highest item-total correlation (.68) was the giving-avoiding contact item. The scale scores ranged from 0 (extremely low intimacy) to 16 (extremely high intimacy). The mean score for the scale was 11.0 (S.d.= 4.1).

Analysis of variance (see Table 7.2) showed that the bereaved after a traffic-fatality felt most intimate with the deceased, while the bereaved after suicide evaluated the relationship as less intimate. The spouses in general felt a somewhat more intimate contact with the deceased than the other kinship groups.

Dominance

The dominance of the deceased over the bereaved was measured with a four-item scale in the same way as the intimacy of the relationship: the respondent was asked to describe the deceased in terms of four dichotomies. These were: authoritarian versus docile, executive versus obedient, aggressive versus gentle, and staying in the background versus in the foreground.

This scale also proved to be sufficiently reliable, with a mean inter-item correlation of .29 and Cronbach's α of .62. The item with the highest item-total correlation (.52) was the authoritarian versus docile item. The scale scores ranged from 0 (extremely submissive) to 16 (extremely dominant). The mean score was 6.2 (S.d.= 3.3).

Women, significantly more often than men, felt the deceased to be dominant, although the absolute difference is only small. There were no differences between the modes of death or the kinship groups in this respect.

Independence

The extent to which the deceased was seen by the bereaved as functioning independently was measured with a three-item scale, constructed in the same way as the Intimacy and Dominance scales. Again, the respondent was asked to describe the deceased in terms of (three) dichotomies: mature versus childish, self-reliant versus dependent and attention demanding versus caring.

The scale proved to be reliable. The mean inter-item correlation was .43 and Cronbach's α .70. The dichotomy with the highest item-total correlation (.57) was the self-reliant versus dependent item. The scale scores ranged from 0 (extremely dependent) to 12 (extremely independent). The mean score was 7.7 (S.d.= 3.4).

In the suicide group, the deceased was often described as being independent, more so than in the other modes of death. Often the bereaved felt that the deceased chose to be on his or her own and to mind his own business. This was often accompanied by a feeling of him or her being 'inaccessible' or 'distant'. This reflects, to some extent, the pattern that was found for the Intimacy scale.

Ambivalent feelings

Ambivalent feelings toward the deceased was measured with two items about which the respondent was asked to what extent he (dis)agreed. The statements were: 'Our relationship was stable', and 'I have conflicting feelings about my relationship with ..[name of the deceased]..'. The respondent was asked to agree or disagree with the statements on a five-point scale ranging from 0: 'disagree completely' to 4: 'agree completely'.

The items correlated -.42 with each other, and after recoding were added up, ranging from 0 (not ambivalent) to 8 (extremely ambivalent). The mean score was 1.9 (S.d.=2.3).

The suicide-bereaved felt more ambivalent about the relationship with the deceased than the others (see Table 7.2). Women showed somewhat more ambivalent feelings than men.

Expectancy of the loss

The extent to which the loss was expected or unexpected was measured with a single question:

'Did you expect the death of ...[name deceased]...?'.

The answer categories were 1: 'not at all' 2: 'slightly' 3: 'yes, but not at that moment' and 4: 'yes, it came not unexpectedly at that moment'. The mean score for the sample was 2.2 (S.d. = 1.2).

As foreseen, the illness-bereaved very often had expected the death (m=2.9, s.d.=1.2). On the whole, death was least expected among the bereaved in the traffic-fatality group (m=1.5, s.d.=.8), while the bereaved after suicide took an intermediary position (m=1.9, s.d.=1.1).

Pre-loss stressors

Apart from the aspects of the relationship, described in the scales above, other factors may aggravate the situation. Three aspects of the pre-bereavement situation were assessed: additive stressors during the year before bereavement, physical health and psychological health problems before the loss.

Additional stressors

The presence of additional problems was measured with a modified version of the AKTPRO and BIOPRO, commented previously by Schippers (1981) and Hosman (1983). The scale consists of 7 items, each of them assessing the presence of problems in a different area of life: financial problems, problems with housing conditions, problems with parents, study problems, problems at work, problems with partner, and problems with friends or family. The answering categories for each item ranged from 0: 'no problem at all' to 3: 'a severe problem'.

The scale was administered at both interviews. At four months, the respondents were asked to answer the questions both for the time before the loss and the situation at that moment. At fourteen months, the respondents were asked to answer the questions for the time between the two interviews and at that moment.

The scale was evaluated separately for each time period The main features of the scale are listed in Table 7.1. As is common with stress scales, the reliability of the scale was quite low at each point in time. The test-retest correlations provide an indication for the stability of the scale over time: they ranged between .42 and .86. The scale-score was formed by adding the scores of the seven items. This resulted in four scores on cumulative stress for each person. In the regression analysis, only the score for the time before the loss was entered.

Table 7.1
Properties of the Additional Stress Scale (AKTPRO-BIOPRO)

	Number of Items	Range	Mean	S.D.	Eigen value	% Expl. variance	α
Year before loss T1	7	0 - 21	2.0	2.5	2.0	28.0	.54
4 Months after loss T1	7	0 - 21	2.0	2.4	1.8	24.8	.44
4-14 Months after loss T2	7	0 - 21	2.3	2.5	1.6	23.4	.40
14 Months after loss T2	7	0 - 21	1.7	2.1	1.6	22.6	.36

From analysis of variance (see Table 7.2), it appeared that on the whole, the highest level of additional stress was mentioned by the siblings and children, less by the parents and least by spouses. This grading can probably be explained by the fact that, because of the immediate importance of the (impending) loss for the entire life situation, of the spouses, other problems may have been pushed into the background and experienced as of minor importance. The same mechanism may have operated among the parents.

Physical health problems

Problems with physical health during the last half-year before the loss were measured with a single question:

'Did you have problems with your health during the last half-year before the death of ..[name of deceased]..?'

The answer categories ranged from 0: 'not at all', 1: 'somewhat', 2: 'quite a few' to 3: 'severe' The mean score for this question in our sample was 1.6 (S.d.= 1.0). Analysis of variance showed that spouses and parents evidenced more health problems before the loss than siblings and children, while the suicide-bereaved reported somewhat more physical problems than the others (see Table 7.2).

Psychological health problems

Problems in psychological functioning were also assessed with a single question, assessing several areas of possible pre-loss psychological dysfunction:

'Did you have problems such as feeling stressed, confused or downcast or problems with the use of alcohol, medicine or drugs during the last half-year before the death of ..[name of deceased]..?'

As with the preceding question, the answer categories ranged from 0: 'not at all', 1: 'somewhat', 2: 'quite a few' to 3: 'severe'.

The mean score for this question was 1.6 (S.d.= 0.9). From ANOVA it appeared that the bereaved after a traffic-fatality generally reported less psychological problems before the loss than the other groups. There were no significant differences between the kinship groups or the sexes.

Available material resources

Financial and socioeconomic resources were measured with two variables, commonly regarded as representing the socioeconomic status of an individual:

* *Educational level* of the respondent
* *Income* of the respondent

Both variables were measured with single items, discussed in Chapter 5. A third variable giving an indication of available material resources, is occupational level. However, since less than half of the respondents were working, the variable has too many missing values to be employed as a predictor, and was omitted from the candidate predictor variables.

7.1.2   Social support for the completion of the tasks

Our interview comprised a measure for emotional support, and a combined measure
for practical and instrumental support. Here, we will look at the extent to which the
received support matches the needs of the bereaved. Whereas the *need* for support is
considered to be an aspect of social functioning of the bereaved, the *sufficiency* of
support (assessed here) pertains to the 'fit' of the support to the needs of the
bereaved.

Experienced Emotional Support Scale

The extent to which the bereaved felt sufficiently supported by the environment in
coping with the situation was measured with the four-item Experienced Emotional
Support Scale (EESS) of our own design.

The EESS exists of four items, whose contents parallel the Need for Emotional
Support Scale, discussed in Section 5.3.1. The bereaved were asked to what extent
they had sufficient opportunity to freely express their feelings and thoughts to others,
to talk with others about the memories of the deceased, about the circumstances in
which the deceased had died, and if they had someone to put an arm around their
shoulder when they needed it. The answer categories were: 0: 'insufficient' 1: 'not
sufficient / not insufficient' and 2: 'sufficient'.

The EESS was administered at both interviews[3]. The inter-item correlations ranged
between .24 and .54 (mean r =.38) at four months, and between .29 and .55 (mean r
=.42) at fourteen months. The EESS turned out to be reliable, Cronbach's α being
.70 at four months and .73 at fourteen months. Analysis of variance on the
Experienced Emotional Support Scale showed no systematic differences between the
modes of death, kinship groups or the sexes in the sufficiency of emotional support.

Experienced Practical and Informational Support

The Experienced Practical and Informational Support Scale (EPISS) consists of seven
items. Two of these assessed the extent to which the bereaved had sufficient support
in practical matters: the sufficiency of help by others in handling practical matters and
help with daily work. Three questions assessed practical help with reorienting life:
help to rearrange things and divide the heritage, the availability of diverting contacts,
and help with making new friends. Two further questions were concerned with the
availability of informational support: help in the form of advice, and help in ordering
their thoughts. The answer categories for each question were: 0: 'insufficient' 1: 'not
sufficient / not insufficient' and 2 'sufficient'.

---

[3]   Only the measurement at four months will be entered in the regression equations.

The inter-item correlations ranged from .00 to .49 at four months, and .01 to .47 at fourteen months. Given the diversity of practical subjects assessed by the EPISS, its reliability can be considered sufficient, coefficient α being .57 at four months and .51 at fourteen months. An analysis of variance on the Experienced Practical and Informational Support Scale indicated no systematic differences between the modes of death, kinship groups or the sexes in the sufficiency of practical and informational support.

7.1.3 Attitude to the loss

Three specific reactions will be evaluated here as reflecting the attribution process and attitude towards the loss. Since these have already been amply discussed in Chapter 5, we will only mention them briefly here.

Anger

The extent to which the bereaved felt anger at four months, measured with the Anger Scale (see also Section 5.5.1)

Guilt

The extent to which the bereaved felt guilty about the death, or the circumstances that lead to the death at four months, measured with the Guilt Scale (see also Section 5.5.2).

Relief

The extent to which the bereaved felt relieved about the death at four months, measured with the Relief Scale (see also Section 5.5.3).

7.1.4 The environment in which the task-demands are carried out

The role of the environment in which the task-demands of bereavement have to be carried out is hard to assess. Its influence is in fact very diffuse. It is difficult to identify the relevant variables, since they may be translated in sets of other resources. For instance: the meaningful difference between 'living in a home for the aged' and 'living with the children' can fairly well be translated in a set of differences in social support, material support, practical and informational support, and perhaps concurrent task-demands. Stripped of these aspects, the difference in environment is largely reduced to the housing situation of the bereaved. One question in the interview assessed this situation (see also Section 4.5). In employing this variable as a predictor, there are however several problems.

In the first place, the variable is a discrete one. This means that in order to enter it into a regression equation, it would have to be recoded in dummies.

In the second place, the variable is not sensitive enough to assess the meaning of the particular housing situation. The meaning of a particular 'formal' situation may differ substantially with the individual. For instance: some of the people living alone did so of their free will, but others falling into this category had lost a partner, either due to the death in question, or to other reasons, such as a divorce. The same confounding situation could be found for the other categories.

In the third place, as can be seen in Table 4.5, the distribution over the categories is very skewed.

The above problems led to elimination of the housing variable, and consequently to omission of assessment of this resource. We considered this to be not much of a problem in view of the conceptual overlap with other resources described above.

7.2   Differences between groups on task-demands and resources

In the preceding sections, we saw that there are a number of systematic differences between the kinship groups and the modes of death in terms of task-demands and resources. The significant results of these analyses will be summarized here and are listed in Table 7.2. Only main effects are listed, since virtually none of the interaction effects were significant.

Differences between the modes of death

In comparison with the other modes of death, the bereaved from suicide in general had had a lower frequency of contact with the deceased before the loss. They tended to be somewhat less satisfied with the relationship, evidenced more ambivalent feelings about it, and felt the relationship to be less intimate. They generally judged the deceased as more independent.

In general, the suicide-bereaved expected the loss somewhat less than the illness-bereaved, but more than the traffic-fatality bereaved. Before the loss, they evidenced more physical health problems than the other modes of death, but equally as many problems with psychological health as the illness-bereaved.

The pre-loss characteristics among bereaved after a traffic-fatality resemble, to a substantial extent, those in the long-term illness bereaved group: relationship satisfaction, dependency and ambivalent feelings are reported at virtually the same level. The frequency of contact during the time before the loss was somewhat higher than among the suicide-bereaved, but lower in comparison with the illness-bereaved. The traffic-fatality bereaved report somewhat more intimacy in the relationship with the deceased before the loss. They evidence the least number of physical and psychological health problems before the loss.

Kinship

As could be expected, there are considerable systematic differences between the kinship groups in pre-loss characteristics. On most measures, spouses and parents resemble each other, differing from siblings and children of the deceased.

The spouses reported the highest frequency of contact before the loss, the highest degree of satisfaction in the relationship and intimacy. They also suffered somewhat more physical health problems, although psychological health seems to be virtually the same in all kinship groups. Interestingly, the spouses report the least cumulative stress in the time before the loss. The parents follow closely behind the spouses in all aspects. Siblings and children of the deceased, in comparison with spouses and parents, generally show a lower (although still a high) level of satisfaction with the relationship and intimacy. They evidence less physical health problems before the loss, but the highest level of cumulative non-bereavement stresses. The siblings report the lowest frequent contact during the time before the loss in comparison with the other modes of death.

Sex differences

There are hardly any significant differences between men and women on pre-loss characteristics. Women only show somewhat more ambivalent feelings towards the deceased, and judged him or her to be somewhat more dominant than the men.

Conclusion

There are considerable differences between the modes of death and the kinship groups in the characteristics of task-demands and resources. This is particularly clear as regards the relationship characteristics. The differences between the kinship groups are in the expected direction. Given the fact that differences exist in frequency of contact, the qualities of the relationship are likely to differ accordingly. This may also explain the inverse order of the kinship groups in their scores on cumulative stress before the loss. The loss, especially when it was to some extent expected and a good relationship existed, was likely to push other problems to the background in the parents and spouses groups[4].

---

[4] This may also explain the findings of Murrell et al. (1988) that concurrent stressors only appeared to some influence on health when the target loss was a non-bereavement loss (see Section 3.3.7).

Table 7.2
ANOVA's on pre-loss variables, with mode of death, kinship and sex independent

Dependent variable:

Independent:	Var.expl.:	Signific.:	Description:
Frequency of contact			
Mode	4.8%	p=.000	Suicide less frequent, illness most frequent
Kinship	18.9%	p=.000	Spouses most frequent, then parents, children and siblings
Sex	0.3%	N.S.	
Relationship satisfaction			
Mode	5.5%	p=.000	Suicide less satisfied than other modes
Kinship	5.1%	p=.001	Largest among spouses and parents
Sex	0.3%	N.S.	
Ambivalent feelings			
Mode	8.1%	p=.000	Suicide more ambivalent than other modes
Kinship	1.5%	N.S.	
Sex	2.1%	p=.008	Women more ambivalent
Intimacy			
Mode	5.5%	p=.000	Suicide least intimate, traffic most intimate
Kinship	3.6%	p=.009	Spouses most intimate, parents & sibs in-between, children least
Sex	0.0%	N.S.	
Independence deceased			
Mode	14.4%	p=.000	Suicide much more independent
Kinship	1.5%	N.S.	
Sex	0.1%	N.S.	
Dominance deceased			
Mode	0.1%	N.S.	
Kinship	0.7%	N.S.	
Sex	1.9%	p=.015	Women judged deceased to be more dominant
Expectancy of loss			
Mode	21.0%	p=.000	Most expected by illness, least by traffic, suicide in between
Kinship	0.4%	N.S.	
Sex	0.3%	N.S.	
Physical health problems			
Mode	2.3%	p=.03	Most problems in suicide, less in illness, least in traffic
Kinship	2.8%	p=.03	Spouses and parents more problems than sibs and children
Sex	0.6%	N.S.	
Psychologic health probl.			
Mode	5.4%	p=.000	Traffic less problems than both other modes
Kinship	1.2%	N.S.	
Sex	0.8%	N.S.	
Cumulative stress before loss			
Mode	1.3%	N.S.	
Kinship	6.3%	p=.000	Highest: siblings and children, less: parents, least: spouses
Sex	0.1%	N.S.	

Note: Not listed in this table are the ANOVA's for *Cumulative stress* (at 4 months), *Sufficiency of Emot. Support*, and *Sufficiency Pract. & Inform. Support*, since no significant effects were found.

The differences between the modes of death are also interesting. It appears that the bereaved after suicide are less satisfied, and more ambivalent about their relationship with the deceased. It must be noted that since the pre-loss characteristics are measured in retrospect, some of the difference may be due to hindsight bias, or avoidance cognitive dissonance: 'Since (s)he committed suicide, our relationship cannot have been very good.'. It will be explored more in detail in the linear regression analysis to what extent these pre-loss differences match or outweigh the importance of mode of death itself.

There appear to be no systematic differences between the modes of death in the extent to which the needs for emotional, practical and informational support were met. From these data, there seems to be no excess insufficiency of support in any of the groups. This finding is in line with other comparative research in this area[5].

These results suggest that a large number of the potential indicators of adaptation are to some extent nested within kinship group or mode of death. As we saw earlier for age (see Chapter 5), not taking into account this nesting may lead to contradictory results. In the next section, we will propose a way to control for this aspect.

7.3   Multiple linear regression: technique and goals

In the present study, multiple linear regression was applied, following the stepwise method. With this method we assessed which combination of task-demands and resources is optimally related to the level of functioning (in terms of Loss-reactions, Health and Social Functioning) and the amelioration or deterioration in functioning between the two interviews. The task-demands and resources which were described in Section 7.1 were evaluated as independent variables.

Multiple linear regression is a technique which attempts to optimally calculate the value of a criterion-variable from a linear combination of a given set of independent variables. The indication for the adequacy of the prediction is the height of the correlation between the predicted (constructed) value of the criterion variable and its actual value.

In regression analysis, when entering the variables with the 'stepwise' method, the procedure first enters the independent variable which has the highest correlation with the criterion variable (thus explaining the largest proportion of variance). Then, the remaining independent variables are examined for their (partial) correlation with the remaining variance of the criterion variable which is not explained by the variable in the equation. If, due to entering the last variable in the equation, the contribution of one of those entered earlier is no longer significant, this one is eliminated again. This

---

5   See Section 3.3.2.4.

procedure is repeated until all independent variables are entered in the equation or until no variable outside the equation significantly improves the adequacy of the prediction. This is indicated by a significance level of the t-test. In the present study, the minimal significance level for entering a variable in the equation was .05.

The criteria to be predicted

There will be two central questions on which the regression procedures followed here are based:

1) *How well can adaptation four months after the loss be predicted from socio-demographic, pre-loss and loss characteristics?*

2) *Given the adaptation at four months, how well can adaptation at fourteen months be predicted on the basis of socio-demographic, pre-loss and loss characteristics?*

In order to answer the first question, independent regression analyses were performed for each aspect of adaptation (Loss-reactions, Health, and Social Functioning). Each analysis was run by entering the independent variables in one block for evaluation in a stepwise manner.

For the second interview, we aimed to predict the *change* in functioning in comparison with four months after the loss. Rather than using raw difference scores to measure this change, the difference score between the *observed* and the *predicted* score at fourteen months was used. With this aim in view, on each functioning scale, the score at fourteen months (Y_{T2}) was predicted from the score at four months (Y_{T1}) by linear regression of Y_{T2} on Y_{T1}:

$$Y'_{T2} = b \cdot Y_{T1} + c$$

where Y'_{T2} = the predicted score at fourteen months
         b = the raw regression weight
         Y_{T1} = the observed score at four months
         c = a constant

Based on this regression formula, the difference between observed and predicted score was computed:

$$Y_{change} = Y_{T2} - Y'_{T2} = Y_{T2} - (b \cdot Y_{T1}) + c$$

where Y_{T2} = the observed score at fourteen months

Since the absolute level of Y$_{change}$ is not important for our purpose, the dependent variable was computed without the constant c :

$$Y_{change} = Y_{T2} - (b.Y_{T1})$$

A change score was computed for each of the three adaptational aspects. Regression analysis was then performed with the constructed variable Y$_{change}$ as the dependent variable, and the aforementioned independent variables as predictors.

The effect of the prediction of this Y$_{change}$ score resembles a regression analysis in which the score at T1 is the first variable to be entered. There, by first assigning a regression weight to he initial level of adaptation, the remaining variance to be explained is the deviation of the individual score from the expected score on the basis of the first measurement. In performing multiple regression in this way, one can also get an indication as to which variables play a role in change (Visser, 1982). A disadvantage of this method is, however, that the regression weight assigned to the score at four months is constantly reevaluated and changed in the equation on the basis of subsequent variables to be entered. In this way, its role as a covariate in the equation is unstable. An advantage of predicting the Y$_{change}$ score (as described above) instead, is that, here, the regression weight of the score at T1 is discounted in the criterion variable, and is thus fixed as representing the truly expected value of the criterion at fourteen months.

Procedure

As an initial to the regression analysis, the candidate predictor variables that did not correlate significantly (p > .05) with the criterion variable were eliminated. Depending on the subsample, this corresponded roughly with a correlation between .20 and .25, thus a variable which did not explain more than 4 to 6% of the variance on the criterion variable was excluded from further analysis.

The treatment of kinship and mode of death

The role of the loss characteristics (mode of death and kinship with the deceased) is more difficult to assess in a regression analysis, since the latter are categorical variables. As was discussed before, many of the sociodemographic variables, such as age of the bereaved and the deceased, as well as the qualities of the relationship are for a substantial part determined by, and contained within kinship and mode of death (see Section 7.2). For this reason, it is important to find a way of taking them into account.

One way to account for the influence of categoric variables in regression analysis is to create dummy variables for each category of these variables (Meerling, 1981). One of the problems is, however, that analyses with a large number of dummy variables are difficult to interpret, especially when interactions between the variables are taken into consideration.

From the analyses in the foregoing chapters, it appears that the largest systematic differences, especially on background characteristics, are found between kinship groups and, to a much smaller extent, between modes of death. Interactions between mode of death and kinship were rare. For these reasons, it was decided to perform parallel regression analyses for each kinship group, and to check for the possible role of mode of death by creating three dummy variables, each one contrasting one mode of death with the other two. The variance of the criterion variable explained by kinship group is examined in a pre-step by a one-way analysis of variance, and will be listed alongside the proportions of variance explained by the regression equation.

Next to this, by way of a comparison, the same regression procedure was performed on the whole sample without splitting up by kinship. This was done in order to get a better view on how each kinship group differs from the overall picture.

To predict change in functioning on a specific dimension between four and fourteen months, the initial scores on the remaining dimensions were added for evaluation as possible predictors.

Explanation of the tables

Listed vertically on the left in each table are the potential predictor variables. Each column in the Tables 7.3 through 7.5 represents a different regression analysis. In each table, predictions are made for each kinship group independently and the sample as a whole: first for the situation at four months after the loss, and secondly for the change in functioning between four and fourteen months. The first five columns list the standardized regression weights ß of the variables that best predict the adaptation at four months on the basis of task-demands and resources. The second group of five columns lists the optimal prediction of the adaptation at fourteen months, *given* the adaptation at four months.

The ß-weights in the first five columns reflect the role of the predictor variable in the absolute height of the score on the criterion in question. The larger ß, the larger the role of the variable in bringing about dysfunction. A large negative value of ß indicates that low values of the variable in question are related to a high level of dysfunction.

The ß-weights at fourteen months (T2) have a slightly different meaning. Since the score at four months is first taken into account, the ß-weights in the prediction equations at T2 reflect the role of the variable in the *change* in score between the two measurements. Here, a large positive ß-weight for a particular variable indicates that a high score on the predictive variable in question is related to an relatively smaller decrease (or increase) of dysfunction in comparison with bereaved scoring lower on the predictor variable, taking into account the general score change in the sample.

In the course of a stepwise regression analysis, the ß-values change as more variables are entered. Listed in the tables are the values of each ß at the end of the analysis. Only those ß-values which significantly ($p<.05$) contributed to the prediction somewhere in the analysis, and thus were entered into the equation, are shown in the table. When a variable was not entered for evaluation because of too low a correlation with the criterion, this is indicated with a point (.). When a variable correlated significantly with the criterion and was entered for evaluation, but *not* entered in the equation, this is indicated with a zero (0).

Listed at the bottom of each table, the correlation of the predicted value on the basis of the equation with the criterion is listed (R), the proportion of variance explained (equivalent to R^2) and the adjusted R^2 (correcting for the number of predictors). In this way, the adequacy of the prediction can be traced.

7.4   Prediction of loss-reactions

In this section, the results of the regression analyses for the Loss-reactions Scale will be discussed. As mentioned in Chapter 7, this scale comprises difficulties with detachment from the deceased, intrusive thoughts and avoidance (shock reactions), and feelings of meaninglessness.

Loss-reactions four months after the loss

Loss-reactions at four months after the loss are to a substantial extent predictable from the task-demands and resources of the bereaved (see Table 7.3). In the regression equation for the whole sample, half of the variance is explained by the task-demands and the resources. In an ANOVA on Loss-reactions with kinship as an independent variable, we find an explained variance of 18%. This is the equivalent of a ß of .42. When we split the sample by kinship, we find the multiple correlations to be in the same range within each kinship group. This means that taking kinship into account yields a surplus in explained variance.

Among the spouses, a high level of the loss-reactions four months after bereavement is predicted by (in order of importance): much anger, high relationship satisfaction, the deceased having died after an unnatural mode of death, and low income level. These aspects together explain 39% of the variance in loss-reactions among the spouses at four months.

For the parents, a high level of loss-reactions at four months was predicted by the absence of relief, the presence of feelings of anger, by the bereaved being mother, and having had physical problems before the loss. Together, these predictors accounted for 46% of the variance in the loss-reactions among the parents.

Among the siblings, the level of loss-reactions is mainly predicted by pre-loss aspects. Stronger loss-reactions are predicted by a high satisfaction about the relationship with the deceased, unexpectedness of the loss, feeling guilty, insufficient practical and informational support after the loss, and the deceased brother or sister having died at a younger age.

Among adult children of the deceased, a higher intensity of loss-reactions is predicted by feelings of anger, by having had a more frequent contact with the deceased, by high satisfaction with the relationship, by the sibling being a daughter of the deceased, and by having insufficient practical and informational support. These variables, together, account for 53% of the variance in the loss-reactions four months after loss of a parent.

At face value, there are no major differences between the kinship groups in the variables that are predictive for adaptation. The best and most stable predictors for the level of Loss-reactions across kinship groups are satisfaction with the relationship, anger, and practical and informational support, which parallels the prediction for the sample as a whole. In the regression equation for the entire sample, age of the deceased plays a relatively larger role. This is probably an artifact since, as was outlined in Chapter 5, age is to a substantial degree contained within the relationship groups.

Not surprisingly, anger, which is often considered as representing the wish to undo the loss or its effects, is related to more intense reactions. Relief among the bereaved, on the contrary, indicates relatively less reactions. Interestingly, we find that there is hardly a unique contribution of mode of death: only among the spouses is the contrast between natural and unnatural death predictive for the level of loss-reactions.

The change in loss-reactions

The change score was computed as described in Section 7.3. The ß weights for the regression of Loss-Reactions at fourteen months on four months ranged between .65 (for the siblings) and .87 (for the parents) The corresponding proportions of variance explained thus ranged between 41% and 76%. Breaking up the sample by kinship, in an ANOVA with multiple classification analysis, resulted in a small but significant regression weight (ß = .23) for kinship, corresponding to an explained variance of 5%. Also, when controlled for the initial score, parents and spouses recovered significantly less quickly than siblings and children.

Table 7.3
Prediction of loss-reactions at four months (T1), and the change in loss-reactions between four and fourteen months for the whole sample and per kinship group.

	Loss-reactions					Change in Loss-reactions				
	(ß Kinship: .42)					(ß Kinship: .23)				
	Spouse	Parent	Sibl.	Childr.	**Whole sample**	Spouse	Parent	Sibl.	Childr.	**Whole sample**
Task-demands										
Nonsuicide - suicide death	.	.	.	.	•	.	o	.	.	.
Nontraffic - traffic death	o	o	o	.	o	.	.	.	.	.
Nonillness - illness death	-.29	o	o	.	**-.10**	.	.	.	.	.
Sex of bereaved	.	.26	o	.24	**.17**	.	o	.	.	.
Sex of deceased	.	.	o	o	.	.	.	.	.31	.
Deceased of same sex	.	o	o	.	o	.	-.31	.	.	.
Age of the bereaved	.	.	o	.	.	.	.	.	.	.
Age of the deceased	.	.	-.18	.	**-.19**	.	.	.	.	o
Frequency of contact	.	.	o	.31	**.12**	.	.	o	o	o
Expectancy of the loss	o	o	-.31	.	.	.	.	.	.	.
Relationship satisfaction	.33	o	.34	.23	**.22**	.	.	.	.	.
Ambivalent feelings	.	.	.	.	•	.	.	.	.	o
Intimacy	o	o	o	o	**.12**	.	o	.	.	.
Independence deceased	.	.	.	o	.	.	o	.	.	.
Dominance deceased	.	.	.	.	.	.	.	o	.23	.
Pre-loss stressors	.	.	.	o	.	.	.	o	.	.
Psychol. probl. (pre-loss)	.	.	.	.	o	.	.	.	.	.
Physical probl. (pre-loss)	.	.24	.	o	**.12**	.	.	.	o	o
Social support										
Emotional support	.	o	o	o	o	.	.	.	.	o
Practical support	.	o	-.22	-.20	**-.15**	.	.	.	.	.
Material resources										
Income	-.20	.	o	o	o	.	.	.	.	.
Educational level	.	.	.	o	o	.	o	o	.	o
Attitude to loss										
Anger (at four months)	.38	.30	.	.33	**.19**	o	.	.	.	o
Guilt (at four months)	.	.	.24	.	**.12**	.	.35	.	.	**.12**
Relief (at four months)	o	-.34	o	.	**-.14**	.	.	.	.	.
*Functioning T1**										
Health						o	o	.27	.	**.23**
Social functioning						.	.	.	o	o
Multiple R:	.63	.68	.67	.73	**.70**	.00	.46	.27	.36	**.28**
Total variance expl. R²:	.39	.46	.45	.53	**.50**	.00	.21	.07	.13	**.08**
Adjusted R²:	.35	.42	.41	.50	**.48**	.00	.19	.06	.11	**.07**

Notes: . = not entered for evaluation as a predictor, o = entered for evaluation as a predictor, no significant contribution (p>.05), * = not entered at T1

In contrast with the absolute level of loss-reactions, the change in reactions between the two interviews generally appeared less predictable from task-demands and resources.

For bereaved spouses, the loss-reactions fourteen months after the loss are for 41% explained by the reactions at four months, but no adequate prediction could be made for the change in loss-reactions.

With the parents, guilt at four months after the loss predicted a relatively persistent level (or increase) of loss-reactions. A smaller decrease was also predicted by the deceased child being of the opposite sex to the parent. The proportion of the change explained by these variables is higher in comparison with the other kinship groups, but is still relatively low (21%).

Among the siblings, a relatively large decrease in loss-reactions at fourteen months is predicted by good health at four months. However, the amount of variance explained is, with 7%, low.

The decrease in loss-reactions between the two interviews is larger for loss of a father than loss of a mother. If the deceased parent had been dominant, there was a smaller decrease in reactions. The total amount of variance in change explained by these variables is quite low (13%).

When predicting change for the entire sample without taking kinship into account, two variables have (some) predictive value. Guilt feelings and bad health at four months predict a somewhat smaller decrease in loss-reactions. Evaluating the results of the regression analyses on change in reactions, we must conclude that the latter is only marginally predictable from task-demands and resources. Only among the parents is a somewhat better prediction possible.

7.5   Prediction of health

The same procedure as was outlined in the preceding section was applied to predict the health of the bereaved. The Health Problems scale, which is described in more detail in Chapter 7, measures physical health problems, in terms of health complaints and medicine use, and psychological problems in terms of depressive symptoms, confidence in the future, and suicidal ideation.

Health problems four months after the loss

As was shown before in Chapter 6, the health problems systematically varied with kinship group. In an ANOVA with multiple classification analysis, there was a significant regression weight ($\beta = .31$) for kinship, corresponding to an explained variance of 10%, with parents evidencing most health problems, followed by

Table 7.4

Prediction of health problems at four months (T1), and the change in health problems between four and fourteen months for the whole sample and by kinship group

	Health problems (ß Kinship: .31)					Change in health problems (ß Kinship: .0)				
	Spouse	Parent	Sibl.	Childr.	Whole sample	Spouse	Parent	Sibl.	Childr.	Whole sample
Task-demands										
Nonsuicide - suicide death	.24	.	.	.	.	.	o	.	.	o
Nontraffic - traffic death	.	.	.	.	o	.	.	-.27	.	o
Nonillness - illness death	o	.	.	.	o	.	.	.	.	.
Sex of bereaved	.	.26	.30	o	.13	.	.	.	.	.
Sex of deceased	.	.	o	o	.	.	.	.	.	.
Deceased of same sex	.	o	.	.18	.	.	.	.	-.25	.
Age of the bereaved	.	.	.	.	.17	.	.	.	.21	.19
Age of the deceased	.	.	.	.	-.19	.	o	.27	.	.
Frequency of contact	.	.	.21	o	o	.	.	.	.	.
Expectancy of the loss	.	.	.	.	.	.	.	.	.	.
Relationship satisfaction	.	.	o	o	o	.	o	.	.	.
Ambivalent feelings	.	.	.	.	.	.	o	.	-.30	.
Intimacy	.	.	.	.	o	o	-.34	.	o	.
Independence deceased	.	.	.	.	.	.	.	.	.	.
Dominance deceased	.	.	o	.	.	.	.	.	.	.
Pre-loss stressors	.	o	.34	o	o	.	.	.	.	.
Psychol. probl. (pre-loss)	o	o	.	.38	.17	.	.28	.	.	o
Physical probl. (pre-loss)	.28	o	.	o	.19	.	.	.	.	o
Social support										
Emotional support	.	.	.	o	o	.	.	.	.	.
Practical support	-.36	o	-.22	-.34	-.22	-.50	.	.	.	-.16
Material resources										
Income	-.19	.	o	-.21	o	.	.	.	.	.
Educational level	.	.	o	.	o	.	.	.	.	.
Attitude to loss										
Anger (at four months)	o	.46	o	o	.24	.	.	.	.	.
Guilt (at four months)	.	.	o	o	o	o	.	.	.	o
Relief (at four months)	-.28	o	.	.	-.18	.	.	.	.	.
Functioning T1*										
Loss-reactions						.	.	.	.	.
Social functioning						.	.	o	.	o
Multiple R:	.66	.55	.61	.71	.63	.50	.32	.43	.44	.24
Total variance expl. R²:	.43	.30	.37	.51	.39	.25	.10	.19	.19	.06
Adjusted R²:	.40	.28	.33	.48	.38	.23	.08	.16	.16	.05

Notes: . = not entered for evaluation as a predictor, o = entered for evaluation as a predictor, no significant contribution (p>.05), * = not entered at T1

spouses, siblings and children. Prediction equations were again made for the whole sample and each kinship group separately to check for possible differential mechanisms (see Table 7.4).

A high level of health problems among the spouses four months after the loss was predicted by little practical and informational support, physical health problems before the loss, little feeling of relief, the mode of death being suicide and low income. The total proportion of variance explained by task-demands and resources is somewhat higher (43%) than for the loss-reactions.

With the parents, health problems at four months are predicted by strong feelings of anger (which correlates .48 with health) and the respondent being the mother of the deceased. These two variables account for 30% of the variance in health for the parents group.

Health problems among the siblings subsample are predicted by pre-loss task-demands, the respondent being the sister of the deceased, a lack of practical and informational support, and frequent contact with the deceased before the loss. These variables together account for 37% of the variance in health among the siblings.

Children's health at four months after the loss is less defined by the task-demands of bereavement than among the other kinship groups. Health problems are predicted by: psychological health problems before the loss, a lack of practical and informational support, low income and the deceased being of the same sex as the bereaved. Together, these variables account for 51% of the variance in health-scores among the children.

When we consider the sample as a whole, we find that (as for loss-reactions) experienced practical and informational support is one of the most stable predictors. Here again, anger and little relief generally are indicative of health problems. The contribution of age of the bereaved and the deceased in the regression equation for the entire sample appears, again, to be related to the nesting within the kinship groups, since they are never significantly related to health within the kinship groups. Mode of death only plays a role in the spouses group, where the suicide-bereaved evidence more health problems.

Change in health complaints

The change in health between four and fourteen months was assessed by computing a change variable (see Section 7.3). The regression weights of T2 on T1 for the Health Problems scale were .72 for the spouses and siblings, .86 for the parents and .73 for the children. The explained variance thus ranged from .52 to .74, indicating that among the parents, in particular, their state of health at four months is a very important indicator for their health at fourteen months.

As can be seen in Table 7.4, among the spouses there is only one major predictor for the change in health problems[6]. A continued high, or increased level of health problems at fourteen months is strongly predicted by a lack of practical and informational support at four months. This variable explains 25% of the variance in change in health problems.

Among parents, the health four months after the loss is highly indicative of health at fourteen months, explaining 74% of the variance. This decreases considerably the variance left to be explained for other predictor variables. Still, a relatively larger decrease in health problems at fourteen months is predicted by higher intimacy with the child before the loss, and the absence of psychological problems before the loss. The amount of the variance in change explained is modest: 10%.

Among siblings, an increase, or only a slight decrease in health problems is predicted by the deceased being older, and cause of death not being a traffic-fatality: the siblings bereaved after a traffic-fatality evidence a larger decrease in health problems than the siblings in the other groups. Together these independent variables explain 19% of the variance in health-change among siblings.

For children of the deceased, a relatively larger decrease in health problems is predicted when the parent of the other sex died: this seems to neutralize the initial higher level of health problems at four months for this variable. A larger decrease in health problems is also predicted for younger bereaved children and when there were relatively strong ambivalent feelings about the relationship with the deceased. The variance in the change between the two interviews is for 19% explained by these predictors.

As was the case for the loss-reactions scale, the change in problems is less predictable from task-demands and resources than the absolute level. The predictor variables vary with each kinship group and, with the notable exception of the spouses, a lot of variance in the change remains unexplained.

7.6   Prediction of social dysfunction

The Social Dysfunction Scale was used as a criterion to predict social functioning among the bereaved from task-demands and resources of the bereaved. This scale, which is also described in more detail in Chapter 7, measures social integration and involvement in social activities. As for loss-reactions and health, the regression procedure was performed both on the sample as a whole and on the individual kinship groups (see Table 7.5).

---

[6]   The analysis reported here omits one of the spouses in the traffic fatality group, whose extreme increase in health problems biased the results.

Table 7.5
Prediction of social dysfunction at four months (T1), and the change in dysfunction between four and fourteen months for the whole sample and by kinship group

	Social dysfunction					Change in social dysfunction				
	(ß Kinship: .17)					(ß Kinship: .18)				
	Spouse	Parent	Sibl.	Childr.	Whole sample	Spouse	Parent	Sibl.	Childr.	Whole sample
Task-demands										
Nonsuicide - suicide death	.33	o	.	.	o	.	.	-.38	.	.
Nontraffic - traffic death	.	o	.	.	o	.	.	.	.	.
Nonillness - illness death	.	.	.	.	.	.	.	o	.	.
Sex of bereaved	.	.	.	.	.	o	.	.	.	.
Sex of deceased	.	.	.	.	.	.	.	.	.	.
Deceased of same sex	.	.	.	.	.	.	.	.	.	.
Age of the bereaved	.	o	.	.	o	.	.	.	o	.
Age of the deceased	.	o	.	.25	.	.	.	.	o	o
Frequency of contact	.	.	.	.	.	.	.	.	.	o
Expectancy of the loss	.	.	.	.	.	.	.	.	.35	.
Relationship satisfaction	.	.	.	.	.	o	.	.	.	.
Ambivalent feelings	.	.	.	.	.	.45	.	.	.	.
Intimacy	.	.	.	.	.	o	.	.	.	.
Independence deceased	.	.	.	.	.	.	.	o	.	.
Dominance deceased	.	.	.	.	.	o	.	.	.	o
Pre-loss stressors	.	.	.	o	.	o	.	.	.	.
Psychol. probl. (pre-loss)	o	o	.	.	o	o	.	.	.	.
Physical probl. (pre-loss)	.	.	.	.	o	.	.	.	.	.
Social support										
Emotional support	o	.	.	o	o	.	o	.	.	o
Practical support	-.30	.	o	-.27	-.24	o	.	.	o	o
Material resources										
Income	.	-.54	.	.	o	.	.	.	.	.
Educational level	.	o	.	.	-.14	.	.	.	o	.
Attitude to loss										
Anger (at four months)	.27	o	.	o	.	.	.	.	.	.
Guilt (at four months)	o	.	.	.	o	.	.	o	.	.
Relief (at four months)	-.22	.	.	.	.	.	.	.	.	.
Functioning T1*										
Loss-reactions	.	.	.	.	.	.	.	.	.	.
Health	.	.	.	.	.	.28	.	.	o	.23
Multiple R:	.60	.54	.00	.35	**.28**	.58	.00	.38	.36	**.23**
Total variance expl. R^2:	.36	.29	.00	.12	**.08**	.33	.00	.14	.13	**.05**
Adjusted R^2:	.33	.28	.00	.10	**.07**	.30	.00	.13	.12	**.05**

Notes: . = not entered for evaluation as a predictor, o = entered for evaluation as a predictor, no significant contribution (p>.05), * = not entered at T1

Social dysfunction four months after the loss

In contrast with the other measures of adaptation, the level of social functioning at four months was hardly divergent for the various kinship groups. From an ANOVA with multiple classification analysis, it appeared that the explained variance by kinship on the scale was only 3% (F=2.8, p=.04). Spouses and parents were slightly more isolated than children and siblings.

Among the spouses, more problems in social functioning at four months after the loss were predicted by the death being suicide in contrast with the other modes of death, by insufficient practical and informational support, feelings of anger and the absence of relief after the loss. Together these variables accounted for 36% of the variance in social dysfunction. Social functioning at four months among the parents is only predicted by income level (the lower the income, the greater the dysfunction). This variable alone explains 29% of the level of dysfunction. For siblings, social functioning cannot adequately be predicted with linear regression analysis from the task-demands and resources: no variables are entered in the equation.

Social dysfunction among the children losing a parent is, to some extent, predicted by age of the deceased (the older the deceased, the more problems), and a lack of practical and informational support, which together, however, account only for 12% of the variance in social functioning.

For the entire sample, the level of functioning can only be predicted to a small extent from practical and informational support and educational level of the bereaved. Altogether, the prediction of the level of social functioning is much less adequate than for health and loss-reactions. A possible reason for this, is that the level of social functioning may be less related to specific task-demands, and may itself act more as a kind of resource.

Change in social dysfunction

Whereas the absolute level of social functioning at four months seems hard to predict from our data, the change in social functioning between four months and fourteen months is relatively better predictable: about the same amount of variance is explained here as for the change in loss-reactions and health discussed in the preceding sections. Regression of the score on social dysfunction at T2 on T1 to construct the change measure reveals that the ß-weights here are relatively small, ranging from .37 (r^2 = .14) among the children to .55 (r^2 = .30) among the parents, indicating that social functioning at fourteen months is less predictable from the situation at four months than is possible for loss-reactions and health. From an ANOVA with multiple classification analysis, it appeared that, taking into account the height of the score at T1, the amelioration in social functioning is somewhat larger among children in comparison with the other groups. Kinship, however, only explains 3% of the variance in change in functioning (F=3.124, p=.03).

For the spouses, a smaller decrease or increase of problems in social functioning are predicted by ambivalent feelings about the relationship with the deceased. Those who evidenced more health problems at four months show slower recovery of social functioning.

For the parents, the change in functioning between the two interviews cannot be predicted from any of the independent variables.

For the siblings, at fourteen months, the variance in social functioning is only for 24% explained by the level of social functioning at four months. A relatively larger improvement of social functioning is found among the bereaved from suicide. This variable accounts for 14% of the variance in the change-variable.

Among the children of the deceased, social functioning at four months only explains 14% of the variance at fourteen months. Improvement in social functioning is relatively greater when the loss was more expected. This last aspect may be related to our observation that, in the case of an expected loss, the children often directed more attention to the dying parent and spent more time with him or her. This frequently led to a retreat from other social contacts and we speculate that there may be an initial temporary impairment of the social network.

The number of task-demands and resources that are related to the change in social dysfunction seems to be limited, and differs strongly according to kinship group.

7.7   Conclusion

From the preceding sections, it appears that, to some extent, we can predict the outcome in different areas of functioning from the task-demands of bereavement and the resources a person has available. In general, we found that, within each kinship group, the predictors for functioning after the loss can be found both in terms of the task-demands of the loss and the resources a person has available.

Reviewing the results of the above analyses, some variables turn up as fairly consistent predictors for adaptation.

In general, more intense initial loss-reactions seem to be predicted by a high intimacy and quality of the relation with the deceased and, except in the spouses group, by the bereaved being a women. Anger in the bereaved is also indicative of stronger loss-reactions. Prediction of the *change* in loss-reactions is more equivocal: the predictors diverge for each kinship group. An interesting finding for the parent group is that feelings of guilt at four months are related to a continued higher level of loss-reactions at fourteen months, and that reactions are more persistent when the deceased child was of the opposite sex.

More health problems in the early period after the loss are generally predicted for bereaved who report a low level of practical and informational support, for bereaved who suffered health problems before the loss, and in some groups for those with a low income level. Characteristics of the relationship here seem to play a smaller role than in the prediction of loss-reactions. Health at four months after the loss is a good predictor for later health. The change in health problems between the two interviews is best predictable in the spouses group, where the widowed who have little practical and informational support at the first interview are prone to suffer continued bad health. In the other kinship groups, the predictors for the change in health can mainly be found in the task-demands of the loss, rather than in the resources of the individual.

Social dysfunction four months after the loss, in general, is somewhat less easily predictable from our set of independent variables. Reasonable prediction seems only possible for the spouses and parents. The lesser predictability may be due to the fact that social functioning can be regarded as a resource variable in itself, which is related to personal efficacy and other individual characteristics. As can be seen in the above analyses, social functioning is somewhat independent of the task-demands of bereavement. Among spouses, however, the suicide-bereaved evidence somewhat more problems at four months after the death. Spouses evidencing a debilitated health at four months are likely to evidence less improvement in social functioning at fourteen months.

It appears that the level of loss-reactions is highly predictable from the task-demands of bereavement and the resources of the bereaved, with proportions of explained variance up to 53%. For health dysfunction, the prediction is only slightly weaker.

Social functioning appears difficult to predict. In view of the task-demand and resources framework this is an interesting finding. Although the state of the social network can be seen as both resource and outcome after the loss, it appears that it may be less influenced by loss-specific variables and thus may be more on the resource, than the outcome side of the equation. In all kinship groups, social functioning at fourteen months is only slightly related to the level at four months.

For the spouses subsample, the absolute level of social functioning as well as the change between the interviews, are better predictable than for the other kinship groups. A possible reason for this finding may be that with the widowed, bereavement is more likely to imply an important drain of resources, and a profound change of one's social position. With the death of the spouse, we see for instance that, more often than in other kinship groups, an important source of comfort and practical support was lost.

In addition, we notice that the predictors for adaptation in the spouses subsample are somewhat different from those in the other groups. It is plausible that, given the greater impact of the loss mentioned above, the widowed face a more profound (practical) reorganization of daily life, which demands skills and forms of adaptation different from the other kinship groups.

Chapter 8

Discussion

In this study we have examined the consequences of a death for surviving family members. In the first chapters, we looked at the available theories and empirical findings to identify possible risk-indicators in bereavement. Some methodological pitfalls for the study of bereavement were discussed and some requirements were formulated which aimed at avoiding them. In the second half of this publication, the method and results of the Leiden Bereavement Study were presented.

In the set up of this presentation, we employed a framework which considers stress, and its negative impact on health, to be the result of the extent to which the individual, material, and social resources of the individual match the task-demands he or she has to cope with.

In this chapter we will take an overall look at the findings of the study, look at some of its limitations, and discuss implications for strategies of prevention and intervention in bereaved families.

In the following sections, we must bear in mind that most of the aspects we studied are interrelated. When discussing the role of specific variables or identifying risk-indicators, we refer to the situation of everything else being equal (controlled for other relevant variables).

8.1 The influence of bereavement on functioning

In looking at adaptation after bereavement, we have focused on three dimensions of functioning. The first concerned the impact of the loss in terms of shock reactions and difficulties with detachment from the deceased. The second involved functioning in terms of psychological and physical health, while the third reflected social integration and activity.

The logical question to ask here is whether all dimensions of functioning are affected equally by the task-demands posed by bereavement itself, or whether some aspects of functioning are less affected by the loss than others. From this study, it appears there are considerable differences between loss reactions, health and social functioning in this respect.

Not surprisingly, we find that the loss-reactions in terms of shock and difficulty with detachment are strongly related to the magnitude of the loss itself, with major determinants such as kinship relationship to the deceased, the satisfaction with the relationship, and the attitude of the bereaved to the loss. These loss-reactions seem somewhat less determined by the other resources of the bereaved, such as pre-loss physical and psychological problems, and material resources.

In contrast with this, the level of social functioning after the loss seems to be hardly related to the task-demands of the loss at all. In general, social functioning seems to be a more or less stable background which seems not to be fundamentally changed by the loss. Among the widowed, however, social functioning is more strongly linked to the attitude to the loss. Anger and absence of feelings of relief, as well as the mode of death being suicide are related to a lower level of social functioning.

Physical and psychological health seem to act as pre and post loss resources, but are also substantially related to the task-demands of the loss, although less strongly than the loss-reactions. It is interesting, however, that the *recovery* of health over time seems to be highly dependent on the aspects related to the loss, and virtually not on resource strength. In other words: the extent to which the bereaved's health improves between four and fourteen months seems to be strongly related to the magnitude and characteristics of the loss, rather than to the strength of his or her resources *per se*.

• *Strong loss-reactions among the bereaved are related to impaired health.*

Bad health is closely related to strong loss-reactions. This means either that impaired health impedes adaptation to the loss, or that failure to come to grips with the loss leads to health problems. The present study provides some evidence that both mechanisms operate simultaneously.

Health after the loss is, not surprisingly, related to pre-loss physical and psychological health. However, there is little evidence here that *improvement* of health between four and fourteen months is dependent on pre-loss health. This means that good health before the loss does not guarantee a quicker recovery of health in this period after bereavement.

On the other hand, we see that at least part of the health condition is directly determined by the *type* of loss. This is most strongly supported by the fact that considerable differences in general health and depression appear between family members on the basis of their kinship relationship to the deceased. Since kinship is a 'formal' characteristic of the type of loss, and therefore cannot be influenced by the loss itself, it follows that the loss, or the circumstances preceding it, influence the health of the bereaved.

• *The state of functioning at four months after the death in terms of loss-reactions and health is a highly reliable indication for adaptation.*

When a person at three to four months after the loss still experiences a high level of shock reactions and difficulty with detachment from the deceased, it is highly probable that these problems will still be relatively persistent more than one year after the loss. For psychological and physical health this relationship is even stronger. From this, we may conclude that future problems are already announced in the first months after the loss.

• *Social functioning is more or less independent of the severity of the loss-reactions.*

Severe social dysfunction was relatively rare in our study. Although many bereaved found their support networks had changed, there was hardly a general direction. After the loss they often went through a reappraisal of their relationships and social activities. In many cases it was felt that the loss had put their relationships to the test. There was frequently a reshuffling of their social pattern, with old friends lost and new friends found. To many bereaved, the extent to which their grief was accepted as a normal and integral part of their being was an important touchstone for the quality of relationships as well as social activities.

8.2 Differences in adaptation related to kinship

Reviewing the results of our study, we may state that kinship relationship to the deceased is a major factor, determining to a substantial degree the level of adaptation after the loss. This aspect has been wrongfully overlooked in most of the research that has hitherto been conducted.

The loss of a spouse, as we have seen, substantially differs from other family relationships on a multitude of pre-loss characteristics. The importance of the other as a provider of security and support, the frequent operation of the couple as a social unit, and the intricate entanglement of daily life are to some extent unique or apply more strongly to the spousal relationship. The almost exclusive concentration on spousal bereavement in empirical research, although highly valuable in itself, has led to a multitude of generalizations about grief in humans, based solely on the study of this specific psychosocial relationship.

At the end of our study, we must ask ourselves whether the picture is really different for spouses as compared to other family members. For a number of aspects the answer must definitely be yes.

Firstly, it appears that for loss of a spouse, the predictors of problematic adaptation often differ from those in the other kinship groups. In general, functioning after the loss of a spouse is more strongly related to one's resources than to characteristics of the relationship. In contrast to other kinship relationships, among spouses, mode of death appears to play a (small) role in the level of adaptation at four months. This may be due to the fact that the spouse is usually the family member who had the most frequent, often daily, contact with the deceased, and is thus is likely to have experienced many aspects of the events leading to, and following the death.

Secondly, the sex difference in functioning among spouses appears to be the reverse of that in the other kinship groups. In the present study, we saw that in all kinship groups the women suffer from more loss-reactions and health complaints than the men, except among the widowed: widowers and widows are generally about equally affected. In terms of social functioning, the widowers do worse than the widows. Interestingly, we found no health difference between older and younger widowed. This finding was essentially the same in the other kinship groups.

- *The level of adaptation, as well as the pace of recovery, in terms of loss-reactions and health, differs between the kinship relationships.*

With most of the bereaved, there is a decrease in loss-reactions over time and an increase in health. Recovery is, however, significantly lesser for bereaved parents. As a group, they show little decrease in preoccupation with their child's death and little improvement in health between four and fourteen months after the loss.

- *Loss-reactions are more strongly related to health among spouses and parents, than among siblings and children of the deceased.*

An interesting, although not surprising, finding is that the level of shock reactions and difficulties with detachment is more closely related to psychological and physical health in spouses ($r=.52$) and parents ($r=.42$) than in siblings ($r=.19$) and children ($r=.21$). This indicates that the impact of the loss-event is less important to general health in the latter two groups. By the same token, stresses occurring during the same period as the loss play a role in post-bereavement health in siblings and children, but not in the spouses and parents groups. It is probable that, if one is confronted with the loss of one's child or spouse, other stresses become less important, and are thus a less important predictor for the health situation.

- *Social functioning is most severely impaired in the widowers and mothers, both contrasting unfavorably with the other kinship groups.*

For most bereaved, an initial withdrawal from social activities appears to take place followed by a gradual reintegration over time. For those who lose their spouse, however, there appears a considerable difference between widows and widowers. The latter in general show a *decrease* in activities and integration between four and fourteen months. The widowed who are angry and feel little relief after the loss have more problems in social integration and social activities.

8.3   Differences in adaptation related to mode of death

In both clinical lore and theory, a sudden and violent loss is regarded as having a more debilitating effect than an expected, natural loss. One of the major concerns of the present study was the search for consistent differences between different modes of death.

• *At four months after the loss, bereaved after a traffic-fatality evidence stronger loss-reactions and are somewhat, but significantly, more depressed than those bereaved after suicide or a long-term illness.*

Initially, we found small but significant differences between the modes of death in the level of adaptation. It must be marked, however that the magnitude of these differences was relatively small. In the case of loss after a long-term illness there are often somewhat less initial shock reactions, such as unexpected intruding images of the deceased intervening with daily functioning and numbness. No differences were found in the majority of the measures of social functioning and health.

• *In the longer run, there is hardly any systematic difference between suicide, death after a traffic-fatality and death after a long-term illness in the level of adaptation of the bereaved.*

At fourteen months, no systematic difference can be found for any of the aspects of functioning. The systematic differences in loss-reactions have also subsided. This means that on the basis of our findings, it is unlikely that longer-term level of adaptation differs fundamentally with the mode of death.

• *The pace of recovery, in terms of detachment and depression differs between the modes of death.*

Bereaved after a traffic-fatality mostly evidence a relatively high level of loss-reactions and depression at four months after the loss, but the pace of recovery is generally somewhat faster, bringing their functioning (as a group) to the same level as the bereaved after suicide and illness.

To conclude, we may state that bereavement after different modes of death is marked more by similarities than by differences. As other studies in the field (as discussed in Chapter 3) have shown, when differences occurred, they were usually related to the *themes* of preoccupation and rumination, but rarely to the *intensity*. In other words, the overall *degree* of preoccupation and affectedness differed only marginally with the modes of death.

A developmental approach to mode of death

Another point that is clearly made by the present study is that we should adopt a developmental approach to the study of bereavement. By this I mean that *the reasons for maladaptation are more likely to be found in the antecedent situation, than in the characteristics of the death itself.*

The most evident indication of this can be found in the health problems dimension. The state of health appeared to be hardly predictable from the loss related variables such as expectancy of the loss or mode of death. Instead, the qualities of the relationship, the attitude to the loss, pre-loss stress and well-being, and need for practical and informational support were the most stable predictors for health.

From the findings discussed in Chapters 6 and 7, it is clear that the history of the bereaved person in relational, social and individual respects plays a central role in adaptation. In looking only at the cause of death for considering and ascribing the effects of the loss, we would limit our perspective. We have already seen that within each mode of death there is an enormous variety of circumstances. In many instances, the suicide struck the bereaved as being expected, while to others it was completely unexpected. For some bereaved, the suicide came undeniably as a solution to an unbearable situation, and created new opportunities and freedom of movement. For others, it meant personal failure or made no sense at all.

Although the modes of death do not seem to essentially differ in the seriousness of their consequences, we can state that for each mode of death some shared, typical characteristics of the antecedents of the loss exist. This is especially clear in the case of suicide bereavement.

Frequently, prior to suicide there were preexisting tensions and problems with the deceased, with not seldom a long history of suicide attempts and hospitalizations in mental health clinics. At the same time, the suicide-bereaved more often feel they 'had no grip' on the deceased, and that he or she had led an independent life. Furthermore, the loss often does not come as a complete surprise and has regularly at least been fantasized about. This does not mean that the shock of death is any less: to many bereaved it is the nightmare come true. Pre-loss physical health also tends to be somewhat worse in suicide bereaved than in the other groups.

Summing up these differences, it is highly probable that even if the suicide had not taken place, we would find these families to be under more stress, especially the spouses and parents. The threat of impaired functioning may thus be determined to a substantial degree by the history of person and family, rather than being solely a consequence of bereavement or the traumatic event of the suicide itself.

Dimensionality of mode of death

When studying the significance of the cause of death in bereavement, we also have to take into account the broader context in which the loss occurred. Different sets of characteristics are associated with each cause of death. In Chapter 4 we distinguished a number of psychologically relevant aspects which are associated with the mode of death: expectedness of the loss, the extent to which the death was natural, responsibility for the death and timeliness. Each mode of death incorporates a combination of these aspects. Other differences may also play in the background: death after a long-term illness is more often associated with older age of the deceased, whereas suicide and traffic-fatalities in particular are often prominent in younger age groups.

Expectancy of the loss, more often present in illness and suicide bereavement, consistently plays a role in the level of loss-reactions but not in health or social functioning. However, expectancy as it was measured in the present study, comprised, in fact, recognition or cognitive acceptance that the deceased was going to die. The finding that expectancy rather than mode of death itself turned out to be a predictor for the intensity of the loss-reactions (cf. Chapter 7), indicates that the way a person recognizes the impending loss is probably a more important aspect than the formal characteristics of the cause of death.

The role of naturalness of the loss (measured by the contrast between illness death and the other modes of death) seems also to be limited to a higher level of initial loss-reactions after the loss. In our study, the unnatural death causes hardly seem to give rise to increased health problems or problems in social functioning in the first fourteen months after the loss.

The role of responsibility for the death (perhaps best reflected in the contrast between suicide death and the other modes of death) seems to be particularly confined to increased self-blame in the bereaved after suicide. There is a relatively higher initial level of health problems and social dysfunction among the widowed after suicide, which disappears in the longer run. Interestingly, self-blame about the death is only slightly related to dysfunction.

The effect of untimeliness of the loss was not directly assessed by the present study. When we look at age of the deceased as an indication of timeliness, this hardly seems to be related to functioning in our study.

To conclude, we may state that the mode of death does not appear to have a consistent influence on adaptation after the loss, although there are many differences between the modes of death in the characteristics of the pre-loss situation. The suicide bereaved more often look back on a less fulfilling relationship and less intimacy with the deceased. The illness and suicide bereaved report more psychological and physical problems before the loss than those bereaved after a traffic-fatality.

After the loss, there is a clear difference in attitude to the loss between the modes of death. The bereaved after suicide or an illness-related death much more frequently experience relief than those who lost a family member in a traffic accident. On the other hand, the family members of a suicide victim experience markedly more feelings of guilt in comparison to both other modes of death.

8.4   Risk-indicators after bereavement

Death of a family member is considered to be an event with a large impact, but for whom, and to what extent is it a devastating experience? The results of this study show that the majority seems to do quite well in terms of adaptation. Still, there is a substantial number of bereaved who evidence long-lasting effects. More than one year after the loss, one-third of the family members still experiences moderate to severe difficulty in detaching from the deceased. Thirteen percent of our sample still show moderate to severe depressive symptoms at fourteen months. In this section, we will summarize the characteristics of those at risk for problems after bereavement.

The assessment of risk-indicators has its practical value in that it offers a direction for monitoring and preventive actions. The earlier we can determine whether a person is at risk, the more time and opportunity there is to intervene, when necessary, and to eventually adapt the situation before it deteriorates. When we are able to adequately predict the situation after the loss from factors that can, in principle, already be assessed before the loss, this offers an even broader scope for preventive action. In the case of death after a terminal illness, this is most clear: interaction with the dying patient is usually still possible and there is still time to solve possible problems in the relationship, while interventions can ameliorate the situation.

The first step in prevention is thus the recognition of specific risk-groups of bereaved, as well as specific individual characteristics that are indicative of dysfunction.

In the subsequent paragraphs, the major risk-indicators that were found in the present study will be summarized.

First of all, our study has clearly shown that some kinship relationships carry a higher risk than others for evidencing problems after the loss. In fact, the kinship relationship appears to be a factor that determines, to a large extent, both the type of task set for the bereaved and the level of problems experienced after bereavement.

- *The relationship groups most at risk for problems after bereavement are the mothers, followed at some distance by widowers, fathers and sisters of the deceased person.*

First and foremost we may expect severe problems for mothers who lose a child. They are the group which is most clearly at risk for developing severe problems after the loss. Regardless the age of their child or their own age, the loss seems to create a permanent vacuum in their lives. The level of loss-reactions, depression and health is higher than in all other groups at both four and fourteen months. Recovery, if possible at all, seems to be slower than for the other relationships. More than three-quarters of the mothers in our study had either a great need for emotional support on both interviews or an increasing need. One-quarter of the mothers evidence unchanged severe depressive symptoms or a significant deterioration of these symptoms.

The fathers of a deceased child are also among the more affected, but seem to form less of a homogeneous risk-group. For a number of them, the reactions to the loss seem to be somewhat postponed. Twenty-five percent of the fathers show an increase in bereavement reactions over time, and one-fifth evidences significant increase in depression. Among the fathers, we find the largest proportion of deterioration over time in comparison with other relationship groups, which also defines them as a risk-group.

The reason for the increasing debilitation among fathers may be related to them initially taking the role of principal comforter and supporter of their wives. It was our impression that the intense reactions of the mother and her strong need for support often formed a considerable additional burden for the father. His attention was not rarely concentrated on his wife's grief, rather than on his own problems with the loss. Perhaps in association with this, among fathers, there is also a relatively low involvement in social activities which hardly increases over time.

Parents felt generally more guilty about the death than other relationship groups. An important theme for the parents was the abnormality, often felt as injustice, of having outlived their child.

A group which also has a relatively high risk for more problematic adaptation are the widowers. It seems their problems mostly lie in maintaining and rebuilding social relationships. The risk of isolation is greatest for this group. They appear to have a worse prognosis than the widows: their reactions to the loss show little decrease, and there is an increase in social isolation and a decrease in social activities which persist a long time after the loss. One quarter of the widowers continues to have severe difficulties with detachment from their wives. In many cases, with the death of their spouse, the major provider of emotional support has been lost, and rebuilding social integration appears difficult for many of them.

Perhaps even more important, especially since less expected, is to watch for problems in women who have lost a brother or sister. Psychological and physical problems occurred even more frequently among them than among widows. Sisters of the deceased often reported having had a special relationship with their deceased brother or sister, and felt strong responsibility for him or her. Something that may possibly contribute to the relatively high level of problems, is that the sisters of the deceased are generally not in the focus of attention after the loss. Practical help and emotional support from the environment seem to center on bereaved spouses and parents rather than on them. They clearly appear here to be a 'forgotten' group.

Interestingly, the brothers of the deceased show a much more favorable adaptation, and, as a group, cannot be considered as being at risk.

The above listing of risk-groups by no means implies that no problems exist in the other relationship groups. The other family members may also suffer severe difficulties. The identification of parents, widowers and sisters simply means that they are *more likely* to have problems after the loss. This means at the same time, of course, that not all the bereaved in the identified risk-groups develop problems[1].

One group that seems to do relatively well are the widows. Many of them become rapidly reinvolved in social contacts and show a quicker decrease in loss-reactions and increase in health after the loss than the other groups. A combination of reasons may be responsible for this. The widows often seemed to be in a state of considerable self-sufficiency before the loss. The impression exists that they are better prepared for a life without their husband than vice versa. It may also be that the relatively better position of the widows can be ascribed to the fact that their widowed position is generally recognized by the environment and caregivers, as well as by the (Dutch) state, which offers financial support to widows and their children. To a certain extent, their needs may be better met than those of other relationship groups in this respect. In addition, since there are considerably more widows than widowers, they have more equal sex models available for adaptation and support than their male counterparts.

Adult children of the deceased generally show the least difficulties after the loss. At four months after the loss they are mostly in good health, and are little occupied with the loss. Although daughters of the deceased initially have a somewhat heightened level of shock reactions and need for emotional support, recovery is fairly quick. Their health seems little affected. The sons, though at four months still sometimes occupied with the loss, evidence the least problems in comparison to all other relationships.

Next to the 'formal' aspect of kinship, we found a number of early indicators for problematic functioning which may be counted among the individual resources of the

---

[1]   This can most clearly be seen for the scales to which the model of change and normscores was applied (see Chapter 5).

bereaved person. We will now discuss the these aspects, more or less in order of predictive value.

• *Bereaved who experience insufficient practical and informational support are prone to have more severe loss-reactions, deteriorated health and problems in social functioning after the loss.*

Satisfactory functioning on all three dimensions of adaptation is most strongly related to the sufficiency of practical and informational support, like help of others in handling practical matters and daily work, availability of diverting contacts and help in the form of advice. However, before drawing conclusions for interventions on this basis, we have to examine the meaning of this finding.

When we look more closely, we find the cause-effect relationship between support and functioning to be ambiguous. There are at least three different mechanisms that may operate here.

The first possible mechanism is that adequate informational and practical support helps the bereaved on the track toward adaptation,. By giving (adequate) advice, creating possible models for adaptation, and by rewarding behaviors that lead to acknowledgement of the reality of the loss and to renewed social integration, the bereaved is put and kept on the right track. The presence of and involvement with others may also provide protection against insufficient reinforcement which might lead to depression.

For a second scenario, we have to look into the meaning of the notion of 'sufficiency of support'. We may speculate that bereaved who are in good physical and mental health generally will be relatively self-sufficient, and consequently will not draw heavily on their support network for assistance. Conversely, since the proof of the pudding is in the eating, those who are in great need of support and make a strong appeal to the members of the support network are more likely to be confronted with a lack of the support available to them. In other words, insufficiency of support in particular is more likely to be experienced by those who need it: those in bad health.

A third alternative relationship is that bad mental health, especially depression, is associated with a perceptual or attributional set of the environment being unhelpful. We must not forget that our measure concerns *perceived* sufficiency of support. Lakey & Cassady (1990) recently found in an experimental design that perceived support, although related to enacted support, operated in part as a cognitive personality variable. They found low levels of perceived support were associated with a negative bias in the evaluation of supportive behaviors. Those who reported low levels of support also remembered less of the supportive behaviors offered to them in an experimental setting. In addition, it is known that depressed persons send out cues that discourage others to provide support, and thus lead to an actual decrease of the support provided (Lewinsohn, 1985).

To conclude, we may state that we cannot be sure whether a lack of this support is the cause of deteriorated health, or a consequence. Environmental support may enhance health, but it is at least as likely that bad physical and mental health is the *cause* of either a need for support which is not easily met by the environment, a devaluation of the support offered, or an attitude that discourages support attempts. The possibility that low perceived-support individuals may have a specific perceptive set of support has implications for the type of intervention needed.

- *Feelings of anger are strongly related to more severe loss-reactions, as well as a higher level of health problems.*

A finding of some importance is that, although anger is strongly related to dysfunction, it does not follow the pattern of the loss-reactions. Systematic differences between the kinship groups and the modes of death are minimal. This indicates that anger (at least at four months) after a loss must be seen as an individually defined way of coping with the loss, rather than a 'typical' part of the loss reaction at this point in time. It is one of the most consistent predictors for a high level of loss-reactions, and to a smaller extent for health and problems with social functioning.

Lasting anger, as an attitude towards the loss, thus appears to be dysfunctional in adaptation. Anger at four months after the loss may be related to a more or less stable cognitive style of leveling (difficulties to integrate new experiences with existing ones) with a tendency to try to change or undo situations rather than adapt to them. This is perhaps partly reflected by the fact that the objects of anger seem to vary considerably between individuals.

- *An intimate and satisfactory relationship with the deceased before the loss is related to a more traumatic impact of the death, but not to more health problems.*

Contrarily to what is sometimes assumed, problematic relationships do not, as a rule, seem to give rise to a problematic bereavement process. Overt ambivalent feelings with regard to the deceased person do not seem to have a systematic negative influence on adaptation. They mostly implied a less frequent contact and a decreased involvement with the deceased before the loss.

In general, we have to be watchful for strong loss-reactions in the bereaved who report having had a good relationship with the deceased rather than to concentrate on those who report a bad relationship.

• *Good health in a person before the loss indicates less physical and psychological problems afterward.*

Those who report having been in good health before the loss are, as could be expected, less liable to experience health problems during bereavement. This means that, although health is influenced by loss-characteristics, pre-loss health also seems to operate as a resource during bereavement.

• *Bereaved after natural, expected deaths run the same risk of developing health problems in the longer-term after the loss as bereaved after an unnatural, unexpected death.*

The results of this study also indicate that certain aspects may *not* operate as risk-indicators. At four months, only in the spouses are there some differences in the level of adaptation between the modes of death. At fourteen months, however, the adaptation has converged. In the longer run, mode of death does, in itself, not generally appear to be a risk-indicator. More severe dysfunction can be found virtually equally spread over bereaved in all modes of death.

On the other hand there are, to a certain extent, themes in bereavement which are specific to each mode of death. It appears that the history of the relationship with the deceased is likely to differ accordingly. The bereaved after suicide in particular contrast with both other modes of death. On the whole, they are less satisfied and more ambivalent about their relationship with the deceased, and report less frequent contact and less intimate contact in the time before death. Self-blame, although in itself not strongly related to impaired functioning, is a more prominent theme in the process among suicide-bereaved. The themes of questions about the circumstances of death, as well as the reasons and subject of relief and anger may also differ[2].

• *Extreme loss-reactions at four months after the loss are a strong indication of future problems in adaptation, rather than a sign of adequately 'working through' the loss.*

The most important predictor for the level of adaptation on a dimension at fourteen months was the functioning of the bereaved on that same dimension at four months. Our findings lead to the conclusion that a vehement reaction at four months after the loss is not only related to impaired health, but also to more intense reactions in the longer run. A bereaved person showing strong emotional release and intense occupation with the event some months after the loss is, by the lay-public, sometimes seen as evidencing adequate coping with the death. The opposite seems to be true.

---

2   See Chapter 5.

Table 8.1

Risk-indicators for problems with adaptation to the loss, health and social functioning, at four months after the loss, and little or no improvement between four and fourteen months. (Risk indicators for each kinship relationship, listed in cells in order of importance)

	Loss-reactions		Health problems		Social dysfunction	
	High level at 4 months	Little Improvement at 14 months	High level at 4 months	Little Improvement at 14 months	High level at 4 months	Little Improvement at 14 months
Spouses	• Feeling angry • High satisfaction with relationship • Death by suicide or traffic accident	---	• Lack of practical support • Pre-loss physical health problems • Feeling no relief • Death by suicide • Low income	• Lack of practical support	• Death by suicide • Lack of practical support • Feeling angry • Feeling no relief	• Strong ambivalent feelings about deceased • Bad health four months after loss
Parents	• Feeling no relief • Feeling angry • Being the mother of the deceased • Pre-loss physical health problems	• Feeling guilty • Deceased child of other sex	• Feeling angry • Being the mother of the deceased	• Little intimacy with child before loss • Psychological problems before loss	• Low income	---
Siblings	• High satisfaction with relationship • Loss came unexpected • Feeling guilty • Lack of practic. support • Deceased died at younger age	• Bad health four months after the loss	• Other stressors before the loss • Being the sister of the deceased • Lack of practic. support • Frequent contact with sibling	• Deceased died at older age • Death by suicide or illness	---	• Death by traffic-accident or illness
Adult children	• Feeling angry • Freq.contact with parent • Being daughter of the deceased • High satisfaction with relationship • Lack of practic. support	• Deceased was mother of the bereaved	• Pre-loss psychological problems • Lack of practical support • Low income • Deceased of the same sex	• Little ambivalent feelings about deceased • Deceased of the other sex • Bereaved being older	• Lack of practical support • Deceased died at older age	• Frequent contact with deceased before death

This also indicates, on the other hand, that 'working through' the loss may not consist of simply reacting to it in terms of emotional discharge and preoccupation.

What it means to 'work through' a loss is still difficult to define, and differs from author to author on the subject (cf. Stroebe & Stroebe, 1990; Wortman & Silver, 1989). Nonetheless, it seems to comprise at least some form of adaptation of one's cognitions and environment. The line between full awareness of the reality and implications of the loss and obsessive rumination about it is vague. Confronting oneself with the loss may not be for every individual the most adequate road to adaptation, and avoidance of certain reminders may even be considered healthy.

In Table 8.1, the risk-indicators for problematic adaptation are summarized for each of the kinship relationships separately. For each dimension, the cells of the first column contain the indicators for a high level of problems at four months after the loss for each kinship group. Each second column lists indicators (measured at four months after the loss) which predict relatively little improvement or a deterioration of the situation at fourteen months[3]. Within each cell, the indicators for problems after bereavement are listed in order of importance.

Conclusion

This study has resulted in the confirmation of a number of beliefs about the consequences of bereavement and gives rise to doubts about a number of others. Since they were described in detail in this section and the preceding chapter, we will not repeat all of them here.

The most important conclusions to remind here are the finding that quite soon after the loss we can make a reliable estimate about longer term outcome of bereavement, the finding that women who lose their (adult) child run the highest risk for problems in adaptation, the somewhat unexpected finding that sisters of the deceased run a relatively high risk of problems after a loss, and the finding that longer-term risk for problems in the bereavement process appears to be equally spread over different modes of death.

8.5   Some post-hoc comparisons with theory

In this section we will look at our findings against the background of some of the theories we discussed earlier in Chapter 2. Since this study was not undertaken to test any specific theoretical framework, our conclusions can only be tentative.

---

3   For the absolute level of adaptation at fourteen months no risk-indicators are listed here. They differ not considerably from those at four months after the loss, although the predictive power is somewhat smaller. Some variables with a low predictive value at four months do not turn up in the prediction at fourteen months.

Psychoanalytical theory

In view of psychoanalytic notions, we could not retrace certain mechanisms that are claimed to play a role in adaptation. Some of our findings seemingly contradict certain psychoanalytic assumptions.

The conclusion drawn by Van der Wal (1988) that guilt and relief are not related to each other among the suicide and traffic-fatality bereaved also holds true for the long-term illness bereaved. In addition, it appears that guilt feelings about the death are also hardly predictive for longer-term adaptation.

The notion that catharsis (exteriorizing feelings about the loss) facilitates longer-term adaptation is not confirmed by the present study. Strong emotionality and high awareness of the loss, as reflected e.g. in the shock reactions and preoccupation with the loss, were related to more instead of less health problems, also in the longer run.

We must be aware, however, as pointed out by Freud (1955), that psychoanalytic notions must be examined and validated at an individual level. The present study has looked at the relationships between factors in bereavement on a macro rather than on a micro level. Nor was the questionnaire designed to assess the psychoanalytic notions of ambivalence, guilt and relief. We measured overt statements about these feelings, rather than their covert or subconscious presence in the mind of the bereaved.

Psychoanalytic-cognitively oriented theory

The present study provides support for the notion that the extent to which the lost person was an attachment figure for the bereaved determines the intensity of the reactions to the loss. This is reflected in the positions of the formal relationship groups, as well as importance of the closeness of bereaved and deceased before the loss. According to Bowlby (1969), the most important early attachment relationship is the one between mother and child.

From our findings it is clear that to a mother, the loss of a child is almost unbearable. In contrast, we see that adult children generally suffer relatively little from loss of a parent. From the point of view of attachment theory, this is also to be expected, since the attachment to the parent is considered to be important at a young age, while later other attachment relationships become more important. In addition, our study shows that loss of mother in adulthood still elicits somewhat stronger loss-reactions than loss of father, while there is also a smaller decrease in loss-reactions over time in mother-loss in comparison to father-loss.

As we saw in Chapter 7, loss-reactions are also strongly determined by the quality of the relationship with the deceased, and the latter's proximity, which can be seen as attachment. This would also be in line with the predictions of the attachment theory.

Our findings, in terms of the theory, suggest that in the spousal relationship, the woman in marriage may be a more central attachment figure for the man than vice versa.

However, in accordance with Van der Wal (1988) we may state that in contrast to the assumptions of Bowlby (1980, p. 86-92) we did not find anger to be a common emotion in the bereaved, and the scores on the Anger Scale did not follow the 'typical' pattern of reactions to the loss. Neither did strong searching behavior occur frequently. Although it was quite common for the bereaved to have (had) visual and auditive delusions about the deceased still being present, actual searching behavior only occurred in some bereaved who showed signs of psychopathology, with compelling hallucinations and loss of contact with reality. These findings could run counter to Bowlby's proposed similarity in processes between a young child's separation from its mother and grief in the adult person.

Another interpretation is, however, possible. It might be that these behaviors were more common in the first weeks after the loss, and quickly subsided afterward. Since our first interview with the bereaved took place three to four months after the loss, we may have missed this part of the process. On the basis of the present study, no reliable conclusions can be drawn as to whether these behaviors were present at an earlier point in time.

In Marris' (1974) view of bereavement, in order to regain control over the situation after the loss, the bereaved may apply two conflicting strategies: one to delusively return to the time before the loss, the other to forget the loss or to concentrate his or her thoughts on the future.

It would follow from Marris' theory that little sense of control implicates a frequent preoccupation with the deceased. Interestingly, we found lack of a sense of control at fourteen months to be quite strongly related to problems with detachment from the deceased ($r=.40$) and difficulty finding meaning in the loss ($r=.43$). In our study we found decreased sense of control also to be strongly related to decreased psychological health and, to a somewhat lesser extent, to impaired physical health. This may imply that, although intensive 'returning to the time before the loss' in one's imagination might be a way to retain cognitive control, it also proves to be maladaptive in terms of health.

Marris postulated that 'externalizing ambivalence' is one means of proceeding to recovery from the loss. In the present study, we measured the level of (overt) ambivalent feelings with regard to the deceased. No unequivocal relationship was found with adaptation.

The importance of mourning rituals, also stressed by Marris, was not discussed in the present publication. Van den Brink (1989), however, studied funeral rituals in a subsample of the present study (the bereaved after suicide). She found virtually no relationship between the characteristics of these rituals and the different aspects of adaptation at four months after the loss. Thus, this aspect of Marris' theory is not corroborated by the present study.

Cognitive stress theory

A number of the mechanisms proposed by cognitive stress theory can be retraced in the present study. Although the instrument did not include specific questions about different types of appraisal, our observations appear to be in line with Lazarus' views on appraisal of stressful situations.

In the first period after the loss in particular, the bereaved reported quickly changing moods and emotions, which closely paralleled their convictions and uncertainties about their abilities to cope. Numbness, intrusive thoughts, avoidance and various emotional states appeared to alternate quickly, rather than follow a chronological (stage or phase-like) pattern. We found this general picture to be in accordance with Lazarus' stress-coping framework. According to his theory, appraisal of an event may change in rapid succession between perceiving it in as a challenge, threat, or pain, whilst each of these appraisals triggers corresponding emotions.

The different types of appraisal and their consequences for behavior were even more clearly observed in events that followed the loss. Appraisal of social events and activities in terms of threat or pain, rather than challenge was related to being socially more withdrawn. This was particularly clear in bereaved spouses coping with (social) events without the presence of their spouse.

The findings with the Impact of Event Scale show that even in the longer run, the reactions of many bereaved could be labeled in terms of post-traumatic stress disorder. An interesting finding is that high levels of post-traumatic stress are by no means confined to bereaved after unexpected deaths. Although the initial shock reaction is more pronounced in bereaved after a traffic-fatality and suicide, the general level is not much lower in bereaved after an illness. The present study thus shows that bereavement *as such* can be seen as having the characteristics of a psycho-traumatic experience.

Behaviorally oriented theories

As discussed in Section 2.3, behavioral theories generally tend to stress the importance of (social) reinforcement for the course taken in adaptation to a loss.

On first glance, there seems to be support for this in the findings of our study. In the Chapter 7 we saw that the sufficiency of informational and practical support in dealing with the consequences of bereavement is one of the strongest predictors for health problems. As we saw in the preceding section, however, the cause-effect relationship is far from clear

This study provides, however, one finding that corroborates the idea that experiencing sufficient informational and practical support is related to enhanced longer-term health in the those who have lost their spouse. The widowed are the group which, as a rule, faces the most substantial change in living arrangements after the loss, while being confronted with a substantial drop of resources. The widowed who experienced sufficient informational and practical support at four months, even when corrected for their level of health at that point in time[4], ten months later showed a stronger decrease in health problems than those for whom less support was available. This means that even taking into account the relationship between support and health (whatever their cause-effect relationship), the initial level of experienced support had substantial predictive value for longer-term health.

On the basis of the present study, no definitive conclusions can be drawn and it is likely that different mechanisms operate together in the relationship between support and health. We may state, however, that a purely behavioral framework is probably not sufficient to explain our findings.

A sociobiological explanation?

The present study, at a first glance, seems to corroborate some of the assumptions of Littlefield & Rushton (1986). They state that the intensity of grief after bereavement is proportional to the extent to which the chances for 'genetic survival' of the bereaved are impaired.

With regard to the kinship groups, in our sample the rank order predicted by Littlefield & Rushton (see Section 2.4) occurs in most of the areas of functioning. The difference between sexes is in the expected direction for parents, siblings and children, but for the spouses it is unclear, and sometimes the reverse. The relatively high level of reactions among sisters of the deceased does not fit into the picture either.

Littlefield & Rushton's predictions that mothers would grieve more than fathers is confirmed in our findings. Another of their predictions is that healthy children would be more grieved for than unhealthy children. In that case, parents of children who have died in a traffic-fatality would be more affected than those bereaved after other modes of death. This is not confirmed in any way by our results. Also, the assertion that male children are more grieved for than female children is not confirmed by our findings.

---

4   See Table 7.4

We have to question whether the observed differences between the kinship groups are a consequence of the described frustration of genetic survival. First of all, there is a considerable amount of variation in loss-reactions and health within each kinship group. There are sizable systematic differences between the kinship groups and between the sexes in terms of qualities and intimacy of the relationship (see also Table 7.2). This indicates that the explanation is perhaps to be found in these aspects rather than in kinship *per se*. Indeed, we saw that for the bereaved, again within each kinship group, intensity of the loss-reactions is strongly related to the qualities of the relationship and the attitude to the loss. This underlines that, although the hypothesis of the impediment of genetic survival may hold true, its role is probably relatively small in comparison with the importance of relational, sociocultural and personal style aspects. In this respect, a better explanation for our findings can be found in attachment theory.

Task-demands and resources

The framework chosen for the present study was a stress-model which considers functioning after bereavement to be determined by the extent to which a persons resources match the task demands he or she is confronted with. In the present study, we distinguished between functioning in terms of three dimensions: loss-reactions, psychological and physical health, and social functioning.

Since there was no *a priory* assumption about what constitutes a balance or unbalance between demands and resources, it is difficult to test the basic assumptions of the demand-resource model.

It was not, however, our objective to test the model itself, but rather to use it as a tool for categorizing the aspects possibly involved in adaptation after bereavement. In fact, an individual's task demands were not *weighted* against his resources, but both were considered alongside each other in their relationship to adaptation.

Still, we can draw some tentative conclusions about the relative importance of the resources available to a person for coping with the demands he or she faces. There is some divergence between the different dimensions of functioning.

An interesting finding is that magnitude and characteristics of the loss (the task-demands of bereavement) appear to have a stronger influence on some dimensions of functioning than on others. Both loss reactions and health are clearly related to the magnitude of the loss *and* to the resources of the bereaved.

Social functioning, on the other hand, seems to be predominantly related to the resources of the bereaved. This is demonstrated clearly in spousal bereavement. In Chapter 3 we saw already that, for men in particular, the wife is often the most important resource for practical, social and emotional support. In our study, the widowers evidenced the lowest level, and the largest drop in level of social functioning, suggesting that the resource itself was severely affected by the death of their spouse. In other kinship relationships, social functioning is much less determined by the task-demands of bereavement.

A fundamental property of reality, which often poses a problem in social scientific research, remains implicit in most theories, but is clearly demonstrated by the current model. A number of variables cannot unambiguously be assigned to either the demands or the resources, but may operate on different sides, depending on our angle of observation and the time period under study. An example are pre-loss health problems. Bad health of the individual at the time of the loss has been considered here as a concurrent task that has to be attended to: one of the task demands for the bereaved. On the other hand, it may be argued that health operates as a resource for coping with the loss. This means that something which can be seen as a task demand at time t, may operate as a resource at time $t+1$. Health and social functioning may thus be considered as both independent *and* dependent variables of themselves (cf. Rutter, 1985).

Conclusion

Some of the theoretical frameworks we discussed appear to provide a better explanatory framework than others. First of all we must, however, keep in mind that the measures we used have their roots in a primarily cognitive approach of stress and bereavement. This makes that our findings will probably more easily corroborate this framework than others.

The Freudian psychoanalytic view of grief is, for instance, not strongly supported by our findings. It must be noted, though, that this may be partially due to our method of study, which is not the one most suited to make valid judgements about the absence or presence of certain dynamics.

Bowlby's attachment-theoretical point of view appears to fit our data somewhat better. Difficulties after the loss appear to be, for the major part, related to the kinship relationship and the intimacy of and satisfaction with the relationship that was lost. Furthermore, difficulty with detachment was closely related to other functioning. We could not retrace, however, specific behaviors of protest, searching and despair at different stages in this process.

The importance of feeling in control and the different ways of regaining control, stressed both by Marris and Horowitz, can clearly be observed in the present study. The mechanisms by which recovery (according to Marris' theory) takes place could not be found.

No conclusive support could be found for the role of (social) reinforcement claimed by the behaviorally oriented theories. Although this may be one of the mechanisms that operates in adaptation after bereavement, it is clear that it is not sufficient to explain our observations. Likewise, the sociobiological perspective, as forwarded by Littlefield & Rushton, appears to be insufficient to explain the diversity of reactions after loss.

The findings of the present study fail to find many of the dynamic and cathartic mechanisms claimed in grief theory. There may be different reasons why this is the case, some related to the character of the present study, others to the character of grief itself.

In the first place, it is important to note that most theories deal with the dynamics or the *process* of grief. Since our study assessed the *state* of this process in the bereaved, albeit at two points in time, a large part of the process itself remains unobserved. There may, however, also be other reasons involved.

An important reason can be found in our own observations. In contrast to the underlying assumption of many theories, the loss of a family member does not automatically have to be a very *relevant* loss to the bereaved. Particularly those who lost their father or mother, while being parents themselves, were often more preoccupied with other problems than with the loss. Processes like 'externalizing ambivalence', 'experiencing anger and guilt' presuppose that there is a considerable amount of energy invested in the relationship which needs to be neutralized. In the present study, strong anger, guilt and ambivalence were only experienced by a few bereaved. It is therefore possible that there is no *general* need in the bereaved to go through these dynamic and cathartic processes.

Another possible reason is the difficulty to distinguish between cathartic expressions of emotion and expressions that appear to be part of a behavioral repertoire of the bereaved. The latter may be an integrated part of the communication with others and a way to define one's new, 'bereaved' identity. In contrast to cathartic expressions, this way of coping may be counterproductive to recovery. Since both mechanisms appear to work in opposite directions, while pertaining to the same type of behavior, the mixed effects of expressing emotions may remain unclear.

8.6   Practical implications

Most of the bereaved seem to adapt quite well after a loss. We may ask ourselves what is the reason that most of the bereaved adapt favorably, although with some difficulty, and what it is that makes a small group of bereaved evidence severe problems.

The risk-indicators listed above form some points of attention on which post-loss interventions and preventive psychological health care could focus. As we saw, the results point to specific groups, as well as to individual aspects which are related to impaired functioning.

Who needs help?

Looking at kinship to the deceased, we found strong differences in health-risk. Virtually no severe health problems are found in the adult children of the deceased, while, of the ten percent of our sample faring worst, more than half are parents of the deceased. It is obvious that special attention should be given to this group.

For the mothers in particular, grief is not likely to wear off. Depression and somatic complaints are common, and in many cases change little over time. Intervention in this group would probably have to be geared quite explicitly towards help with detachment from their child.

Widowers are at a higher risk for developing health problems and also for becoming socially isolated. To many, their wife was the principal provider of emotional and practical support. With her death, they seem to suffer a loss which affects all areas of their life. More than for widows, their social support network appears to be particularly affected. Widowers quite often had difficulties taking up the daily practical chores which were formerly looked after by their wife. It thus seems that in this group there is a greater need for help at a practical level, as well as interventions aimed at stimulating their practical and social skills.

Special attention should be given to women who lose a brother or sister. Sisters of deceased are a relatively strongly affected, but forgotten group. Especially in our society, their grief may stay in the shadow of that of spouses and parents. Giving more attention to their plight by training professionals and informing the lay public should be considered.

As we saw, not all of the bereaved in these groups are at risk. A number of individual characteristics were found to be related to more severe problems. Experiencing insufficient practical and informational support, looking back on a fulfilling relationship and feeling guilty, angry, and more isolated at three to four months after the loss, are often signs of more severe physical and psychological health problems. The presence of health problems four months after the loss is also a reliable indication for future problems.

At this point, we want to stress the importance of being aware of the health risks in *all* modes of death. Since the circumstances of an unnatural death often appeal strongly to the imagination, we may tend to overemphasize its debilitating long-term impact on the bereaved. Death after an illness, which is a much more frequent phenomenon than unnatural death, may thus be underestimated in its consequences. It is, of course, desirable to be watchful for problems in a family when an accident or suicide has struck. The findings of this study indicate, however, that it is necessary to be as alert for problems after other, more common, natural deaths.

What type of help?

Although much remains to be learned about the effects of different types of support and interventions in the bereaved, the fact that a number of the bereaved express a need for assistance justifies attention to the subject.

A perceived lack of practical and informational support is generally strongly related to problematic adaptation after the loss. However, adequate intervention may not consist of merely providing these types of support. As we saw in Section 8.4, evaluating support as being insufficient may bear little or no relationship to the support that is actually available. The bereaved with more severe problems will probably be less inclined to seek the help of friends or relatives or professional caretakers on their own. Depression and dysfunctional attitudes towards others may render a person sceptical about whether he or she can be helped at all, and impede reception of the support offered. It seems that, the worse the psychological health of the bereaved, the less they are able to organize and profit from the support of others. Without an active, more or less outreaching approach on the part of the environment, it is likely that those who are most in need of help will not receive or profit from it.

The bereaved's attitudes to the loss and coping processes are closely related to the level of dysfunction. Changing dysfunctional attitudes, learning that it is possible to look at the loss and oneself in a different way can take place in different settings.

The first one could of course be the existing social network of the bereaved. In our study, it appeared that support given by familiar sources of support, such as relatives and friends, was readily accepted by most of the bereaved and sufficient for most of them. The type of support was, however, often on a practical and informational level. Emotional support appeared to be given more easily in response to feelings of sadness. The environment generally seemed to have more problems in dealing with anger and guilt in the bereaved. An additional problem to many bereaved was that the other relatives, otherwise an important source of help, were grieving themselves and they felt that extensive talking to them about their own problems would not be appropriate.

For many of those who suffer problems after loss, it seems unnecessary to engage in psychotherapy. It appears that companion self-help groups often provide the necessary informational and emotional support the bereaved need. They offer recognition and understanding of the problems the bereaved is dealing with, but also provide role models of adequate ways to deal with the loss. (cf. De Boer & Van der Wal, 1987; Lund, Caserta, & Dimond, 1989). In our study, these groups formed an important source of support to some bereaved, especially to those who found they needed to talk about the loss, but could or wanted no longer to burden their environment with their pain and grief.

A third source of help are professional caregivers. For a limited number of bereaved, help in an individual or groupwise psychotherapeutical setting is needed. This type of support may deal with dysfunctional attitudes towards the loss most directly, and can be geared toward active detachment from the deceased, bringing about and guiding changes in the bereaved. The focus may also be more explicitly on broader personal change.

Although there seems no need to focus on a specific mode of death when looking for the *presence* of problems, the *type* of problems the bereaved are struggling with may differ considerably. This means that interventions will differ accordingly in terms of themes and contents. This also implies that in groupwise interventions with a goal of sharing experiences, it may prove to be difficult to mix bereaved after, for instance, suicide death and long-term illness death because of differences in preoccupation.

Offering help

This study shows that as early as three or four months after the loss, we may have a fairly good indication of which bereaved are likely to need help. Stable patterns of dealing with the loss have generally crystalized, and appear to change little over time. Adequate early assessment of problems appears possible, and it would be possible to offer interventions to those who need them in a relatively early period after the loss. The question is: do the bereaved want them?

Frequently, we found the bereaved were opposed to seeking help. There was much mistrust about professional psychological health care in particular. Some of this resistance was based on negative stories about experiences of others, in other cases it was the fear of being seen as 'insane' or 'abnormal', or fearful images about what 'happened there'.

We found the social network to be an important mediator between the bereaved and external sources of voluntary or professional help. Many of the bereaved who had sought psychological assistance or took part in companion groups, did so after being stimulated by friends and relatives. The strongest motivator appeared to be accounts of other bereaved who had benefitted from such help.

Bereaved thus appear to benefit most from adequate and detailed information about what types of support are available, handed to them through sources which are seen as reliable. People who are involved in the situation surrounding the death, such as the family doctor, hospital personnel, members of the police force, or the undertaker may play a role in providing the bereaved with adequate information. Although their attention is often directed towards the deceased, and has a more or less 'technical' character, it is important to give the bereaved at least informational support.

In the case of an unnatural death, it is often the police who first get in contact with the bereaved, usually to break the bad news to them. This heavy burden brings at the same time a responsibility and opportunity to be of help to the bereaved family with information about the death, and about possible sources of help[5].

In the case of a natural death, personnel from the hospital or district nursing service may be in the most appropriate position to perform this role. When counselors and volunteer caretakers (such as people from the Hospice movement) are involved in the terminal phase of the illness, follow-up on the bereaved is easier.

A successful initiative of providing adequate informational support in the Netherlands is the 'Guide after a death', a book issued by the Dutch Back-up Center for Bereavement Counselors (LSR). It contains information about all sorts of practical affairs the bereaved may be confronted with after a loss, information about the many aspects of grief, and gives addresses of bodies which can provide assistance in each of these areas. A number of large organizations of undertakers now distribute this book to every bereaved family as part of their standard service.

It is encouraging that, in recent years, more initiatives have developed to provide low threshold structures of bereavement care. A good example of an organization that works well in Great Britain, in this respect, is Cruse, which provides support to the widowed and their children. In the Netherlands, an organization strongly providing informational support to bereaved, as well as people who deal with the bereaved, is the Foundation Dutch Back-up Center for Bereavement Counselors (LSR).

8.7   Limitations of the present study

Some remarks can be made about the limitations and general validity of the present study.

First of all, we must note that the interval between the death and the first interview is relatively long. The bereaved have already gone through a period of changing affects, cognitions and social processes. It may thus be that the state of adaptation of our bereaved at four months is already a more or less crystalized pattern. The finding that the pattern of adaptation does not change very much between four and fourteen months corroborates this. Impaired functioning at four months may be the result of dysfunctional coping strategies during the time before and shortly after the loss and part of this remains hidden from our view.

---

5   For a more elaborate discussion on the role of the police see Van der Wal & Cleiren (1990).

In being a systematic time-sample survey (see Section 4.2) and having a relatively low refusal rate (25%) the present study contrasts favorably with others. Even here though we must be cautious about extending the absolute percentages of bereaved evidencing problematic adaptation to the loss to population figures. The non-response analyses (see Chapter 4) form an indication that the percentage of bereaved showing dysfunction in the population may be higher. In this respect, we can repeat the conclusion of Van der Wal (1988) that the percentages of bereaved evidencing problems in this study form a lower limit for the problems evidenced in the bereaved population.

A possible problem in the present study is the high attrition rate for the second interview among the spouses bereaved after suicide. They did not systematically differ at the first interview in terms of health problems or loss-reactions. This may indicate that there were at least no early signs of impaired functioning for the drop-outs.

The response percentage for first contacts with the families was somewhat lower than for the second step approach of subsequent family members. The exact implications of this are not entirely clear. There were no signs, however, of specific drop-out for a specific mode of death or kinship group. We may thus suspect that most of the comparative analyses between groups are less affected and more generalizable.

A more fundamental problem is the retrospective character of part of the present study. All the aspects of the pre-loss situation were assessed *after* the loss. In particular, the validity of their perspectives on the relationship with the deceased, pre-loss health and resources may be influenced by hindsight bias (cf. Fischoff, 1975). Retrospective assessment of expectation of the loss may also be exaggerated (cf. Campbell & Tesser, 1983). A recent study of pregnancy loss by Toedter et al. (1990) suggests, however, that retrospective assessment hardly leads to bias in ratings of mental health and anxiety (see also Section 8.8)

We do not know to what extent retrospective bias influenced our results. Suspicion is that the magnitude and direction of the bias may differ with individuals, and depend on a number of motivational and cognitive mechanisms.

8.8   Suggestions for further research

As is often the case, the findings of the present study lead to a range of new questions. Here, we will only offer some suggestions for further research, which could clarify some of the preliminary findings here.

In the first place, researchers should be aware that the widowed are not the only, and generally not even the most seriously affected member of a bereaved family. The finding that the widows contrast rather favorably with some other groups is somewhat surprising in view of the fact that widows have up till now been the most elaborately studied group in bereavement research.

• *More comparative, research into the role of relationship to the deceased is desirable. Special attention should be given to cross-cultural differences in this respect*

The present study is one of the first to make a systematic comparison between kinship relationships in the consequences of loss. In the first place, corroboration of the present study is hardly available but necessary.

Cross-cultural study in this area could bring more decisive insight into which aspects have to be ascribed to social role rather than purely genealogical differences between kinship groups. Although the biological position of the kinship relationship is fixed, its social and cultural connotations differ considerably between societies.

• *More attention should be given to the study of bereavement in parents and siblings of the deceased. Future research should in particular concentrate on the detection of mechanisms that lead to dysfunction in mothers and sisters.*

The parents and siblings groups have in common that little large-scale systematic research has hitherto been undertaken, while the present study shows that a considerable percentage may be expected to face long-lasting debilitating effects upon bereavement. In particular, much remains to be learned about the situation of sisters of the deceased. Earlier research among siblings has mostly concentrated on the effects of sibling loss in early childhood. It would be wise to elaborate this to loss of a brother or sister in adult life.

• *In order to better understand the consequences of bereavement, studies should include (non-bereaved) 'surrogate' comparison groups of family members.*

Toedter et al.(1990) recently suggested an interesting method that serves to isolate the effect of bereavement as such, as well as to tackle the problem of retrospectivity in bereavement studies. They applied, what they call, a 'retrospective pretest design' in a study of bereavement-outcome following pregnancy-loss. Their solution to the problem of retrospective assessment of the situation before the loss was to include a 'surrogate comparison group'. They define this as '...a group that has not experienced the traumatic event, but is as similar as possible to what the [bereaved] group was like before the event. Hence a 'surrogate' for the pretest, and a check for the accuracy of retrospective data...' (p. 78). The comparison group was questioned about the same time periods as the bereaved group. The only difference was, that their report on the period of the pregnancy were 'current' data, while those in the loss-group were retrospective data. In their study, Toedter et al.(1990) found virtually no difference between current and retrospective ratings of mental health. It appeared, however, that those in the loss group who had an early suspicion of loss of their child had a biased perception towards a higher level of anxiety during the pregnancy[6].

Especially in suicide and long-term illness bereavement it is not clear to what extent the mental and physical health condition of the bereaved is the consequence of the loss itself. By including the suggested matched 'surrogate' non-bereaved groups in the design, more insight into the role of antecedent stress can be obtained as well. In the case of bereavement after suicide, one may interview a matched group of family members of suicide-attempters, while for bereaved after an illness, a comparison group of family members of chronically ill may be selected.

- *Where possible, prospective survey research of the consequences of bereavement should be effected.*

Most importantly, prospective research of the consequences of loss would lead to a more reliable assessment of risk-indicators. Systematical prospective, observational, in-depth study of interaction patterns between bereaved and terminally ill, the qualities of their relationship, and the health condition before the loss, might also afford a better view on the sources of problems after bereavement.

Families where a member suffers from a probably fatal disease are virtually the only target group where prospective research of this type seems feasible. There is the possibility to follow the family members throughout the time of the illness and the dying process, as well as bereavement. Even communication patterns between bereaved and terminally could be studied in observation, for instance to assess the structure of the relationship and ambivalent feelings. Research in this area remains, however, a very delicate and difficult enterprise and is subject to ethical questions.

Even more difficult is the prospective study of sudden, unexpected losses. Although important, for many researchers prospective research of bereavement after sudden losses and unnatural modes of death remains a noble wish, since both in terms of cost and time investment, this is often hardly feasible.

One possibility to prospectively study the consequences of sudden, unexpected losses would be to base a study of bereavement on a bereaved subsample of large population samples which are followed through time, like in ongoing national survey programs. This type of study may contain subsamples who become bereaved during

---

6   Similarly, we may suspect that this bias will be more likely to occur in those who lost someone after an illness which in the later stages appeared to be fatal. In the case of long-term illness, we thus could still opt for a longitudinal, prospective method.

or after the time of the study. Under condition that valid measures of physical and mental health form an integral part of these studies, these data may be combined with a more elaborate survey concentrating on bereavement. This type of prospective design, necessarily, offers less specific information about the pre-loss period than the retrospective pretest design mentioned above. In general, it is thus difficult to tell whether a prospective method is to be preferred over the use of surrogate comparison groups. The choice for one design or the other will depend on the specific interest of the researcher, as well as the means in terms of time and money available for the study.

References

American Psychiatric Association (1987) *Diagnostic and Statistical Manual of Mental Disorders.* (Third revised edition). Washington D.C.: American Psychiatric Association.

Archer, J. (1988) The sociology of bereavement: a reply to Littlefield & Rushton. *Journal of Personality and Social Psychology, 55(2)*, 272-278.

Arens, D.A. (1982-1983) Widowhood and well-being: an examination of sex differences within a causal model. *International Journal Aging and Human Development, 15*, p 1.

Atchley, R.C. (1975) Dimensions of widowhood in later life. *The Gerontologist, 15*, 176-178.

Averill, J.R. (1968) Grief: its nature and significance. *Psychological Bulletin, 70*, 721-748.

Averill, J.R. & Nunley, E.P. (1988) Grief as an emotion and as a disease: a social-constructionist perspective. *Journal of Social Issues, 44(3)*, 79-95.

Babri, K.B., & Kitson, G.C. (1988) *Who's worse off? Economic problems and mental health consequences for widowed and divorced women.* Case Western University, unpublished.

Bahr, H.M., & Harvey, C.D. (1980) Correlates of morale among the newly widowed. *Journal of Social Psychology, 110*, 219-233.

Balkwell, C. (1981) Transition to widowhood. *Family Relations, 30*, 117.

Ball, J. F. (1976-1977) Widow's grief: The impact of age and mode of death. *Omega, 7(4)*, 307-333.

Bank, S.P., & Kahn, M.D. (1982) *The sibling bond.* New York: Basic Books.

Bankoff, E.A. (1985) Aged parents and their widowed daughters: a support relationship. *Journal of Gerontology, 38*, 226-230.

Baron, R.S., Cutrona, C.E., Hicklin, D., Russell, D.W. & Lubaroff, D.M. (1990) Social support and immune function among spouses of cancer partients. *Journal of Personality and Social Psychology, 59(2)*, 344-352.

Barraclough, B.M., Holding, T., & Fayers, P. (1976) Influence of coroners' officers and pathologists on suicide verdicts. *British Journal of Psychiatry, 128*, 471-474.

Barraclough, B.M., & Shepherd, D.M. (1976) Public interest: private grief. *British Journal of Psychiatry, 129*, 109-113.

Barraclough, B.M. & Shepherd, D. M. (1977) The immediate and enduring effects of the inquest on relatives of suicides. *British Journal of Psychiatry, 131*, 400-404.

Barrett, C.J., & Schneweis, K.M. (1980-1981) An empirical search for the stages of widowhood *Omega,11(2)*, 97-104.

Barrett, T.W., & Scott, T.B. (1987) *Suicide vs other bereavement recovery patterns.* Paper presented at the combined meeting of the American Association of Suicidology and the International Association for Suicide Prevention. San Francisco

Beck, A.T., & Beck, R.W. (1972) Screening depressed patients in family practice. *Postgraduate Medicine, december,* 81-85.

Beekman, A.J. & Maillette de Buy Wenniger, W.F. (1989) De betekenis voor life-events in de anamnese en in het bijzonder het verlies van een ouder tijdens de puberteit. *Tijdschrift voor Psychiatrie, 31(6).*

Berardo, F.M. (1968) Widowhood status in the United States: perspective on a neglected aspect of the family life-cycle. *The Family Coordinator, 17,* 191-203.

Berardo, F.M. (1970) Survivorship and social isolation: the case of the aged widower. *The Family Coordinator, 19,* 11-25.

Bertalanffy, L. von (1952) Theoretical Models in Biology & Psychology. In: D. Krech & G.S. Klein, *Theoretical Models and Personality Theory.* Durham: Duke University Press.

Bertalanffy, L. von (1968) *General Systems Theory.* New York: Braziller.

Biewenga, H. (1989) *De betekenis van het geloof en de kerkelijke gemeente bij rouwverwerking.* Paper to obtain masters degree. Leiden, unpublished

Bloom, B.L., Asher, S.J., & White, S.W. (1978) Marital disruption as a stressor: a review and analysis. *Psychological Bulletin, 85,* 867-894.

Boer, O.F. de, & Wal, J. van der (1987) *Geholpen worden door te helpen. Een onderzoek naar het functioneren van rouwgroepen.* Rapport voor het Landelijk Steunpunt Rouwbegeleiding, Vakgroep Klinische en Gezondheids Psychologie, Leiden University.

Bogdan, R.C. & Knopp Biklen, S. (1982) *Qualitative research for education.* Boston

Bojanovsky, J. & Bojanovsky, A. (1976) Zur Risikozeit des Selbstmordes bei Geschiedenen und Verwitweten. *Nervenarzt, 47,* 307-309.

Bolton, Ch. & Camp, D.J. (1986-1987) Funeral rituals and the facilitation of grief work. *Omega,17,* 343-352.

Bornstein, P.E., Clayton, P.J., Halikas, J.A, et.al. (1973) The depression of widowhood after thirteen months. *British Journal of Psychiatry, 122,* 561-566.

Bouman, T.K., Luteyn, F., Albersnagel, F.A., & Ploeg, F.A.E. van der (1985) Enige ervaringen met de Beck Depression Inventory (BDI). *Gedrag, 13,* 13-24.

Bourke, M.P (1984) The continuum of pre- and post-bereavement grieving. *British Journal of Medical Psychology, 57,* 121-125.

Bowlby, J. (1969) *Attachment and Loss. Vol.1: Attachment.* New York: Basic Books.

Bowlby, J. (1980) *Attachment and Loss. Vol 3: Loss Sadness and Depression.* New York: Basic Books.

Bowling, A. (1987) Mortality after bereavement: a review of the literature on survival periodsnd factors affecting survival. *Social Sciences Med. ,24(2) ,* 117-124.

Boyden, S. (1987) *The biological basis of Western civilisation.* Oxford: Oxford University Press.

Breckenridge, J.N., Gallagher, D., Thompson, L. W. Peterson, J. (1986) Characteristic depressive symptoms of bereaved elders. Journal of *Gerontology, 41(2),* 163-168.

Brink, M. v.d. (1989) *Houvast bij afscheid. Een onderzoek naar de waardering van het uitvaartritueel door nabestaanden van suicideslachtoffers.* Leiden paper to obtain masters degree (unpublished).

Brom, D. & Kleber, R.J. (1985) De Schok Verwerkings Lijst. *Nederlands Tijdschrift v.d. Psychologie, 40*, 164-168.

Brown, G.W., & Harris, T. (1978) *Social origins of depression: a study of psychiatric disorder in women.* New York: Free Press.

Bugen, L.A. (1977) Human grief: a model for prediction and intervention. *Journal of Orthopsychiatry, 47*, 196-206.

Bunch, J. (1972) Recent bereavement in relation to suicide. *Journal of Psychosomatic Research, 16*, 361-366.

Burks, V.K., Lund, D.A., Gregg, C.H. & Bluhm, H.P. (1988) Bereavement and remarriage for older adults. *Death Studies, 12*, 51-60.

Calabrese, J.R., Kling, M.A., Gold, P.W. (1987) Alterations in immunocompetence during stress, bereavement and depression: focus on neuroendocrine regulation. *American Journal of Psychiatry, 144(9)*, 1123-1134.

Campbell, J. M. (1988) *The role of hardiness and self-actualisation level in resolution of grief.* Paper presented at the Second International Conference on Grief and Bereavement in Contemporary Society. London, 12th-15 July.

Campbell, J.D. & Tesser, A. (1983) Motivational interpretations of hindsight bias: an individual difference analysis. *Journal of Personality, 54(4)*, 605-620.

Carey, R. G. (1977) The widowed: A year later. *Journal of Counseling Psychology, 24(2)*,125-131.

Carey, R. G. (1979-1980) Weathering widowhood: Problems and adjustment of the widowed during the first year. *Omega, 10(2)*, 163-174.

Carlson, M. & Miller, N. (1987) Explanatioon of the relation between negative mood and helping. *Psychological Bulletin, 102(1)* , 91-108.

Carr, A.C. (1975) Bereavement as a relative experience. In: B. Schoenberg,I. Gerber, A. Wiener e.a. (Eds.), *Bereavement. Its psychosocial aspects.* New York: Columbia University Press.

Caserta, M.S., Lund, D. A., Dimond, M. F. (1985) Assessing interviewer effects in a longitudinal study of bereaved elderly adults. *Journal of Gerontology, 40(5)*, 637-640.

Caserta, M.S., Lund, D. A., Dimond, M. F. (1989) Older widows early bereavement adjustments. *Journal of Women and Aging, 1(4)*, 5-27.

Caserta, M.S., Lund, D. A., Dimond, M. F. (1990) Understanding the context of perceived health ratings: the case of spousal bereavement in later life. *Journal of Aging Studies, 4*, 231-243.

Centraal Bureau voor Statistiek (1984) *De leefsituatie van de Nederlandse bevolking 1980. Kerncijfers.* Den Haag, Staatsuitgeverij/CBS-publikaties.

Central Bureau of Statistics (1980) *Statistical Yearbook of the Netherlands 1979.* The Hague: Staatsuitgeverij.

Central Bureau of Statistics (1983) *Statistical Yearbook of the Netherlands 1982.* The Hague: Staatsuitgeverij.

Central Bureau of Statistics (1986) *Statistical Yearbook of the Netherlands 1985.* The Hague: Staatsuitgeverij/cbs-publications.

Central Bureau of Statistics (1989) *Statistical Yearbook of the Netherlands 1988.* The Hague, Staatsuitgeverij/SDU Publishers/CBS-publications.

Clayton, P., Halikas, J., & Maurice, W.L. (1972) The depression of widowhood. *British Journal of Psychiatry, 120,* 71-78.

Clayton, P.J. (1982) Bereavement. In: Paykel, E.S. (Ed.) *Handbook of affective disorders.* London: Churchill Livingstone.

Clayton, P.J., Halikas, J.A., Maurice, W.L., & Robins, E. (1973) Anticipatory Grief and Widowhood. *British Journal of Psychiatry, 122,* 47-51.

Clayton, P.J., Herjanic, M., Murphy, G.E., Woodruff, R. (1974) Mourning and depression: Their similarities and differences. *Canadian Psychiatric Association Journal , 19(3)* 309-312.

Cleiren, M.P.H.D. (1986) *De dynamiek van waarneming en konstruktie. Een interaktioneel model voor aandacht.* Leiden: paper to obtain masters degree, unpublished.

Cleiren, M.P.H.D. (1988) Anticipatie op een overlijden: een onderzoek naar rouw na een langdurige ziekte. *Nieuwsbrief LSR, 3/4,* december 1988. LSR-Diemen.

Cleiren, M.P.H.D. (1988) *Death after a long term disease: effects on the bereaved.* Paper presented at the International Conference on Grief and Bereavement In Contemporary Society. London, 12th-15th July 1988.

Cleiren, M.P.H.D. (1988) Leven met MEN-2A In: *Gebundelde lezingen Landelijke Dag MEN-2A.* Utrecht: STOET.

Cleiren, M.P.H.D. (1988) *MEN-2, Leven met een erfelijke vorm van kanker. Een onderzoek naar de ervaringen en behoeften van MEN-2A patiënten.* Report for the Foundation for the Detection of Hereditary Tumors. Utrecht: STOET.

Cleiren, M.P.H.D. (1989) Behoefte aan hulpinitiatieven bij nabestaanden. *Nieuwsbrief LSR, 4 (december),* 11-13.

Cleiren, M.P.H.D. (1989) Enkele ideeën over pathologische versus normale rouw. *Nieuwsbrief LSR, 3 (september),* 22-24.

Cleiren, M.P.H.D. & Wal, J. van der (1987) Het Leidse Nabestaandenprojekt: rouw in kaart gebracht. *Nieuwsbrief LSR, 0.*

Cleiren, M.P.H.D., Wal, J. van der, & Diekstra, R.F.W. (1988a) Death after a long term disease: anticipation and outcome in the bereaved. Part I. *Pharos International, 54 (3),* 112-114.

Cleiren, M.P.H.D., Wal, J. van der, & Diekstra, R.F.W. (1988b) Death after a long term disease: anticipation and outcome in the bereaved. Part II. *Pharos International, 54(4),* 136-139.

Cohen, J (1977) *Statistical power analysis for the behavioral sciences.* New York & London: Academic Press.

Cowan, M. E., Murphy, S.A. (1985) Identification of postdisaster bereavement risk predictors. *Nursing Research , 34(2),* 71-75.

Coyne, J.C., Aldwin, C., Lazarus, R.S. (1981) Depression and Coping in stressful episodes. *Journal of Abnormal Psychology, 90(5),* 439-447.

Coysh, W.S., Johnston, J.R., Tschann, J.M., Wallerstein, J.S. & Kline, M. (1989) Parental postdivorce adjustment in joint and sole physical custody families. *Journal of Family Issues, 10,* 52-71.

Cronbach, L.J. (1975) Beyond the two disciplines of scientific psychology. *American Psychologist, 34,* 141-150.

Demi, A.S. (1984) Social adjustment of widows after a sudden death: suicide and non-suicide survivors compared. *Death Education, 8,* 91-111.

Diekstra, R.F.W. (1990) Jobstress en gezondheid in de gezondheidszorg: implicaties van het coherentiemodel. *Gedrag en Gezondheid, 17(4),* 155-161.

Diekstra, R.F.W. (1991) *Bedreigde jeugd?* Wetenschappelijke Raad voor het Regeringsbeleid, Den Haag.

Dill, D., Feld, E. Martin, J., Beukema, S., & Belle, D. (1980) The impact of the environment on the coping efforts of low-income mothers. *Family Relations, 29,* 503-509.

Dimond, M.N., Lund, D.A., Caserta, M.S. (1987) The role of social support in the first two years of bereavement in an elderly sample. *The Gerontologist, 27(5),* 599-604.

Dirken, J.M. (1969) *Arbeid en stress: het vaststellen van aanpassingsproblemen in werksituaties.* Groningen: Wolters.

Dowling, W.J. & Roberts K. (1974) The Historical and Philosophical Background of Cognitive Approaches to Psychology. In: Carterette, E.C., & Friedman, M.P., (Eds.) *Handbook of Perception, Vol 1.* New York: Academic Press.

Duckit, J. (1984) Social support, personality and the prediction of psychological distress: an interactionist approach *Journal of Clinical Psychology, 40(5),* 1199-1205.

Edwards, A.L. & Cronbach, L.J. (1952) Experimental design for research in psychotherapy *Journal of Clinical Psychology, 8,* 51-59.

Egmond, M. van (1988) De beoordeling van suiciderisico door de huisarts. Leiden: doctoral dissertation.

Egmond, M. van, Diekstra, R., & De Graaf, A.C. (1983) Suicide onder patiënten in de huisartsenpraktijk. *Tijdschrift voor Sociale Gezondheidszorg, 61,* 934-937.

Elizur, E., & Kaffman, M. (1983) Factors influencing the severity of childhood bereavement reactions. *American Journal of Orthopsychiatry, 53(4),* 668-676.

Farberow, N.L., Gallagher, D.E., Gilewski, M.J. & Thompson, L.W. (1987) An examination of the early impact of bereavement on psychological distress in survivors of suicide. *The Gerontologist,* in press

Farnsworth, J., Pett, M.A. & Lund, D.A. (1989) Predictors of loss-management and well-being in later life widowhood and divorce. *Journal of Family Issues, 10(1),* 102-121.

Feinson, M.C. (1986) Aging widows and widowers: are there mental health differences? *Int. Journal of Aging and Human Development, 23(4),* 241-255.

Fish, W.C. (1986) Differences of grief intensity in bereaved parents. In: T.A. Rando (Ed.), *Parental loss of a child.* Champain, Illinois: Research Press.

Fischhoff, B (1975) Hindsight ≠ foresight: the effect of outcome knowledge on judgement under uncertainty. *Journal of Experimental Psychology: Human Perception and Performance, Vol. 1(3),* 288-299.

Flesh, R. (1977) Mental health and bereavement by accident or suicide: a preliminary report. In: Danto, B.L & Kutscher, (Eds.) *Suicide and bereavement.* New York: Information Corporation.

Forceville-van Rossum, J. (1978) *Dagen van na-bestaan. Dagboek van een rouwproces.* Baarn: Ambo Uitgeverij.

Forceville-van Rossum, J. (1982) *Oud blauw. Dagen van voort-bestaan.* Baarn: Ambo Uitgeverij
Forgus, R. en Shulman, B.H. (1979) *Personality: A Cognitive View.* London: Prentice-Hall.
Fransella, F., (Ed.) (1981) *Personality; theory, measurement and research.* New York: Methuen.
Freud, S. (1955) »Psychoanalyse« und »Libidotheorie« In: *Gesammelte Werke, Vol 13. Werke aus den Jahren 1909-1913.* London: Imago Publ. Co..
Freud, S. (1957) Mourning and Melancholia. In: J. Strachey (Ed.), *The standard edition of the complete psychological works of Sigmund Freud. Vol 14.* London: Hogarth Press.
Friedman, S.A., Chodoff, P., Mason, J.W., & Hamburg, D.A. (1963) Behavioural observations on parents anticipating the death of a child. *Pediatrics, 23,* 610-625.
Fulton, R., & Gottesman, D.J. (1980) Anticipatory grief: a psychosocial concept reconsidered. British Journal of Psychiatry, 137, 45-54.
Gallagher D.E., Breckenridge J.N., Thompson L.W. & Peterson J.A. (1983) Effects of bereavement on indicators of mental health in elderly widows and widowers. *Journal of Gerontology, 8(5),* 565-71.
Gass, K.A., & Chang, A.S. (1989) Appraisals of bereavement, coping, resources, and psychological health dysfunction in widows and widowers. *Nursing Research, 38(1),* 31-36.
Gauthier, J., & Marshal, W.L. (1977) Grief: a cognitive-behavioral analysis. *Cognitive Therapy Research, 1,* 39-44.
Gazendam, A. & Egmond, M.van, (1987) De validiteit van de VOEG onderzocht bij een groep depressieve vrouwelijke patienten in de huisartspraktijk. *Nederlands Tijdschrift voor de Psychologie, 42,* 149-152.
Geer, J.P. van de. (1985) *HOMALS* University of Leiden, Department of data theory.
Gentry, M. & Schulman, A.D. (1988) Remarriage as a coping response for widowhood. *Psychology and Aging, Vol.3(2),* 191-196.
Gerber, I., Rusalem, R., Hannon, N., Battin, D., Arkin, A. (1975) Anticipatory grief and aged widows and widowers. *Journal of Gerontology, 30,* 225-229.
Gifi, A. (1985) *PRINCALS.* University of Leiden, department of data theory.
Glick, I.O., Weiss, R.S., & Parkes, C.M. (1974) *The first year of bereavement.* New York: Wiley.
Gove, W.R. (1972a) Sex, marital status and suicide. *Journal of Health and Social Behavior, 13,* 204-213.
Gove, W.R. (1972b) The relationship between sex roles, marital roles and mental illness. *Social Forces, 51,* 34-44.
Gove, W.R. & Shin, H.C. (1989) The psychological well-being of divorced and widowed men and women. An empirical analysis. *Journal of Family Issues, 10(1)* , 122-144.
Greenblatt, M. (1978) The grieving spouse. *American Journal of Psychiatry, 135,* 43-47.
Greene, R.W. & Feld, S. (1989) Social support coverage and the well-being of elderly widows and married women. *Journal of Family Issues,10(1),* 33-51.
Hansson, R.O. & Remondet, J.H. (1988) Old age and widowhood: issues of personal control and independance. *Journal of Social Issues, 44 (3).* 159-174.
Hansson, R. O., Stroebe, M.S., & Stroebe, W. (1988) In conclusion: current themes in bereavement and widowhood research. *Journal of Social Issues, 44 (3),* 207-216.

Hardt, D.V. (1978-1979) An investigation of the stages of bereavement. *Omega, 9(3)*, 279-285.

Harré, R. (1978) Accounts, actions and meanings- the practice of participatory psychology. In: M. Brenner, P. Marsh & M. Brenner, *The social contexts of method*. London.

Harvey, C.D. & Bahr, H.M. (1974) Widowhood, morale and affiliation. *Journal of Marriage and the Family, 36*, 97-106.

Hays, W.L. (1981) *Statistics*. New York: Holt Rinehar & Winston.

Helsing K.J., Comstock G.W. & Szklo M. (1982) Causes of death in a widowed population. *American Journal of Epidemiology, 116(3)*, 524-532.

Helsing, K.J., & Szklo, M. (1981) Mortality after bereavement. *American Journal of Epidemiology, 114*, 41-52.

Henslin, J.M. (1970) Guilt and guilt neutralization: response and adjustment to suicide. In: Douglas, J.D. (Ed.) *Deviance and responsability: The social construction of moral meanings*. New York: Basic Books.

Hettema, P.J. (1979) *Personality and Adaptation*. Amsterdam: North-Holland.

Heyman, D.K., & Gianturco, D.T. (1973) Long-term adaptation by the elderly to bereavement. *Journal of Gerontology, 28*, 359-362.

Hilgard, E.R., Atkinson, R.L., & Atkinson, R.C. (1979) *Introduction to Psychology, 7th edition*. New York: Harcourt Brace Jovanovich.

Hill, C.D., Thompson, L.W., & Gallagher, D. (1988) The role of anticipatory bereavement in older women's adjustment to widowhood. *The Gerontologist, 28(6)*, 792-796.

Hinton J. (1971) *Dying*. Aylesbury: Pelican Books.

Hobfoll, S.E. (1989) Conservation of resources. A new attempt at conceptualizing stress. *American Psychologist, 44(3)*, 513-524.

Holahan, C.J., & Moos, R.H. (1986) Personality, coping and family resources in stress resistance: a longitudinal analysis. *Journal of Personality and Social Psychology, 51*, 389-395.

Horowitz, M.J. (1979) Psychological response to serious life events. In: H.J. Parad, H.L.P. Resnik, & L.G. Parad (Eds.), *Emergency and disaster management: a mental health sourceback*. Bowie, Maryland: Charles Press, 259-269.

Horowitz, M.J. (1989) A model of mourning: change in schemas of self and other. *Journal of the American Psychoanalytic Asosciation, 38(2)*, 297-324.

Horowitz, M.J., Wilner, N., & Alvarez, W. (1979) Impact of Event Scale: a measure of subjective stress. *Psychosomatic medicine, 41*, 209-218.

Horowitz, M.J., Wilner, N. , Kaltreider, N., & Alvarez, W. (1980) Signs and symptoms of posttraumatic stress disorder. *Archives of General Psychiatry, 37*, 85-92.

Hosman, C.M.H. (1983) *Psychosociale problematiek en hulpzoeken. Een sociaal epidemiologische studie ten behoeve van de preventieve geestelijke gezondheidszorg*. Lisse: Swets & Zeitlinger.

Huston, P.E. (1971) Neglected approach to cause and treatment of psychotic depression. *Archives of General Psychiatry, 24*, 505-508.

Hyman, H. H. (1983) *Of time and widowhood: nationwide studies of enduring effects*. Durham North Carolina: Duke University Press, Duke Press Policy Studies.

Ipso Facto (1987) *Leren leven met het Damoclessyndroom*. Leiden: Stichting Ipso Facto.

Irwin, M., Daniels, M., Weiner, H. (1987) Immune and neuroendocrine changes during bereavement. *Psychiatric Clinics of North America, 10*, 449-465.

Jacobs, S.C., Brown, S.A., Mason, J., Wahby, V., Kasl S.V., & Ostfeld, A.M. (1986) Psychological distress, depression and prolactin response in stressed persons. *Journal of Human Stress, Fall 1986*, 113-118.

Jacobs, S.C., Kosten, T.R. ,Kasl, S.V., Ostfeld, A.M., Berkman, L., Charpentier, P. (1987-1988) Attachment theory and multiple dimensions of grief. *Omega, Vol.18(1)*, 41-53.

Jacobs, S.C., Mason, J.W., Kosten, T.R., Kasl, S.V., Ostfeld, A.M., & Wahby, V.S. (1987) Urinary free cortisol and separation anxiety early in the course of bereavement and threatened loss. *Biological Psychiatry, 22*, 148-152.

Jacobs, S., Kasl, S., Ostfeld, A. ,Berkman, L., Charpentier, P. (1986) The measurement of grief: age and sex variation. *British Journal of Medical Psychology, 59*, 305-310.

Jacobs, S., Nelson, J.C., & Zisook, S. (1987) Treating depressions of bereavement with antidepressants. *Psychiatric Clinics of North America, 10*, 501-510.

Janoff-Bullman, R. & Frieze, I.H. (1983) A theoretical perspective for understanding reactions to victimization. *Journal of Social Issues, 39*, 1-17.

Johnson, R.J., Lund, D.A., Dimond, M.F. (1986) Stress, self esteem, and coping during bereavement among the elderly. *Social Psychology Quarterly, 49*, 273-279.

Jones, D.R. (1987) Heart disease mortality following widowhood: some results of the OPCS longitudinal study. *Journal of Psychosomatic Research, 31*, 325-333.

Kaffman, M. & Elizur, E. (1983) Bereavement responses of kibbutz and non-kibbutz children following the death of the father. Journal of Child *Psychology & Psychiatry & Allied Disciplines , 24(3)*, 435-442.

Kaffman, M. & Elizur, E. (1984) Children's bereavement reactions following death of the father. Special Issue: Family psychiatry in the kibbutz. *International Journal of Family Therapy , 6(4)*, 259-283.

Kaprio J., Koskenvuo M. & Rita, H. (1987) Mortality after bereavement: A Prospective Study of 95.647 Widowed Persons. *American Journal of Public Health, 77*, 283-287.

Kastenbaum, R. (1969) Death and bereavement in later life. In: A.H. Kutsher (Ed.), *Death and bereavement*. Springfield, Illinois: C.J. Thomas.

Kelly, G.A. (1963) *A Theory of Personality: The Psychology of Personal Constructs*. New York: Norton.

Kerkhof, A.J.F.M. (1985) *Suicide en de geestelijke gezondheidszorg*. Lisse: Swets & Zeitlinger.

Kessler, R.C., Price, R.H., & Wortman, C.B. (1985) Social factors in psychopathology: Stress, social support and copin processes. *Annual Review Psychology, 36*, 531-572.

Kim, J. & Mueller, C.W. (1978) *Introduction to factor analysis. What it is and how to do it*. Beverly Hills: Sage publications.

Kitson, G.C., Babri, K.B.,Roach, M.J., Placidi, K.S. (1989) Adjustment to widowhood and divorce. *Journal of Family Issues, 10(1)*, 5-32.

Kitson G.C. & Zyzanski S.J. (1987) Grief in widowhood and divorce. *Psychiatric Clinics of North America ,10(3)*, 369-86.

Kivett, V.R. (1978) Loneliness and the rural widow. *Family Coordinator, 27(4)*, 249-258.

Klass, D. (1986-1987) Marriage and divorce among bereaved parents in a self-help group. *Omega, Vol. 17(3)*, 237-249.

Klass, D. (1987) John Bowlby's model of grief and the problem of identification. *Omega, 18(1)*, 13-32.

Kleber, R., Brom, D., Defares, P.B. (1986) *Traumatische ervaringen, gevolgen en verwerking*. Lisse: Swets & Zeitlinger.

Knapp, R.J. (1987) When a child dies. *Psychology Today, July*, 60-67.

Kobasa, S.C., & Puccetti, M.C. (1986) Personality and Social resources in stress resistance. *Journal of Personality and Social Psychology, 45*, 839-850.

Koocher, G.P. (1986) Coping with a death from cancer. *Journal of Counseling & Clinical Psychology, 54*, 623-631.

Krant, M.J., & Johnson, L. (1978) Family members' perceptions of communication in late stage cancer. *International Journal of Psychiatry in Medicine, 8*, 203-216.

Kraus, A.S., & Lilienfeld, A.M. (1959) Some epidemiological aspects of the high mortality rate in the young widowed group. *Journal of Chronic Diseases, 10*, 207-217.

Kübler-Ross, E. (Ed.) (1982) *Reif werden zum Tode*. Gütersloher Verlagshaus Mohn.

Lakey, B., & Cassady, P.B. (1990) Cognitive processes in perceived social support. *Journal of Personality and Social Psychology, 59(2)*, 337-343.

Lane, R.D., Jacobs, S.C., Mason, J.W., Wahby, V.S., Kasl, S.V., & Ostfeld, A.M. (1987) Sex differences in prolactin change during mourning. *Journal of psychosomatic research, 31*, 375-383.

Laudenslager, M. M. (1988) The psychobiology of loss: lessons from humans and nonhuman primates. *Journal of Social Issues, 44 (3)* ,175-190.

Lazarus, R.S. (1966) *Psychological stress and the coping process*. New York: McGraw-Hill.

Lazarus, R.S. (1967) *Patterns of Adjustment* (Third edition). New York: McGraw-Hill.

Lazarus, R.S., & Folkman, S. (1984) *Stress, appraisal and coping*. New York: Springer Publishing.

Lazarus, R.S., & Launier, R. (1978) Stress-related transactions between person and environment. In: Pervin, L.A., & Lewis (Eds.), *Perspectives in Interactional Psychology*. New York: Plenum Press.

Lehman, L.R., Wortman, C.B., Williams, A.F. (1987) Long-term effects of losing a spouse or child in a motor vehicle crash. *Journal of Personality and Social Psychology, 52*, 218-231.

Levav, I. (1982) Mortality and psychopathology following the death of an adult child: An epidemiological review. *Israel Journal of Psychiatry & Related Sciences ,19(1)*, 23-38.

Levav, I., Friedlander, Y. , Kark, J.D., Peritz, E. (1988) An epidemiologic study of mortality among bereaved parents. *New England Journal of Medicine, 319(8)* , 457-461.

Lewinsohn, P.M., Hoberman, H., Teri, L. & Hantzinger, M. (1985) An integrative theory of depression. In: S. Reiss & R. Bootzin *Theoretical issues in behavior therapy*. Orlando, FL.: Academic Press.

Liem, R., & Liem, J.V. (1978) Social class and mental illness reconsidered: the role of economic stress and social support. *Journal of Health and Social Behavior, 19*, 139-156.

Lindemann, E. (1944) Symptomatology and management of acute grief. *American Journal of Psychiatry, 101,* 141-148.

Lipowski, Z.J. (1973) Life events as stressors: a methodological inquiry. *Comprehensive Psychiatry, 14 (3),* 203-215.

Littlefield, C.H., & Rushton, J.P. (1986) When a child dies: the sociobiology of bereavement. *Journal of Personality and social psychology, 51,* 797-802.

Lopata, H.Z. (1972) Social relations of widows in urbanizing societies. *Sociological Quarterly, 13,* 259-271.

Lopata, H.Z. (1973a) Living through widowhood. *Psychology Today, 7,* 87-92.

Lopata, H.Z. (1973b) *Widowhood in an American city.* Morristown, New Jersey: General Learning Press.

Lopata, H.Z. (1979) *Women as widows: support systems.* New York: Elsevier.

Lopata, H.Z. (1988) Support systems of American widowhood. *Journal of Social Issues, 44,(3) ,* 113-128.

Lund D.A., Caserta, M.S., Dimond, M.F. (1986) Gender differences through two years of bereavement among the elderly. *The Gerontologist, Vol. 26(3),* 314-320.

Lund D.A., Caserta, M.S., Dimond, M.F. (1988) A comparison of bereavement adjustments between Mormon and non-Mormon older adults. *Journal of Religion and Aging, 5,* 75-92.

Lund D.A., Caserta, M.S., & Dimond, M.F. (1989) *Effectiveness of self-help groups for older bereaved spouses.* Paper presented at the 42nd annual meeting of the Gerotological Society of America, Minneapolis, Minnesota, November 17-21, 1989.

Lund D.A., Caserta, M.S., Dimond, M.F., Gray, R.M. (1986) Impact of bereavement on the self-conceptions of older surviving spouses. *Symbolic Interaction, 9(2),* 235-244.

Lund D.A., Caserta, M.S., van Pelt, J., Gass, K.A. (1990) Stability of social support networks after later-life spousal bereavement. *Death Studies, 14,* 53-73.

Lund, D.A., Dimond, M.F., Caserta, M.S., Johnson, R.J., Poulton, J.L. & Connelly, J.R. (1985-1986) Identifying elderly with coping difficulties after two years of bereavement. *Omega, 16,* 213-224.

Lund, D.A. (Ed.), (1989) *Older bereaved spouses: research with practical implications.* New York: Hemisphere.

Lundin, T. (1984a) Morbidity following sudden and unexpected bereavement. *British Journal of Psychiatry,144,* 84-88.

Lundin, T. (1984b) Long-term outcome of bereavement. *British Journal of Psychiatry , 145,* 424-428.

Luteijn, F. Starren, J. & Dijk, H. van. (1975) *Nederlandse Persoonlijkheids Vragenlijst, Handleiding.* Lisse: Swets & Zeitlinger.

MacMahon, B. & Pugh, T.F. (1965) Suicide in the widowed. *American Journal of Epidemiology, 81,* 23-31.

Maddison, D.C. & Walker, W.L. (1967) Factors affecting the outcome of conjugal bereavement. *British Journal of Psychiatry, 113,* 1057-1067.

Marris, P. (1958) *Widows and their families.* London: Routledge & Kegan Paul.

Marris, P. (1974) *Loss and Change*. London: Routledge & Kegan Paul.

McCrae, R.R., & Costa, P.T. (1986) Personality, coping, and coping effectiveness in an adult sample. *Journal of Personality, 54(2)*, 385-405.

McCrae, R. R., & Costa, P.T. (1988) Psychological resilience among widowed men and women: a 10-year follow up study of a national sample. *Journal of Social Issues, 44, (3)*, 129-142.

McNiel, Dale A., Hatcher, C., & Reubin, R. (1988) Family survivors of suicide and accidental death: consequences for widows. *Suicide and Life-Threatening Behaviour, 18(2)*, 137-148.

Meerling (1981) *Methoden en technieken van psychologisch onderzoek, deel 1, Model, observatie en beslissing*. Meppel: Boom.

Methorst, G.J. (1988) Verdriet bij chronisch zieken en hun partners. In: J Bennebroek, R.F.W. Diekstra en K. Gill (Eds.) *Verdriet, verliesverwerking en gezondheid*. Boerhaave Commissie voor Postacedamisch Onderwijs in de Geneeskunde. Leiden.

Miles, M.S. & Demi, A.S. (1983-1984) Toward the development of a theory on bereavement guilt: sources of guilt in bereaved parents. *Omega, 14*, 299-314.

Mor, V., McHorney, C., & Sherwood, S. (1986) Secondary morbidity among the recently bereaved. *American Journal of Psychiatry, 143(2)*, 158-163.

Morgan, L.A. (1976) A re-examination of widowhood and morale. *Journal of Gerontology, 31*, 687-695.

Morgan, L.A. (1981) Economic change at mid-life widowhood: a longitudinal analysis. *Journal of Marriage and the Family, 43*, 899-907.

Morgan, L.A. (1989) Economic well-being following marital termination: a comparison of widowed and divorced women. *Journal of Family Issues, 10*, 86-101.

Moss, M. S. & Moss, S. Z. (1984-1985) Some aspects of the elderly widow(er)'s persistent tie with the deceased spouse. *Omega, 15(3)*, 195-206.

Murphy, P.A. (1986-1987) Parental death in childhood and loneliness in young adults. *Omega, 17(3)*, 219-228.

Murphy, S.A. (1986) Stress, coping and mental health outcomes following a natural disaster: bereaved family members and friends compared. *Death Studies, 10*, 411-429.

Murrell, S.A., Himmelfarb, S. , Phifer, J.F. (1988) Effects of pre-bereavement loss and pre-event status on subsequent physical health in older adults. *Int. Journal Aging and Human Development, 27(2)*, 89-107.

Neisser, U. (1967) *Cognitive Psychology*. New York: Appleton-Century.

Neisser, U. (1976) *Cognition and Reality*. San Francisco: W.H.Freeman & co.

Nisbett, R.E. & Wilson, T.D. (1977) Telling More Than We Can Know: Verbal Reports on Mental Processes. *Psychological Review, 84 (3)*, 231-259.

Norris, F.H. & Murrell, S.A. (1987) Older adult family stress and adaptation before and after bereavement. *Journal of Gerontology, 42(6)*, 606-612.

Osterweis, M., Salomon, F., Green, M. (Eds.) (1984) *Bereavement. Reactions, consequences and care*. Washington D.C.: National Academy Press.

Owen, G., Fulton, R. & Markusen, E. (1982-1983) Death at a distance: a study of family survivors. *Omega, 13*, 191-225.

Parker, G. & Manicavasagar, V. (1986) Childhood bereavement circumstances associated with adult depression. *British Journal of Medical Psychology, 59*, 387-391.

Parkes, C.M. (1970) The first year of bereavement. *Psychiatry, 33*, 444-467.

Parkes, C.M. (1975a) Determinants of outcome following bereavement. *Omega, Vol.6(4)*, 303-323.

Parkes, C.M. (1975b) Unexpected and untimely bereavement: A statistical study of young Boston widows and widowers. In: B. Schoenberg, A.C. Carr, A.H. Kutcher, et. al. (Eds.). *Anticipatory grief.* New York: Columbia University Press.

Parkes, C.M. (1987) *Bereavement. Studies of grief in adult life.* New York: Penguin Books Publishers.

Parkes, C.M. (1988) Bereavement as a psychosocial transition: processes of adaptation to change. *Journal of Social Issues, 44(3)*, 53-65.

Parkes, C.M., & Brown, R. (1972) Health after bereavement: a controlled study of young Boston widows and widowers. *Psychosomatic Medicine, 34*, 249-461.

Parkes, C.M., & Weiss, R.S. (1983) *Recovery from Bereavement.* New York: Basic Books.

Parkes, K.R. (1986) Coping in stressful episodes: the role of individual differences, environmental factors, and situational characteristics. *Journal of Personality and Social Psychology, 51(6)*, 1277-1292.

Parry, G. (1986) Paid employment, life events, social support and mental health in working-class mothers. *Journal of Health and Social Behaviour, 27*, 193-208.

Pennebaker, J.W., & O' Heeron, R.C. (1984) Confiding in others and illness rate among spouses of suicide and accidental death victims. *Journal of Abnormal Psychology, 93*, 473-476.

Perkins, D.V. & Tebes, J.A. (1984) Genuine versus simulated responses on the impact of event scale. *Psychological Reports, 54*, 575-578.

Pierce, R.C. (1982) Antecedents of symptom expression during marital separation. *Journal of Clinical Psychology, 38*, 732-741.

Plewis, I. (1985) *Analysing change measurement and explanation using longitudinal data.* Chichester: Wiley & Sons.

Ploeg, H.M. van der, Defares, P.B., & Spielberger, C.D. (1982) *Handleiding bij de Zelf-Analysevragenlijst.* Lisse: Swets & Zeitlinger.

Radloff, L. (1975) Sex differences in depression: the effects of occupation and marital status. *Sex Roles, 1*, 249-265.

Ramsay, R.W. (1979a) Rouwtherapie. De gedragstherapeutische behandeling van pathologische rouwproblemen. In: *Handboek gedragstherapie- Afl. 5 (may).*

Ramsay, R.W. (1979b) Bereavement: a behavioral treatment of pathological grief. In: Sjoden, P.O., Bates, S. & Dorkens, W.S. (Eds.), *Trends in Behavior Therapy.* New York: Acedemic Press.

Rando, T.A. (1983) An investigation of grief and adaptation in parents whose children have died from cancer. *Journal of Pediatric Psychology , 8(1)* , 3-20.

Range, L.M., Niss, N.M. (1990) Long-term bereavement from suicide, homicide, accidents and natural deaths. *Death Studies, 14*, 423-433.

Raphael, B., & Maddison, D. (1976) The care of bereaved adults. In: Hill, O.W. (Ed.). *Modern trends in psychosomatic medicine.* London: Butterworth.

Raphael, B. & Nunn, K. (1988) Counseling the bereaved. *Journal of Social Issues, 44,(3)*, 191-206.

Rees, W., & Lutkins, S. (1967) Mortality of bereavement. *British Medical Journal, 4*, 13-16.

Reissman, C.K. & Gerstel, N. (1985) Marital dissolution and health: do males or females have greater risk? *Social Science and Medicine, 20*, 627-635.

Remondet, J.H., Hansson, R.O., Rule, B., & Winfrey, G. (1987) Rehearsal for widowhood. *Journal of Social and Clinical Psychology, 5*, 285-297.

Richards, J. & McCallum, J. (1979) Bereavement in the elderly. *The New Zealand Medical Journal, 89*, 201-204.

Roach, M.J., & Kitson, G.C. (1989) The impact of forewarning on adjustment in widowhood and divorce. In: D.A. Lund (Ed.), *Older bereaved spouses: research with practical implications*. New York: Hemisphere.

Rosenblatt, P.C. (1988) Grief: the social context of private feelings. *Journal of Social Issues, 44(3)*, 67-78.

Rosenblum, L.A. (1984) Monkeys responses to separation and loss. In: M. Osterweis, F. Salomon, M. Green (Eds.), *Bereavement. Reactions, consequences and care*. Washington D.C.: National Academy Press.

Rutter, M. (1985) Resilience in the face of adversity. Protective factors and resistance to psychiatric disorder. *British Journal of Psychiatry, 147*, 598-611.

Rynearson, E.K. (1987) Psychotherapy of pathologic grief. Revisions and limitations. *Psychiatric Clinics of North America, 10(3)*, 487-499.

Sanders, C.M. (1979-1980) A comparison of adult bereavement in the death of a spouse, child, and parent. *Omega, 10*, 303-322.

Sanders, C.M. (1981) Comparison of younger and older spouses in bereavement outcome. *Omega, 11*, 217-232.

Sanders, C.M. (1982-1983) Effects of sudden vs. chronic illness death on bereavement outcome. *Omega, 13*, 227-241.

Sanders, C. M. (1988) Risk factors in bereavement outcome. *Journal of Social Issues, 44(3)*, 97-111.

Sarafino, E.P. (1990) *Health psychology: biopsychosocial interactions*. New York: Wiley & Sons.

Sarason, B.R., E.N. Shearin, G.R. Pierce, I.G. Sarason (1987) Interrelations of social support measures: theoretical and practical implications. *Journal of Personality and Social Psychology, 52*, 813-832.

Schippers, G.M. (1981) *Alkoholgebruik en alcoholgerelateerde problematiek*. Lisse: Swets & Zeitlinger.

Schuchter, S. R. (1986) *Dimensions of grief*. San Francisco/ London: Jossey Bass Publishers.

Schut, H.A.W., Keijser, A. de, Bout, J. van den (1988) *Gender differences in coping with loss and health in conjugal bereavement*. Paper presented to the 2nd International Conference on Grief and Bereavement in Contemporary Society. London, 12th-15th July, 1988.

Schwab, J.J., & Schwab, M.E. (1978) *Sociocultural roots of mental illness: an epidemiologic survey*. New York: Plenum.

Schwarzer, C. (1984) Stressful life events and emotions in the elderly In: R. Schwarzer (Ed.) *The self in anxiety, stress and depression*. Amsterdam: Elsevier

Seitz, F.C. (1971) Behavior modification techniques for treating depression. *Psychotherapy, Theory, Research and Practice, 8*, 181-184.

Seitz, P. M., & Warrick, L.H. (1974) Perinatal death: The grieving mother. *American Journal of Nursing, 74(11)*, 2028-2033.

Seligman, M.E.P. (1975) *Helplessness.*San Francisco: Freeman.

Sen, A. (1988) Bereavement and the family: some personal experiences. *Bereavement Care,7(3)* , 26-29.

Shackleton, C.H. (1984) The Psychology of Grief. *Advances in Behaviour Research and Therapy: an international review, 6*, 153-205.

Sheldon, A.R., Cochrane, J., Vachon, M.L., Lyall, W., Rogers, J. & Freeman, S. (1981) A psychosocial analysis of risk of psychological impairment following bereavement. *The Journal of Nervous and Mental Disease, 169*, 253-255.

Shepherd, D., & Barraclough, B.M. (1974) The aftermath of suicide. *British Medical Journal, 2*, 600-603.

Shuchter, S. R., & Zisook, S. (1986) Treatment of spousal bereavement: A multidimensional approach. *Psychiatric Annals, 16(5)*, 295-305.

Silverman, Ph. D. (1974) Anticipatory grief from the perspective of widowhood. In: Schoenberg, B., Carr, A.C., Kutcher, A.H. et. al. (Eds.), *Anticipatory grief.* New York/London: Columbia University Press.

Silverman, Ph. D. (1987) The impact of parental death on college age women. *Psychiatric Clinics of North America, 10(3)*, 387-404.

Smith, K.R. (1990) *Risk of mortality following widowhood: sex differences between sudden and expected widowhood.* Revised paper presented at the 1990 Annual Meetings of the Society for Epedemiologic Research, Birmingham, AL.

Spiegel, Y. (1973) *Der Prozess des Trauerns: Analyse und Beratung.* Kaiser, Grunewald.

Stein, Z, & Susser, M.W. (1969) Widowhood and mental illness. *British Journal of Preventive and Social Medicine, 23*, 106-110.

Stroebe, M.S., & Stroebe, W. (1983) Who suffers more? Sex differences in health risks of the widowed. *Psychological Bulletin, 93(2)*, 279-301.

Stroebe, M.S., & Stroebe, W. (1989-1990) Who participates in bereavement research? A review and empirical study. *Omega, 20*, 1-29.

Stroebe, M.S., & Stroebe, W. (1990) *Does 'grief work' work? A review of empirical investigation.* Tübingen: Report psychological institute University of Tübingen.

Stroebe, M.S., Stroebe, W., Gergen, K.J., & Gergen, M. (1981-1982) The broken heart, reality or myth? *Omega, 12*, 87-105.

Stroebe, M.S., Stroebe, W., & Hansson, R.O. (1988) Bereavement research: an historical introduction. *Journal of Social Issues, 44(3)*, 1-18.

Stroebe, W., & Stroebe, M.S. (1987) *Bereavement and Health. The psychological and physical consequences of partner loss.* Cambridge: Cambridge University Press.

Stroebe, W, Stroebe, M.S., & Domittner, G. (1988) Individual and situational differences in recovery from bereavement: a risk group identified. *Journal of Social Issues, 44(3)*, 143-158.

Toedter, L.J., Lasker, J.N., & Campbell, D.T. (1990) The comparison group problem in bereavement studies and the retrospective pretest. *Evaluation Review Vol 14*, 75-90.

Trolley, B.C. (1986) Suicide parents and sudden death parents: The grief process, the nature of help, the role of the professional, and methodological issues. *Dissertation Abstracts International46(7-B)*, 2449-2450.

Turner, R.J., & Gartrell, J.W. (1978) Social factors in psychiatric outcome: toward the resolution of interpretive controversies. *American Sociological Review, 43*, 368-382.

Uniken Venema-van Uden, M. (1990) *Hartrevalidatie. Over het bepalen en voorsepellen van herstel.* Utrecht, Doctoral dissertation.

Vachon, M. L. (1976) Grief and bereavement following the death of a spouse. Canadian *Psychiatric Association Journal, 21(1)*, 35-44.

Vachon, M.L., Lyall, W., Rogers, J., Freedman-Leftovsky, K., & Freeman, S. (1980) A controlled study of self-help intervention for widows. American *Journal of Psychiatry, 137*, 1380-1384.

Vachon M.L., Rogers J., Lyall W.A., Lancee W.J., Sheldon A.R. & Freeman S.J. (1982) Predictors and correlates of adaptation to conjugal bereavement. *American Journal of Psychiatry, 139(8)*, 998-1002.

Vachon, M.L.S., Freedman, K. , & Freedman, S.J.J. (1977) *Cancer and bereavement.* Paper presented at a symposion on coping with cancer, Toronto, April 24-26. Toronto.

Vachon M.L., Sheldon A.R. Lancee W.J., Lyall W.A., Rogers J. & Freeman S.J. (1982) Correlates of enduring distress patterns following bereavement: social network, life situation and personality. *Psychological Medicine, 12(4)*, 783-788.

Vachon, Mary L.S., & Stylianos, S.K. (1988) The role of social support in bereavement. *Journal of Social Issues, 44,(3)*, 175-190.

Valanis, B., Yeaworth, R.C., & Mullis, M.R. (1987) Alcohol use among bereaved and nonbereaved older persons. *Journal of Gerontological Nursing, 13(5)*, 26-32.

Vargas, L.A., Loya, F., & Vargas, J. (1984) *Grief across modes of death in three ethnic groups.* Paper presented at the 92nd Annual Convention of the American Psychological Association, Toronto, Canada.

Videka-Sherman, L. (1982) Coping with the death of a child: A study over time. *American Journal of Orthopsychiatry, 52(4)*, 688-698.

Visser, A. Ph., (1983) De betekenis van de VOEG: enkele gegevens over de begripsvaliditeit. *Gezondheid en Samenleving, 4*, 177-188.

Visser, R.A. (1982) *On quantitative longitudinal data in psychological research.* Leiden: doctoral dissertation.

Wagner, K. & Calhoun, L.G. (1990) *Perceptions of Social Support by Suicide Survivors and their Social Networks.* article in press.

Wal, B. van der (1988) *Opvang na overlijden.* Paper to obtain Master degree English summary Unpublished

Wal, J. van der (1987) *Geholpen worden door te helpen. Een onderzoek naar de ervaringen van nabestaanden met rouwgroepen.* Report. Leiden: Repro-press Psychologie.

Wal, J. van der (1988) *De nasleep van suicides en dodelijke verkeersongevallen. Een onderzoek naar de psychische en sociale gevolgen voor nabestaanden.* Leiden: DSWO-press.

Wal, J. van der (1989-1990) The aftermath of suicide: a review of empirical evidence. *Omega, 20(2),* 149-171.

Wal, J. van der, & Cleiren, M.P.H.D. (1990) *Politie en nabestaanden. Een handreiking voor het werk van de politie in rouwsituaties.* Schiedam: Report for the Ministry of the Interior.

Wal, J. van der, Cleiren, M.P.H.D., & Diekstra, R.F.W. (1988) Grief reactions of survivors of suicide; results of a sample survey study. In: R.I. Uffit (Ed.), *Combined 1987 Proceedings: twentieth annual meeting of the American Association of Suicidology and 19th international congress of the International Association of Suicide Prevention. San Francisco, May 25-30. 1987.*

Wal, J. van der, Cleiren, M.P.H.D., Diekstra, R.F.W., & Moritz, B.J.M. (1988) The early impact of bereavement after suicide or fatal traffic accident. In: S.D. Platt & N. Kreitman, *Current researh on suicide and parasuicide. Selected proceedings of the Second European Symposium on Suicidal Behaviour. Edinburgh 29 May - 1 June 1988.*

Wal, J. van der, Cleiren, M.P.H.D., Han, R., & Diekstra, R.F.W. (1988) *Verslag van het nabestaandenprojekt. Deel 2. Psychometrische evaluatie van enkele vragenlijsten, afgenomen tijdens de eerste meting onder nabestaanden van suicides en verkeersslachtoffers.* Internal report, Vakgroep Klinische en Gezondheids Psychologie, R.U. Leiden

Wallace, S.E. (1973) *After suicide.* New York: Wiley.

Weiss, J.M. (1984) Behavioral and psychological influences on gastrointestinal pathology: experimental techniques and findings. In: Gentry, W.D. (Ed.) *Handbook of behavioral medicine.* New York: Guilford.

Weiss, R.S. (1988) Loss and recovery. *Journal of Social Issues, 44(3),* 37-52.

Wingard, D.L. (1984) The sex-differential in morbidity, mortality and lifestyle. In: Breslow, J.E. et. al. (Eds.), *Annual Review of Public Health, 5.* Palo Alto: Annual Reviews Inc.

Worden, J.W. (1982) *Grief counseling and grief therapy.* London & New York: Tavistock Publications.

Wortman, C.B. & Silver, R.C. (1989) The myths of coping with loss. *Journal of Consulting and Clinical Psychology, 57,* 349-357.

Young, M., Benjamin, B., & Wallis, C. (1963) Mortality of widowers. *Lancet, 2,* 254-256.

Zilberg, N.J. , Weiss, D.S., & Horowitz, M.J. (1982) Impact of Event Scale: a cross validation study and some empirical evidence supporting a conceptual model of stress response syndromes. *Journal of Consulting and Clinical Psychology, 50,* 407-414.

Zisook, S. (Ed.) (1987) *Biopsychosocial aspects of bereavement.* Washington: American Psychiatric Press.

Zisook, S. & Lyons, L. (1988) Grief and relationsip to the deceased. *International Journal of Family Psychiatry, 9,* 135-146.

Zisook, S., Schuchter, S.R., & Lyons, L.E. (1988) Grief and relationship to the deceased. *Int. Journal of Family Psychiatry, 9(2),.* 135-146.

Zisook, S., Schuchter, S.R., & Lyons, L.E. (1988) Predictors of psychological reactions during the early stages of widowhood. *Psychiatric Clinics of North America, 10(3)*, 355-368.

Zisook, S. Shuchter, S.R. (1986) The first four years of widowhood. *Psychiatric Annals,16(5)* , 288-294.

Zisook S., Shuchter S.R., Lyons L.E. (1987) Predictors of psychological reactions during the early stages of widowhood. *Psychiatric Clinics of North America ,10(3)*, 355-368.

Properties of the measures of adaptation

Scale		Number of items	Range	Mean	S.D.	Eigen value	% Expl. variance	α
Leiden Detachment Scale	T1	7	0 - 21	8.9	5.6	3.4	48.8	.82
	T2			6.7	5.2	3.4	48.8	.82
Impact of Event Scale -Intrusions	T1	7	0 - 35	16.9	8.2	3.2	45.1	.79
	T2			14.2	8.8	3.6	50.8	.84
Impact of Event Scale -Avoidance	T1	8	0 - 40	10.4	8.4	2.8	35.2	.73
	T2			7.5	7.6	3.0	36.9	.74
Anger Scale	T1	5	0 - 15	1.4	2.4	3.2	63.1	.83
	T2			1.0	1.8	2.6	51.9	.75
Guilt Scale	T1	2	0 - 8	.85	1.8	--	–	.57
Relief Scale	T1	3	0 - 12	4.2	4.8	2.6	86.3	.92
Beck Depression Inventory	T1	13	0 - 39	4.0	4.7	5.1	39.5	.87
	T2			3.4	4.6	5.5	42.1	.88
Suicidal Ideation List	T1	10	0 - 20	.3	1.1	3.3	33.2	.69
	T2			.3	1.1	2.9	29.2	.67
VOEG General well-being	T1	21	0 - 21	5.4	4.9	6.3	30.1	.88
	T2			4.5	4.4	5.8	27.8	.86
Concurrent Stress		7	0 - 21					
(Year before bereavement)	T1			2.0	2.5	2.0	28.0	.54
(3 Mths. after bereavement)	T1			2.0	2.4	1.8	24.8	.44
(3-14 Mths. after bereavement)	T2			2.3	2.5	1.6	23.4	.40
(14 Mths. after bereavement)	T2			1.7	2.1	1.6	22.6	.36
Sense of Control Scale	T1	5	0 - 10	7.6	2.2	1.9	38.4	.59
	T2			7.8	2.2	2.0	40.5	.62
Medicinal Consumption Scale	T1	5	0 - 20	2.5	4.3	2.8	55.4	.72
	T2			2.3	4.7	3.2	63.2	.80
Social Activity Scale	T1	6	0 - 12	7.4	2.9	2.3	38.7	.67
	T2			7.7	2.8	2.2	37.3	.65
Social Integration Scale	T1	3	0 - 12	9.7	2.3	1.9	63.7	.71
	T2			9.9	2.2	1.9	64.3	.72
Need for Emotional Support Scale	T1	4	0 - 8	4.3	2.1	1.9	48.3	.64
	T2			3.8	2.0	1.9	46.8	.62
Aggravating Reactions Scale	T1	5	0 - 15	3.8	3.3	2.1	42.2	.65
	T2			3.5	3.2	2.1	42.4	.64

Correlations between the measures of adaptation at four months (upper triangle) and at fourteen months (lower triangle) On diagonal: correlations between scores at four months and fourteen months

	QaC	SfM	LDS	IES-I	IES-A	BDI	Suic	Cntrl	VOEG	Med.	Alc.	Smo.	NESS	SIS	SAS	EvalR	Anger	Guilt	Relief
QaC Questions ab. cause	.35	.36	.30	.29	.13	.18	.11	-.09	.13	.10	-.06	-.07	.22	.04	.08	.06	.12	.20	-.21
SfM Search for meaning	.33	.43	.39	.39	.16	.21	.08	-.20	.16	.08	-.12	.00	.21	.02	.04	.04	.18	.15	-.19
LDS Detachment	.36	.51	.71	.68	.45	.44	.20	-.27	.35	.09	-.13	-.02	.37	-.01	.07	.20	.21	.18	-.34
IES-I Intrusions	.36	.54	.70	.67	.43	.49	.17	-.17	.45	.15	-.19	-.04	.36	.00	-.03	.11	.29	.14	-.19
IES-A Avoidance	.19	.39	.45	.52	.57	.43	.10	-.16	.39	.15	-.20	.07	.12	.16	.08	.19	.17	.22	-.13
BDI Depression	.28	.44	.47	.49	.47	.72	.41	-.39	.64	.29	-.06	.08	.23	.25	.18	.19	.37	.27	-.13
Suic. Suicidal ideation	.09	.15	.16	.10	.16	.36	.74	-.20	.20	.01	.04	.00	.11	.07	.08	.06	.23	.07	-.05
Ctrl. Sense of Control	-.24	-.43	-.40	-.38	-.20	-.47	-.15	.57	-.16	-.17	-.06	-.06	-.12	-.17	-.28	-.10	-.11	-.15	.19
VOEG General health	.24	.33	.26	.35	.37	.70	.29	-.25	.69	.29	-.07	.18	.18	.12	.03	.21	.40	.16	-.06
Med. Medicine use	.13	.15	.11	.10	.17	.39	.02	-.12	.30	.69	-.17	.05	-.05	.10	.13	.05	.03	.13	.01
Alc. Alcohol use	.07	-.11	-.06	-.08	-.17	-.01	.10	.05	-.05	-.14	.73	.23	-.04	-.02	-.08	.05	.02	-.02	.08
Smo. Smoking	.07	.03	-.03	-.06	-.01	.09	.12	-.05	.13	-.04	.24	.85	.00	.04	.02	.09	.11	.10	.01
NESS Need emotion. supp.	.28	.29	.37	.45	.15	.17	.10	-.12	.21	-.04	.04	-.01	.57	-.19	-.14	.20	.21	.25	-.07
SIS Social integration	.00	.12	.14	.06	.16	.33	.30	-.31	.26	.02	.10	.25	-.05	.46	.26	.04	.11	.12	.01
SAS Social activity	-.03	.14	.07	-.01	.10	.24	.14	-.33	.17	.18	-.07	.13	-.20	.38	.40	-.08	-.08	.08	-.05
Eval Negative reactions	.19	.31	.32	.29	.27	.21	.17	-.24	.10	.05	.09	.07	.27	.24	.11	.38	.26	.25	.01
Ang. Feelings of Anger	—	—	—	—	—	—	—	—	—	—	—	—	—	—	—	—	—	.10	-.02
Guil. Feelings of Guilt	—	—	—	—	—	—	—	—	—	—	—	—	—	—	—	—	—	—	-.08
Relie. Feelings of Relief	—	—	—	—	—	—	—	—	—	—	—	—	—	—	—	—	—	—	—

Request for lectures and research information should be addressed to:

Marc P. H. D. Cleiren, Ph.D.
Dept. of Clinical and Health Psychology
Leiden University
Wassenaarseweg 52
P.O. Box 9555
2300 RB Leiden
The Netherlands